Meaning and Mental Representations

ADVANCES IN SEMIOTICS

General Editor, Thomas A. Sebeok

,/2007

MEANING AND MENTAL REPRESENTATIONS

EDITED BY

Umberto Eco
Marco Santambrogio
Patrizia Violi

Indiana University Press
Bloomington and Indianapolis

Printed by arrangement with Gruppo Editoriale Fabbri,
Bompiani, Sonzogno, Etas S.p..A.

© 1988 by Indiana University Press
All rights reserved

Manufactured in the United States of America

Library of Congress Cataloging-in-Publication Data

Meaning and mental representations / edited by Umberto Eco, Marco
   Santambrogio, Patrizia Violi.
        p.   cm.   — (Advances in semiotics)
      Includes bibliographical references.
      ISBN 0-253-33724-0; 0-253-20496-8 (pbk.)
      1. Semantics. 2. Semantics (Philosophy) 3. Semiotics.
   I. Eco, Umberto. II. Santambrogio, Marco. III. Violi, Patrizia.
   IV. Series.
   P325.M38 1988
   415—dc19   88-9251
                                                           CIP

1 2 3 4 5 92 91 90 89 88

Contents

Meaning and Mental Representations

Marco Santambrogio - Patrizia Violi

Introduction

There is little or no overlapping at all, save for a few minor points, between European semiotics and Anglo-American philosophy of language, as far as the historical origins and the theoretical presuppositions are concerned. It is thus all the more remarkable that, in the past few years, more and more points of contact have emerged between these two traditions of intellectual research on the issue of linguistic meaning and its mental representation — an issue which is clearly crucial both for semiotics and for analytic philosophy, as well as for linguistics, psychology and artificial intelligence. Such a convergence will be apparent to semioticians, we believe, from the majority of the contributions to the present volume, which — with the sole exception of Eco's paper — all belong in the Anglo-American world.

That one can distinguish these two traditions of thought (among others) in the wealth of studies devoted to linguistic meaning does not in the least imply that they should be seen as unitary theories or complexes of theories, with no tensions between opposing views existing within either of them. On the contrary, the whole field of research is rich in conflicts, bearing even on the most fundamental issues. We are proud to bring together here ten original sharply diverging papers, which significantly contribute to the current debate.

It is mainly for the benefit of those among our readers who are not entirely familiar with the Anglo-American perspectives on the problem of meaning that we shall try in the following introductory pages to give an idea of the antecedents of the present debate, and in particular of the pervasive influence of the analytic philosophy of language. Towards the end of this paper, we shall in turn sketch some of the historical background and of the main theoretical assumptions of European semiotics for those readers who are unfamiliar with it.

Modern logic and the philosophy of language which accompanied it (partly as a motivation, partly as a result) were conceived in a deep dislike for "psychologism". According to Frege, no confusion is admissible between the psychological process of thinking and the pure thought "of which mankind has a common store, transmissible from one generation to another ".[1] Logic and philosophy have no concern whatsoever with the

---

[1] G. Frege, "On Sense and Reference", in *Translations from the Philosophical Writings of Gottlob Frege*, by P. Geach and M. Black, Oxford, Blackwell, 1970, p. 59.

processes actually going on in the individual mind, and in any case those processes are simply irrelevant when it comes to exploring the realm of meanings and their cognates, mathematical objects.

In this vein, the two fundamental concepts on which Frege constructed his philosophy of language, those of sense and reference, were both sharply distinguished from their mental accompaniment in the individual mind, the idea. The latter is subjective: "one man's idea is not that of another; while the sign's sense may be the common property of many and therefore is not a part or a mode of the individual mind." [2]

At its birth and for several decades to follow, modern logic was also associated with a deep mistrust for natural language. The artificial languages invented by logicians were conceived of as substitutes for natural language, whose imperfections tend to cloud, rather than disclose, the thoughts which it expresses. It took logicians a long time to realize that there are obvious differences, but no principled *opposition* between formal and natural languages. Richard Montague even denied that any important theoretical difference exists between them and was successful in showing that fragments of the latter are amenable to a rigorous and formal treatment. [3] But even before Montague, it had become increasingly clear in the logically-minded quarters of philosophy that the opposition between these two kinds of language could best be viewed as that between a theory and the field of phenomena it endeavours to explain and to systematize. When one conceives of formal languages as a theoretical aproximation to the richness of linguistic natural phenomena, one soon realizes that there is nothing sacrosanct in the particular theoretical concepts, such as material implication, or the quantifier/variable notation, which are employed in the formal approach. They are tools, which can be substituted without abandoning the logical approach. Just as Frege's and Russell's mistrust in natural language was at least in need of qualification, so is their anti-psychologism. Certainly, it cannot mean that the problem of explaining how the individual mind comes to grasp the meanings of linguistic expressions and to acquire linguistic competence is spurious or irrelevant. As a mere confusion between psychology and logic, psychologism is out, but this is not to say that a theory of meaning, as conceived for example by Frege, is totally unrelated to the actual use we make of language. On the contrary, one can very well argue that it is precisely *because* a theory of meaning is a theory of the practice of using a language that the notion of sense is not a psychological one. [4] It is the very objectivity of the notion of sense which raises the problem of explaining how the individual mind can grasp

[2] *Ibid.*

[3] R. Montague, *Formal Philosophy*, edited by R. Thomason, New Haven and London, Yale University Press, 1974, and particularly ch.6, "English as a formal language", p. 188 ff.

[4] This point has been made by M. Dummett, in *Frege*, London, Duckworth, 1973; see especially ch. 5, "Sense and Reference".

senses; for it is by no means obvious for example how a mental entity, such as an idea in our mind, can become associated with one Platonic entity instead of another. The answer may well be found in the fact of our taking part in a common practice, but in any case one tends to feel that no principled opposition between the logical and the psychological approach to language ought to exist.

Nevertheless, as some of the contributions to this volume testify, a strong reaction to the logical approach is currently occurring in some quarters of contemporary research in semantics. The charge against it is not just that it is too abstract and not sufficiently concerned with the actual practice of speaking and understanding a language, but that it is seriously misconceived as an account of what meaning and linguistic competence are. Meaning, in particular, is totally unrelated to truth and reference, which have always been taken by the logically-minded philosophers to be the cornerstone of semantic theory. Clearly, this is a head-on attack aiming at the heart of that well-established tradition of research.

The present collection of papers is meant to exemplify this reaction against the formal approach to meaning while exploring some of the most recent proposals within the formal camp itself.

Apparently, the notion of meaning is approached at present from two widely diverging viewpoints, roughly corresponding to two groups of disciplines dealing with language in general: logic and logically-oriented philosophy which is almost entirely dominated by the Fregean heritage, on the one hand, and general linguistics, cognitive psychology, artificial intelligence on the other. The two perspectives are so divergent that it is difficult even to say whether the notions of meaning they employ have any relation to one another. It is precisely on the problem of whether meaning is primarily a psychological or logical notion that they are most directly opposed.

Within the logico-philosophical camp, Montague grammar has been, until recently, one of the most active areas of research in natural language. Most of its basic concepts and methods were originally put forward by Frege, Tarski and Carnap; Montague brought them to bear directly on natural language, but the very aims of his program − "Like Donald Davidson, I regard the construction of a theory of truth [...] as the basic goal of serious syntax and semantics"[5] − are entirely consonant with theirs. In particular, the notion of truth employed here is a totally *objective* one, in the sense that sentences are true or false in a model or interpretation entirely independently of whether we recognize them as true or false − independently even of whether anybody has ever thought of them. *A fortiori*, meaning is independent of *individual* minds. This fits in perfectly well with Frege's realism. Similarly, the notion of reference

---

[5] R. Montague, *op. cit.*, p. 188.

is objective in that expressions refer to whatever objects they refer to in the world independently, for example, of the criteria we may use in picking them out and of the conceptions we form of them in our minds. No wonder that, in this perspective, meaning too has an objective character. The meaning of a sentence is taken here to be *what primarily determines the conditions for its truth*. The way meaning (more precisely, the cognitive or designative component of meaning) is formally represented within the Montague framework is by means of the Carnapian notion of intension.[6] Basically, the meaning of a referring expression is the range of its references in all possible circumstances or worlds, or, as it is now customary to represent it, the function associating to each possible world the extension of that expression in that world. As sentences are here taken to refer to truth values, the meaning of a sentence in particular simply turns out to amount to a set of possible worlds, namely those in which the sentence is true. *Prima facie* at least, this is totally unrelated to what goes on in our mind when we hear and understand a sentence: the conditions for the truth of a sentence are those features that the world must have in order for the sentence to be true in it.

Montague grammar has sometimes been criticized on the ground that the models it posits, in order to define truth and meaning, are psychologically unrealistic; for one thing, they are too large and too numerous "to fit within the human brain" and therefore understanding the meaning of a sentence cannot be taken to consist of a capacity to grasp such models or to perform operations on them. It has been claimed, however, that this criticism is not entirely fair, for it was never Montague's aim to give a psychologically realistic notion of meaning. Rather, he thought his main responsibility was towards the theory of truth, objectively conceived. In this he was fairly successful, as will emerge clearly if we consider how linguistic competence is accounted for within the Montague framework: understanding a sentence simply amounts to knowing its intension. It follows from what was said above about intensions that, in order to show that one understands a sentence or is semantically competent with respect to it, it is a necessary and sufficient condition that whenever presented with that sentence and a situation, one is able to say whether the former is true in the latter or not. Consider for example the sentence "John is married". A competent speaker of English should know that s/he must judge this sentence to be true in any circumstance in which John is married and false in any other circumstance. His/her competence then simply amounts to knowing that "John is married" is true if and only if John is in fact married. But this is precisely Tarski's

---

[6] R. Carnap, *Meaning and Necessity. A Study in Semantics and Modal Logic*, Chicago, University of Chicago Press, 1947; see especially ch. 1, "The method of extension and intension", par. 5.

convention T, presented as an account of semantic competence.[7]

For a while, Montague grammarians hoped that this account of semantic competence would be acceptable to linguists. For instance, Katz, Fodor and Postal had singled out entailment, synonymy, contradictoriness and superordination as the basic semantic relations;[8] now, the theory of intensions was meant from its Carnapian beginning to account precisely for these. One can therefore understand why a Montague grammarian, Max Cresswell, once stated that "The only other detailed attempt at linguistic semantics, viz. that inspired by Katz, Fodor and Postal can be seen as a partial answer which can be completed and given content by a truth conditional approach".[9]

It was soon to be realized, however, that semantic competence is not easily accounted for within such a framework. For one thing, the notion of intension was meant to be a rigorous explication of Frege's notion of sense, but it clearly misses some crucial differences in sense. Logically and mathematically equivalent sentences have the same intensions, and yet they can obviously differ in sense. Intension seems to be too coarse a notion to be able to discriminate between many linguistic items which to the competent ear sound entirely different semantically. Attempts have been made to remedy this unwelcome situation. Carnap's notion of intensional isomorphism and the more recent notion of "meaning" proposed by David Lewis must be mentioned in this connection, although we shall not go into any detail here.[10] In any case, other reasons for dissatisfaction soon emerged.

Although logical semantics does not aim at giving a psychologically plausible representation of meaning, it would be seriously mistaken, in our view, to think that it is indifferent to "what goes on in our minds" when we understand a sentence. Logical semantics has in fact at least one good reason to take this into account — and therefore it is in fact committed to some degree of psychological realism. What has come to be known (after Russell) as the class of propositional attitude verbs — i.e. those involving some kind of intentionality, such as "thinking", "seeking", "believing" etc. — is a very large and important class. All these verbs seem to refer to some relation holding between a person and a mental content, either his own or someone else's. Truth theoretical semantics must specify what the truth conditions are for sentences containing

[7] This way of putting the matter can be found, for example, in M. Cresswell, "Semantic Competence", in F. Guenthner and M. Guenthner-Reutter (eds.), *Meaning and Translation*, London, Duckworth, 1978.

[8] J.J. Katz and P.M. Postal, *An Integrated Theory of Linguistic Description*, Cambridge, Mass., 1964; J.J. Katz and J.A. Fodor, "The Structure of a Semantic Theory" in *Language*, 39 (1963), pp. XXX

[9] M. Cresswell, *op. cit.*

[10] Carnap, *op. cit.*, ch. 1, par. 14; D.K. Lewis, "General Semantics" in D. Davidson and G. Harman (eds.), *Semantics of Natural Language*, Dordrecht, Reidel, 1972.

such verbs. But take the sentence "John understands what George said"; in order to give its truth conditions, one must be able somehow to say what it is to understand a sentence or a discourse.

If Montague grammar could give an adequate treatment of propositional attitude verbs, then an important step would be taken in bridging the gap that separates it from cognitive semantics. On the other hand, it is felt among Montague grammarians that, if no adequate solution could be found, then this failure would threaten the very foundations of the whole enterprise.[11]

Not many people would nowadays claim that that challenge has been satisfactorily met. The most formidable problems — by no means the only ones — have originated within the logical camp itself. The "new theory of reference" originally proposed by Kripke, Kaplan, Putnam and others, has pointed out that proper names and indexicals, contrary to what happens with descriptions, seem to refer to whatever objects they refer to *directly*, without the mediation of anything like a Fregean sense; as a consequence, they do not change their referents in passing from one possible world to another. It follows that for these expressions equality of actual extension amounts to equality of intension. Now, possible worlds semantics predicts that equi-intensional expressions can freely be substituted *salva veritate* in all contexts, including indirect and belief contexts; but, despite the fact that the names "Hesperus" and "Phosphorus" are actually equi-extensional — and therefore equi-intensional, being rigid designators — there is considerable difference between, say, "John believes Hesperus to be the planet Venus" and "John believes Phosphorus to be the planet Venus". "Hesperus" and "Phosphorus" are not intersubstitutable *salva veritate* after all.

There is another, even deeper, source of dissatisfaction, however, which must be mentioned. Having semantic competence was equated with knowing the intensions of propositions and the relations (e.g. of inclusion. exclusion, etc.) holding among them. Now, in most cases we seem to be totally unable to recognize whether or not such relations hold; what is more, no procedure is available which could reveal in a finite time whether or not for instance two intensions are the same — this immediately follows from the indecidability of first order logic. Is this to mean that none of us really has semantic competence in any language, not even one's own native language? And even apart from this problem, it is difficult to understand what it is to know the intension of a sentence, which is in general an infinite set of possible worlds, apart from being able to characterize it (entirely vacuously) as that set of worlds in which the given sentence is true. It might be thought that some finite or infinite sets,

[11] See for example, B. Partee, "Belief-sentences and the Limits of Semantics", in S. Peters and E. Saarinen (eds.), *Processes, Beliefs and Questions*, Dordrecht, Reidel, 1982, pp. 87-106.

namely the recursive and the recursively enumerable ones, are in fact more tractable than the rest and that it is not too difficult to say what it is to know them — it could amount, for example, to mastering some procedure which generates them. But then one possible rejoinder is that it is none too clear what knowing an effective procedure amounts to, apart from understanding an associated set of (verbal) instructions: we then seem to be back to square one. It must be added that this is a very general problem, which is by no means confined to possible-worlds semantics.

In recent years, several attempts have been made within truth theoretical semantics at solving these problems without jettisoning the fundamental ideas of model theoretic semantics. Situation semantics figures prominently among these proposals. It has been proposed by Jon Barwise and John Perry, who have argued for it in detail in their book *Situations and Attitudes*.[12]

Situation semantics takes from Montague the idea of focusing attention "on developing a genuine semantics for natural language, rather than some artificial language invented by logicians" and it owes a great deal to the work done in possible worlds semantics. However, its general conception of what meaning is certainly appears to be very far from that adopted within the Carnapian tradition. In *Situation and Attitudes*, meaning is viewed as being located in the interaction of living things and their environment, it is "more in the world and less in the head than the traditional view of meaning assumed".[13] Quite a few of such traditional notions as intension, meaning postulate, possible world, rigid designator, and the like have disappeared from the theory, together with one of Frege's most typical assumptions, namely that sentences have truth values as their references. Barwise's paper in the present collection breaks down the notion of meaning and focuses on the complex relation holding between symbols, their content, the circumstances of their use and the conventions of the language community within which communication takes place. It points out that the current image of the content being determined by the other factors is inadequate, mainly because it ignores the fact that each one of these ingredients can give information about all the others. This feature is shown by Barwise to be crucial in understanding the meaning of literary texts. It comes as a welcome surprise (to us, at least) that the Fregean and Carnapian tradition in semantics proves to contribute significantly to basic questions of literary interpretation — an area well beyond its original interests.

Several proposals now exist as to the notion which is to replace the Leibnizian one of possible world. It is worth noting that almost all the

---

[12] J. Barwise and J. Perry, *Situation Semantics*, Cambridge, Mass., M.I.T. Press, 1983.
[13] *Ibid.*, p. x.

proposals agree on one point. Possible worlds are "complete" in the intuitive sense that to each question concerning any one of them there is a definite answer: for any sentence A, either A holds in a world or it fails to hold in it (and therefore not-A holds). This is not so in the case of situations. It is even clearer that no mind could possibly entertain, for every conceivable proposition, either it or its negation — minds being what Bas van Fraassen suggests we should substitute for possible worlds, in his contribution to this volume. This is especially interesting from our point of view, in that the objectivity associated with logic from its very beginning seems to turn into its opposite, thus making semantics subjective. However, not an iota of its formal character is given up and full use is made of its technical apparatus. A substantial step forward is thus taken in clarifying the epistemic notion of *a priori* and distinguishing it from the metaphysical notion of *necessity*. This is crucial in order to clarify the puzzling status of identities, such as "Phosphorus is Hesperus".

Cognitive semantics, as we are using the term here, is not itself a well-defined theory of meaning, or even a program for such a theory; it is rather a way of construing the notion of meaning. Meaning is not here taken primarily as what determines the truth conditions of a sentence or the reference of a term, but rather as what is converted into speech by a speaker and conveyed to a hearer. Accordingly, the notions of truth and reference seem to lose almost all of their interest. Cognitive semantics is first of all a theory of understanding and of language use, as opposed to a theory of abstract entities called "meanings". As such, it is clearly sensitive to empirical constraints of various kinds; it must depict what actually "goes on in our mind" (psychological realism), and it must explain how language can be so efficiently learned by human beings — which is a stricter constraint than merely requiring, as also truth theoretical semanticists like Davidson do, finite representability of meaning.

Such an outlook is widely shared in various areas of intellectual research such as theoretical linguistics, artificial intelligence and cognitive psychology, and is embodied in a number of specific theories of meaning. Basically, one can discern here several main trends: there are on the one hand, the decompositional theory, the meaning postulates theory and the view based on semantic nets — which, being historically and conceptually closely related, may be viewed as forming one main family — and, on the other hand, the approaches based on the notions (bearing strong similarities among them) of prototype, stereotype and frame. In addition to this, there is a perspective in artificial intelligence which takes the notion of a procedure as the keystone of a yet-to-be-constructed theory of meaning. It is, however, debatable whether "procedural semantics" itself constitutes a theory of meaning or even the core thereof. Finally, the notion of mental model, whether or not it is distinguishable from the previous notions, has also been taken as the fundamental notion in several proposed theories.

We shall assume some familiarity with all these approaches and merely review some of the problems they face relating to the present issue of mental representation. We are already familiar with some of these from the logical tradition. For instance, it is a much debated point whether semantic primitives have any measure of psychological reality; widely divergent views have been upheld. For instance, according to some authors, semantic primitives are not just psychologically real, but even innate and universal, whereas according, for example, to Katz they are no more than theoretical constructs.[14] But in the latter case, one may ask, what is it that sets them apart from other kinds of abstract and objective entities, such as Fregean senses?

It was precisely the alleged psychological unreality of decompositional theories which prompted some of the most effective criticism of them, such as that made by Fodor, Fodor and Garrett, which originated the theory based on meaning postulates.[15] (Whether or not a real conflict exists here is a debated issue; some, such as Katz, have claimed that the theory of meaning postulates is a mere notational variant of the decompositional approach).[16]

In these approaches, the conflict with the logical tradition − apart from the lack of psychological concern of the latter − cannot be due to the notion of meaning postulate itself, since this was originally proposed by Carnap and it naturally fits in with the framework of truth theoretical semantics, in any of its versions.

What does seem to constitute a sharp difference is the lack of interest for the notions of truth and reference. So much so that some authors from within the logical tradition have claimed that simply because of this lack of concern with the two semantically fundamental (for them) notions, those theories have no right to the status of theories of meaning: all they do is to relate words to other words (this is all semantic nets ever purported to do), or to provide translations from one language to another (this is what the decompositional approach, assuming a translation into Markerese, in fact does). "But we can know the Markerese translation of an English sentence without knowing the first thing about the meaning of the English sentence: namely the conditions under which it would be true. Semantics with no treatment of truth condition is not semantics".[17]

This point is so important that at least three papers in the present col-

---

[14] See J.J. Katz, *Semantic Theory*, New York, Harper, 1972.

[15] See J.D. Fodor, J.A. Fodor, and M.F. Garrett, "The Psychological Unreality of Semantic Representations" in *Linguistic Inquiry*, VI, (1975), pp. 515-531.

[16] See J.J. Katz and R.I. Nagel, "Meaning Postulates and Semantic Theory", in *Foundations of Language*, 11, (1974), pp. 311-340.

[17] D.K. Lewis, *op. cit.*

lection directly or indirectly deal with it. Johnson-Laird endorses Lewis' criticism and even gives a name to the alleged misunderstanding: it is the "symbolic fallacy", about which more later on; while Wilks and Lakoff, for all their divergences, agree in taking the opposite stand.

Almost entirely original with the cognitive tradition is the stress placed on the related notions of prototype and frame. They originated on philosophical (Wittgenstein) and psychological grounds and embody a view of how people actually understand and recognize word meanings and natural categories. The basic idea underlying prototypes is that belonging to a natural kind or a category is not so much a matter of necessary and sufficient conditions as of similarity with exemplars or prototypical instances, that is, central members of a category or idealizations built in our own minds. Both because it seems that we have here an entirely original device, unknown to the logically-minded semanticist, and because prototypes clearly are sensitive to our own, peculiarly human, way of categorizing the world, it has sometimes been thought that it is on this point that the two traditions differ most sharply. The cognitive tradition is sometimes viewed as an extension to the semantic field of one of Gestalt theory's most fundamental insights, namely that perceptual recognition is the result of an interaction between environmental inputs and active principles in the mind that impose structure on them.

Frames have proved their usefulness and their flexibility in artificial intelligence. There is a whole family of related notions taking their origin from them. In the paper by Schank and Kass in the present collection, it may be discovered how Schank came to realize the partial nature of conceptual dependency as a tool, especially in accounting for inferencing (surely a primary component of understanding). Accordingly, scripts were first introduced as "pre-packaged inference chains relating to a specific routine situation", and then plans, MOPs (modular devices, breaking scripts into smaller units or scenes, which are easily combinable) and finally Explanation Patterns (chains of inferences about MOPs). A particularly interesting feature of this enterprise is its capability of taking into account the development of knowledge, and of investigating the mechanisms by means of which we deal with novel, previously unheard of situations. The learning issue is explicitly addressed in Lehnert's paper. Focusing on the question of nominal compounds, a problematic natural language construct much studied by linguists, Lehnert shows the inadequacy of purely linguistic methodology. Nominal compounds cannot be correctly interpreted without a general conceptual representation which is able to account for global memory organization as well.

According to Lehnert, the memory access problem is strictly connected to knowledge acquisition; consequently the model of memory structure which we need to account for nominal compounds must be able to learn from what it reads, and so increase its knowledge. Such a perspective exhibits an interesting evolution from previous models, in that representation systems are no longer seen as static structures but become dynamic organizations which are able to add new information in a learning process. Undoubtedly, such a model is a much closer simulation of the real human process than a static model would be.

That serious differences exist between the two traditions, this much is clear. But how are we to characterize them? and is it possible for them to coexist and be part of an overall enterprise, or are they intrinsically incompatible? In 1982, Barbara Partee sketched two possible answers to these questions: the Separatist position and the Common Goal position.[18] According to the former, the two traditions have different goals, different assumptions and different criteria of adequacy. There is therefore no genuine conflict between them and it may be expected that a complete picture of how language works and is used in communication will emerge by pursuing both enterprises in parallel and completely independently. Putnam, for one, seems to adopt this position in his 1977 paper "Reference and Understanding".[19] In this paper, he says that "the theory of language understanding and the theory of reference and truth have much less to do with one another than many philosophers have assumed" and he offers the following argument: the only viable idea leading to a theory of language understanding is that understanding a language consists entirely in being able to use it. But we already have a model of language use; in an admittedly oversimplified form, it is foreshadowed in the work done by Carnap and Reichenbach.

This is the model of the speaker/hearer as possessing an inductive logic ... a deductive logic, a preference ordering ... and a rule of action. And the better the inductive logic, the better the deductive logic, the more realistic the utility function, the more the behaviour of these creatures will resemble "understanding a language".

The correspondence between words and things, or sentences and states of affairs − in other words, reference and truth − will not come into the picture at all. Not that such a correspondence does not exist, but it has no role to play within the model itself. It will be crucial in explaining the highly interesting phenomenon of the *success* of verbal communication, but this is an entirely different phenomenon from linguistic behaviour itself, which might very well exist even if we had entirely wrong ideas about the world and other speakers in it. Truth and knowledge of truth conditions is not therefore presupposed in understanding a language and we have no reason to hold that truth is prior to meaning or that meaning is to be equated with truth conditions.

Even if one is not convinced by this argument, it certainly has the

---

[18] B. Partee, *op. cit.*

[19] H. Putnam, "Reference and Understanding" reprinted in *Meaning and the Moral Sciences*, London, Routledge and Kegan Paul, 1978.

merit of giving a clear-cut answer to our questions. The Common Goal position, on the other hand, considers cognitive semantics and truth theoretical semantics as parts of a common enterprise, sharing goals and assumptions. It must be admitted, however, that it is not easy to detect any deep similarity in the resulting theories. Partee herself advocated this position conditionally on the feasibility of solving the problems that we sketched above concerning propositional attitudes and semantic competence. Unfortunately, it seems that a solution to these problems still remains to be found. Neither Separatism nor the Common Goal position, however, has any doubt that model-theoretic semantics is an entirely legitimate, if psychologically irrelevant, enteprise. But in recent years a third position seems to have emerged, which might be termed Abandonism, claiming that the whole enterprise of model theoretical semantics should best be abandoned as irrelevant and misconceived from the very beginning. The very notions of truth and reference as conceived within model theory are under heavy attack.

Ray Jackendoff claims that the notion of reference which is of interest to semantics cannot be that concerning an independently existing reality; people have things to talk about only by virtue of having mentally represented them and whatever is not represented is simply not available and thus cannot be referred to in an utterance. What is transferred by verbal means from speaker to hearer is, according to him, an information structure *which is about our own construal of the external world*, not about things as they are in themselves. Accordingly, semantics should mainly be concerned with "what information and processing must be ascribed to an organism to account for its categorization judgment — what is involved in grasping an atomic sentence".[20] It follows from this as an immediate consequence that research on the nature of human mental representation is relevant to semantic theory and is a source of constraints and enrichments for it. One cannot then expect the traditional logical approach to provide any interesting theory of meaning, given that it pays no attention to such constraints.

Furthermore, there are other areas in which formal semantics is not so much wrong as simply silent. For instance, it is not usually considered to be any of its business to establish what kinds of entities there are. Once the universe of discourse has been characterized as any set, over which variables are to range, formal semantics does not bother to introduce distinctions among its denizens. Ontology, in other words, is not viewed as part of semantics. Jackendoff, on the contrary, considers pragmatic anaphora and the behaviour of idioms of identity and difference to be evidence that in the universe of discourse at least the following major ontological categories must be countenanced: places, directions,

---

[20] R. Jackendoff, *Semantics and Cognition*, Cambridge, Mass., M.I.T. Press, 1983, pp. 14-15.

actions, events, manners and amounts. Such entities are not to be thought of as independently existing in Reality — in the world as independent from our cognition — if only because manners, for example, do not exist segregated from the actions of which they are the manners. But they are *psychologically* real, for they are in the world as we construe it.

Reference to the independently existing reality is then at best irrelevant to semantics, according to some critics. But is reference *tout court* needed at all?

This is the crucial question raised by Johnson-Laird in his contribution, which deals extensively with the contrast between model theoretical and cognitive meaning. One aspect of the conflict is in fact the attitude taken with respect to reference; it is, says Johnson-Laird, a decisive objection against most theories in the cognitive tradition — semantic networks, semantic decomposition, meaning postulates — that "they say nothing about how words relate to the world". All they do is to tell how words are related to words, or how sentences can be paraphrased by other sentences; but it is a fallacy — the "symbolic fallacy" — to assume that meaning is merely a matter of relating one set of symbols to another. The meaning of a sentence, what we grasp when it is uttered in particular circumstances can, for example, guide our movements and help us in orienting ourselves in the physical world; but there is nothing in the theories committed to the symbolic fallacy to explain how this could possibly happen, given that they are silent on how words relate to the world.

Even though Johnson-Laird's work is primarily concerned with modelling mental representations and processes and accordingly falls entirely within the cognitive camp, his argument could very well amount to a powerful, if partial, defence of logical semantics — though not in the Fregean form, since he claims that *reference* either determines or interacts with *meaning*, contrary to the one-sided dependence of the former upon the latter posited by Frege. Where logical semantics has gone wrong is in supposing that sentences refer to truth values. The correct picture, according to Johnson-Laird, is rather that sentences refer to states of affairs, which can be modelled in our minds by what he calls "mental models". Truth values arise out of the comparison between mental models and states of affairs. Most of what counts as semantic competence is to be accounted for in terms of mental models.

The critical part of Johnson-Laird's work — namely his rejection of the autonomy of semantics — has been criticized in turn, notably by Yorick Wilks in his contribution to this volume, which refers to a 1981 paper by Johnson-Laird.[21] Wilks points out a similarity between Johnson-Laird's (and Lewis') criticism of the "autonomy of semantics" and Fodor's and Searle's criticism of the "autonomy of syntax". In both

---

[21] P. Johnson-Laird, "Mental Models of Meaning" in Joshi et al. (eds.) *Elements of Discourse Understanding*, Cambridge, Cambridge University Press, 1981.

cases, it is claimed that attachment to real world entities is essential in order to confer meaning upon symbols. Clearly, this raises once again the difficult and much debated question of how syntax and semantics differ (every significant step taken in the theory of meaning seems to force us to reconsider this question as well as the parallel one concerning syntax and semantics on the one hand and pragmatics on the other). But in both cases, according to Wilks, one fails to realize that "symbolic processes can only be brought into contact with other symbolic processes". It is simply illusory that "one can in language, or mental representations, or programs escape from the world of symbols to some formal but nonsymbolic realm that confers significance". Referents in formal semantics cannot themselves be but symbols and both syntax and semantics are within "the autonomy of symbol processing". None of the arguments put forward by Johnson-Laird in favor of "an interactive theory of sense and reference" is accepted as conclusive by Wilks. What is most interesting, however, is his claim to the effect that all the work "reference" should do can already be done entirely within "autonomous semantics", and he takes the work done in A.I. in the last fifteen years – within the decompositional, semantic networks or meaning postulate approaches – to show just that.

Whether or not the case against the autonomy of semantics is won, the notion of mental model cannot easily be dismissed. Even if one does not accept the particular twist Johnson-Laird has given to this notion, it must be admitted that some version of it has a role to play in any cognitive theory of meaning. For another version of the notion, one can for example look at Fauconnier's theory of "mental domains" or "mental spaces". The picture that Fauconnier draws in his contribution (as well as in his recent book, *Mental Spaces*)[22] is appealing to anyone trying to chart the criss-crossing of logically and cognitively oriented theories in semantics in that it singles out a specific level at which cognition enters. According to Fauconnier, "language does not link up directly with a real or metaphysical world; in between takes place an extensive process of mental construction, which does not mirror either the expressions of language responsible for setting it up, or the real world target situations to which it may be intended to apply". It is this intermediate level, where most of the mental construction takes place, which can best be called cognitive; it is distinct from objective content, but it is also at least in part independent from the linguistic structure. Fauconnier is not alone in positing such an intermediate level; Hans Kamp's theory of discourse representation, offering yet another candidate for the role of mental model, must also be mentioned in this connection.[23]

[22] G. Fauconnier, *Mental Spaces*, Cambridge Mass., M.I.T. Press, 1985.
[23] See for example H. Kamp, "Discourse representation and truth" in *Amsterdam Papers on Formal Grammar*, vol. III, Amsterdam 1982.

The attack brought by George Lakoff against logical semantics is much more radical. Not only is the language of first-order logic syntactically unfaithful to natural language, not only is model theoretical semantics insensitive to cognitively important constraints, but the very apparatus of set theory is inappropriate to model the real world. Worse still, objectivist — that is, traditional logical — semantics incorporates a fundamentally wrong way of taking "what human beings are like in the most fundamental sense", for it takes rational thought as the "algorithmic manipulation of arbitrary abstract symbols that are meaningless in themselves but get their meaning by being associated with things in the world". Objectivist semantics holds that meaning is based on reference and truth, that truth consists in a correspondence between symbols and states of affairs in the world and that there is an objectively correct way to associate symbols with things. These philosophical doctrines can stand only if grounded on a suitable (objectivist) metaphysics which guarantees that the world is structured in the appropriate way for those doctrines to hold, and in particular that reality admits of set-theoretical modelling. This is the basis for holding that natural kinds, for example, can be modelled as sets defined by the essential properties shared by their members, which in turn justifies applying "the mathematical apparatus of objectivist cognition — algorithms and models". But natural kinds are simply *not* sets.

It has been somewhat of a commonplace in the past few years to assert that the unitary notion of meaning has been replaced by a number of different and unrelated notions. Meaning has disintegrated and there is no way in sight of putting the pieces back together again to form a unitary picture.

However, this might be after all too gloomy a picture, and one can also claim that some hints towards a re-unification are already in the air. Even more, some of the contributions to the present collection already give some hints as to how a possible new unitary picture might be reconstructed.

As we said before, the main charge brought against model theoretical semantics by these recent attacks is that the notions of truth and reference employed in it do not take any notice of what the human mind clearly contributes to the world as we see it. It is not therefore a mere rejection, as being irrelevant, of the notions of truth and reference, but only of a particular way of construing them. Such a construal amounts to taking sentences as true or false in themselves, depending on how the world is, but independently of us and of our recognizing them as such. As we said above, this is precisely what the Fregean tradition in semantics has taken the objectivity of the notions of meaning, as well as truth and reference, to consist in.

Subjectivism, from this point of view, therefore consists in stressing that no sentence can be true if we cannot recognize it as true, just as no word can refer to any piece of external reality if we do not have criteria to apply so as to see what it refers to. Words are not magically associated with things, so to speak, without our intervention. The evidence we have, or can have, which makes us see that a sentence is true or a word refers to something in the world, enters therefore as an essential ingredient in the fundamental notions of semantics, in the subjectivist perspective. In this sense, subjectivism has little to do with psychologism: it is no more concerned with our individual minds than objectivism is; the evidence and criteria it brings in are the common possession of a community of speakers, variously interacting in a social interchange, and are construed in a normative, not a factual sense.

It seems to us that most of the attacks brought against the logical or truth theoretical tradition in semantics are in fact subjectivist in this sense, and therefore one can claim that what they directly oppose is not so much the formal character of the logical tradition as its objectivist twist. Now, if it could be shown that objectivism is not essential to it, and that a subjectivist theory of meaning can in fact be built which would meet all the logicians' requirements, then many reasons offered for the current conflict would perhaps evaporate. Even the idea of taking the meaning of a linguistic expression as determined by its reference conditions, should no longer grate to the cognitive ear, if reference is understood in the appropriately subjective way. If reference to an independently existing world gives way to reference to "a projected world", i.e., to the world as organized by our (collective) mind, there can be little objection to taking meaning as consisting in the information conveyed about the projected world.

The core of such a subjectivist perspective amounts to the well known doctrines of anti-realism and internalism, argued at length by Michael Dummett and Hilary Putnam.[24] If the suggestion put forward above is viable, then it seems to us that the lively debate between realism and anti-realism which has attracted the attention of many philosophers since the beginning of the Seventies can now bear fruit in a much wider area than the one in which it was originally confined.

Umberto Eco's contribution to this issue presents a series of problems which have been considered from a different perspective in the other articles. As will be seen, these differences are evident not so much in the conclusions which are reached but rather in the background disciplines and cultural tradition from which Eco's article springs. It may thus be necessary to present here a brief introduction to this European tradition in order that the article may be more readily understood in its context

---

[24] Dummett's anti-realism has been argued for in a number of papers, notably those included in *Truth and Other Enigmas*, Duckworth, London, 1980; a thorough presentation of Putnam's internalism can be found in his *Meaning and the Moral Sciences*, quoted above, and in *Reasons, Truth and History*, Cambridge, Cambridge University Press, 1981.

by those who come rather from the Anglo-American tradition which has so far provided the main point of reference for the articles in this issue. Such an introduction will also demonstrate the many points which the two traditions have in common and reveal numerous points of convergence between the European semiotic tradition, represented by Eco, and a large sector of the research being carried out in language within the cognitive field. Such points of convergence are far from coincidental.

Semiotics is essentially a European discipline which moves off from several branches of Continental Philosophy and Linguistics. Its relationship to Structuralism is close and is very important here especially in its strictly linguistic form which starts from the founding work of Saussure and covers the tradition up to Hjelmslev's glossematics. However, it is by no means only Linguistics which has been profoundly influenced by structuralist methods. Lévi-Strauss'. work on myth in the field of Anthropology and Vladimir Propp's seminal work on the narrative structure of folk tales opened up an extremely wide and complex field of research in which attention to both the linguistic level and lexical semantics are integrally bound up with the analysis of narrative structures and the textual component.[25]

Structural Semantics has always held as its central interest of research the definition of the relationships between individual lexical items rather than the study of sentences and their truth conditions. In this way, it has remained apart from the more analytical Anglo-American tradition. Starting from Saussure's early studies, this approach has in particular elaborated various conceptual schemes designed to distinguish and classify semantic relationships between lexical items both within the same syntactic categories and from different syntactic categories.

The value of each lexical item is determined by the position the item holds in the *language* system, or, to put it another way, by the network of relationships which the term has with other items. (The idea of links between paradigmatic semantic relationships and syntagmatic semantic relationships is at the root of the concept of a semantic or lexical field. This concept has been developed by several linguists beginning in the 1920s.)

Both the idea of decomposition and semantic network models were implicit in the structuralist approach right from its beginnings in the early years of this century. However, many of the other ideas which have had major influence on the cognitive side are also to be found in the European Structuralist tradition. The problem of categorization, first studied by Gestalt theory in relation to the perception of forms, has been broad-

---

[25] One of the most interesting developments of this approach has been Greimas' theory of Semiotics. See A.J. Greimas and J. Courtés, *Sémiotique. Dictionnaire raisonné de la théorie du langage I, II*, Paris, Hachette, 1979 and 1986.

ly developed by the European semiotic approach. In particular, the function of categories in structuring the world we perceive has been extended to cover not only perceived data, but the entire organization of meaning, seen as the product of both a cultural and social process.

Within this perspective, the rôle of the subject who observes and describes the world through language is central. There can be no external objective reality which is independent of the activity of the subject who proposes it and represents it through language. In the same way, there can be no objective meaning based on an objectively determined relationship between language and the world.

The importance given to the question of subjectivity in relation to language is one of the most interesting and characteristic aspects of European semiotics and stems perhaps from the more important rôle played by the notion of subjectivity in the Continental philosophical tradition as compared with Anglo-American empiricism. This consideration has led to several important developments. From the more strictly linguistic point of view, Benveniste's theory of *énonciation* which was later treated also by other scholars, has been particularly noteworthy.[26] In more general terms, the problem of subjectivity is inextricably linked to the problem of interpretation which is a central theme of Hermeneutics. Semiotics has confronted this problem from its own perspective and has re-elaborated it within the context of its own methodology.

Eco's semiotic theory thus forms part of this tradition but adds to it the philosophical contribution of Charles Sanders Peirce with especial reference to his theory of *unlimited semiosis*. This theory confronts the problem of interpretation of the sign (or of the nature of meaning) by means of the continuous, infinite and circular reference to other signs which thus form its interpretants. This solution gives rise to results which are particularly close to many of the conclusions drawn in the area of cognitivism. It has many similarities, for example, to the polemic set up between Johnson-Laird (and, by implication, Lewis) on the one hand and Wilks on the other. In an interpretative semiotics such as that represented by Eco, the fact that each semantic representation is simply a translation into another symbolic system, far from being seen as a limit to the model, becomes rather an essential and intrinsic part of the way in which language works as a semiotic process.

The attack on the "logical" tradition which is made by several of the authors present in this issue also offers certain interesting points of contact with the basic theoretical assumptions of the semiotic tradition. The "circular" nature of the semiotic process which prevents language from being "anchored" to the world by truth values has already been mentioned. What is more, the same kind of arguments which led analytic

---

[26] See E. Benveniste, *Problems in General Linguistics*. I (1966), Coral Gables, University of Miami Press, 1971, and *Problèmes de linguistique générale* II, Paris, Gallimard, 1974.

philosophers to deny that meanings can be given as sets of necessary and sufficient conditions is also at the root of the rejection, in the Semiotic quarter, of any distinction between dictionaries and encyclopaedias, a not unwelcomed conclusion to many analytic philosophers.

In a model proposed by Eco,[27] there is no need, except for local instrumental necessities, to distinguish analytical components or purely linguistic components from the larger groupings of our encyclopaedic knowledge of the world. For all these components are present to an equal degree in the process of understanding which language activates. The refusal to make theoretical distinctions between dictionary knowledge and encyclopaedia knowledge is analogous to the way in which Artificial Intelligence deals with the problem of knowledge representation. Here too, the distinction between world-based knowledge and language-based knowledge is not central. The problem is in fact that of representing the whole heterogeneous range of types of knowledge which are linked to a certain linguistic expression and which enable the understanding of it even in different contexts. In other words, the model must be able to take account of the entire complex background of knowledge which we habitually take for granted and which plays a central rôle in the way in which we understand and interpret texts. In this way, Semiotics, Hermeneutics and Artificial Intelligence are very close in their common concern to connect lexical meaning to textual interpretation, as well as in their recognition of the necessity which this implies of representing the whole range of the different types of knowledge involved in the interpretative process. Whether this background knowledge be called encyclopaedia, knowledge basis or pre-understanding makes no difference whatsoever.

It is thus by no means a coincidence that in the A.I. community the problem of background has recently been explicitly linked to the hermeneutic perspective and to the European philosophical tradition.[28]

It should at this point be clear how the idea of a semantic theory within the semiotic approach, differs from logical semantics. In the semiotic perspective, the concept of truth as an "objective" correspondence to a real or possible world is not considered useful or important.

Meaning is the result of a complex social process of production and is a cultural unit, according to Eco's definition, the representation of which may be understood only through reference to other cultural units according to the process of infinite transcoding which is *unlimited* semiosis.

It is noticeable that psychological issues are given very little importance in the semiotic model where attention is rather focused on the

---

[27] U. Eco, *A Theory of Semiotics*, Bloomington, Indiana University Press, 1976.
[28] T. Winograd and F. Flores, *Understanding Computers and Cognition*, Norwood, N.J., Ablex, 1986.

socio-cultural nature of the semiotic process and on the communicative function of language. In this sense, the encyclopaedia is not a psychological concept and does not represent the (actual or ideal) semantic competence of an individual speaker, it is rather the cultural repertoire of a given society, its historical memory. The semiotic encyclopaedia model is based on the conviction that there can be no meaning, or language or culture outside and independently of the community in which the speakers are defined and exist.

Jon Barwise

On the Circumstantial Relation between Meaning and Content*

The Locus of Meaning

Where *is* meaning anyway, in the mind of the speaker or author, or in the world shared by a speaker and his audience and an author and his readers? There would seem to be an almost irresolvable conflict in the facts of language use. On the one hand, there is the fact of linguistic communication, people conveying information to other people by telling them things, and by writing things down. For many of us, much of what we know about the world we learned in just this way. On the other hand, for any given sentence or text, there is, in general, a wide range of things it could mean, with the "right" one being some function of what the author means, and so of something only the author has access to. Some (like Hirsch 1967) would say the correct meaning of any text is the author's meaning. (Others (like Mailloux 1982) deny that there is any such thing as the correct meaning at all.)

The world oriented tradition in semantics, from Tarski on, has focused on the public aspect of meaning by trying to identify the meaning of a sentence or text with its truth conditions, the conditions on the actual world that are needed to insure its truth (Davidson 1967 and Montague 1974, e.g.). The psychological tradition, by contrast, has focused on the private aspect by trying to identify meaning with an intrinsically meaningful mental representation of the "logical form" of the expression (Fodor 1975 or Jackendoff 1983, e.g.). The speech act school (Searle 1969, e.g.) has focused on yet a third aspect of language: the fact that utterances are actions and have consequences like other actions. This tradition sees meaning as stemming from these effects of speech acts.

Nowhere is this conflict more keenly felt than in the theory of literary interpretation. This is not surprising, since both the public and the private aspects are vital to understanding how literature works at all. As applied to the meaning of a rich and subtle fictional text, worldly truth conditions are not a very plausible candidate for meaning. And so within this field one frequently encounters the claim that the meaning of a text is simply whatever it was that the author meant, or some representation of these authorial intentions. But the best intentions do not constitute

* I would like to thank Paul Schacht for many interesting discussions of the relation between philosophical theories of meaning and the interpretive enterprise. The preparation of this paper was supported by an award from the System Development Foundation.

literature; they must lead to a text which honors the intentions in an appropriate way, that is, a text whose meaning respects those intentions. But this brings us full circle. We need an independent characterization of the meaning of a text to measure against the author's intentions.

This basic dilemma is nicely illustrated by Borges' famous story "Pierre Menard, Author of the *Quixote*". Recall that Menard rewrote portions of Cervantes' *Don Quixote*, but did so faithfully: "His admirable intention was to produce a few pages which would coincide — word for word and line for line — with those of Miguel de Cervantes." (p. 66) In this he succeeded, through much effort, but in his real intention he failed. He came to see that his work meant something quite different. "Cervantes's text and Menard's are verbally identical, but the second is almost infinitely richer. (More ambiguous, his distractors will say, but ambiguity is richness.)" (p. 69) From the worldly perspective, this seems a logical fantasy, since the two texts (or text-instances) are instances of the same text type, with a fixed meaning, as given by the rules of Spanish. So they must mean the same thing. However, the narrator of Borges' story claims that the two texts mean quite different things. For example, truisms from the pen of Cervantes are astounding claims from the pen of the 20th century Menard. Also, from the authorial intention perspective, Borges' story makes perfect sense, since Menard's intentions were merely to copy the master, while the master's intentions were those of a genius.

When we turn from the big picture to the details of a semantical theory, a different aspect of the dilemma appears. Since Frege, one of the challenges used to judge any semantic theory is that of accounting for the productivity of language. How is it that we can produce meaningful expressions that have never before been uttered? And how do we explain the meaning of a new expression being whatever it is? How is this meaning related to the meanings of the parts of which it is made?

World oriented approaches to meaning typically tackle the problem of productivity by assigning basic meanings to basic words, and associating composition rules that construct the meanings of wholes from the meanings of their parts. But this so-called compositional approach always presupposes some theory of syntax. One seems to need a theory of sentences and their parts, and how they can be put together, to get the story started. This makes the results terribly brittle. Consider the beginning of *Riddley Walker*, a novel about interpretation:

On my naming day when I come 12 I gone front spear and kilt a wyld board he parbly ben the las wyld pig on the Bundel Downs any how there hadnt ben none for a long time befor him nor I aint looking to see none agen. (Hoban 1980)

Compositional accounts fare badly with even mild variations from grammatical usage. Truly creative uses of language like the above are completely beyond the pale. What meaning would any such account give to the verb phrase *gone front spear*, let alone this whole sentence? And even if it could assign truth conditions to the sentence, how could any such account even begin to tell us how this string of characters achieves the effect of drawing us into the dark future age inhabited by Riddley Walker?

In this essay I reflect on some of these issues in meaning and mind, and on their relation to the activity of literary interpretation. Only if we can get clear about the basic structure of meaning, and its relation to mind and world, can we hope to understand the nature of interpretation. My reflections are taken from the perspective of situation semantics, a semantical theory expounded in Barwise and Perry 1983, hereinafter referred to as *S&A*. This theory grew out of the worldly tradition, but also out of dissatisfaction with the tools provided by that tradition for the analysis of meaning. This dissatisfaction was not rooted in its inadequacies for a theory of interpretation, but in simpler (though related) considerations having to do with propositional attitude reports. So, while Perry and I are not literary critics, I think that the tools provided by situation semantics begin to clear the way for a common grounds for the various camps. It seems to me that the basic dilemma shows that neither approach has come to grips with perhaps the most basic fact about meaning: the circumstantial relationship between meaning and content. Only if we understand this can we hope to sort out the dilemma in a way that accounts for all the facts.

From Meaning to Content

Let us look at an extremely simple example of the use of language to convey information. *A* says to *B*, "I am a philosopher". Part of the dilemma discussed above rests in a confusion caused by the meaning of *meaning*. In this example there are at least three things that English identifies with the word *meaning*. There is the sentence *I am a philosopher*, a meaningful sentence of English. Then there is the event of *A*'s using it to say something to *B*, a specific action which means something. And finally there is whatever it is that *A* means. These are three related but distinct things, and so must be kept separate in any theory of meaning. Let us here use "meaning" for the first, that is, for the meaning attached to sentences and other symbols *S*. Thus meanings are to be associated with reasonably abstract objects and can be expected to be rather abstract themselves. In particular, we cannot expect such a sentence to mean anything much at all about any particular speaker, like our *A* above. If a person *A* uses a sentence or other symbol *S* in particular circumstances *c*, let us use "content" for what that particular event means.[1] In our ex-

---

[1] What we here call the content of an utterance was called its "interpretation" in *S&A*. Sadly, that use of "interpretation" is somewhat at odds with the use of the term in the analysis of literary texts, as we will see below.

ample, we may suppose that the content is that the speaker A is a philosopher. Finally, let us use "user meaning" for what the user A of S in c actually meant, that is, for what it was he intended to convey.

Consider *Hamlet* and what it might be said to mean. There is the actual text, a linguistic object of English. As such, it has a certain meaning. This text was presumably written by Shakespeare but would have had the same meaning if it had been written by Bacon.[2] But consider a particular performance of the play. It too will mean something, or, on our terminology, have content. Different performances have different contents, depending on the circumstances of the production: gestures, staging, intonation, and all the facets of the actors' and director's art. And then there is whatever it was that Shakespeare actually meant, something which the content of a particular performance may or may not approximate. This is author's meaning.

For a more mundane example of the difference between meaning and content, suppose that after A says "I am a philosopher" to B, B then says to C, referring to A, "She is a philosopher". C then says to A, "So you are a philosopher". The sentences each person uses are different. Furthermore, the sentences have different meanings. But *something* is the same, namely what each of these statements meant, or indicated, about A, namely *that A is a philosopher*. This claim, some abstract property of the three utterance situations, is what we mean by their (common) content. It is this common content that is preserved throughout the episode, and there is simply no way to understand the episode without recourse to this content. Intuitively, each utterance situation s has the content it does in virtue of two factors, the sentence S used and the circumstances c in which it is used. Thus, let us introduce a little notation and write $C(S, c)$ for this content, whatever it is. So the three distinct sentences S_1, S_2, S_3 used in the three distinct circumstances c_1, c_2, c_3, all have the same content, that is, $C(S_1, c_1) = C(S_2, c_2) = C(S_3, c_3)$.

Just what is this content $C(S, c)$? It is what one might call a realist proposition: the proposition P that A is a philosopher at the time t of the assertion. In *S&A* we characterized this proposition P with an abstract object that classifies the way some real situation would have to be in order for the proposition P to be true. We represented possible facts with ordered sequences and possible situations with sets of possible facts. These possible situations we dubbed "courses of events". In the simple case here, we could get by with a single possible fact, represented by the set-theoretic quadruple

$$< t, \text{philosopher}, A; 1 >,$$

---

[2] I set aside the question as to whether it would have meant the same thing had it been written by a monkey pounding randomly at a typewriter, or by the accidental motions of the waves on the beach. I think there is a real issue as to whether a monkey or a wave could produce anything we should call even a sentence of English, let alone *Hamlet*. This seems to me the real moral of Knapp and Michaels' example in Knapp and Michaels (1982).

where t is the time of the utterance. This represents the type of situation in which A is a philosopher at time t.[3] The constituents of this type are the real individual A, the real time t, and the property of being a philosopher. In order for the proposition $C(S, c)$ to be true, there would have to be a real situation of this type. More generally, we can identify a propositional content P of the form $C(S, c)$ with a type of situation, and say that the proposition is true if there is a real situation of this type.[4]

Simple as our little example was, it nicely illustrates some aspects of the basic dilemma. First, notice that if we vary either factor S or c, the propositional content $C(S, c)$ changes. For example, had B said "I am a philosopher" rather than "She is a philosopher", he would have said something with a different content, namely *that B is a philosopher*, represented by $<t, philosopher, B; 1>$. And B's statement would have had this content regardless of what his intentions were. The rules of English just would not permit him to say something about A with this sentence.

More to the point, changes also occur if the sentence is held fixed but the circumstances of an utterance are varied: for example, if C had used just the sentence he did, but in addressing B rather than A, the content of his statement would have been different, in this case *that B is a philosopher*. In this case something akin to speaker meaning plays a role in determining the content of the utterance. If C utters the sentence "You are a philosopher" in the presence of both A and B, there may be nothing observable about C that determines whom he is addressing, and so nothing observable that determines exactly what the content of his utterance is.

The underdetermination of propositional content exhibited here does not tempt us to posit distinct meanings for the sentence *You are a philosopher*. Rather, it requires us to recognize that the meaning of the sentence underdetermines the content of any particular statement made with it. The approach to meaning in *S&A* is to take the meaning of a *sentence S* to be a relation $[\![S]\!]$ between those circumstances c in which it can be used, on the one hand, and the situations s of the described type, on the other. We can relate this to the above notation by means of the equivalence:

$$c [\![S]\!] s \text{ if and only if } s \text{ is of type } C(S, c).$$

In our example, the different possible contents force us to recognize that there is a fact of the matter about whom C is addressing, A or B, that plays a key role in determining the content of his assertion. This fact is crucial to interpreting the utterance correctly, that is, to getting

---

[3] The sequence $\langle t, philosopher, A; 0 \rangle$ represents the type of situation in which A is not a philosopher at time t.

[4] This oversimplifies things in ways pointed out in *S&A*, 159-161, 319, but it is good enough to make the points here.

at its true content. But since there is nothing in the sentence itself that specifies which person it is, it must be a part of the circumstance situation c. Thus, in the notation of $S\&A$, what matters here is whether $\langle t,\ addressing,\ C,\ A;\ 1\rangle$ or $\langle t,\ addressing,\ C,\ B;\ 1\rangle$ is a fact of c. If $\langle t,\ addressing,\ C,\ x;\ 1\rangle$ is a fact of c, then the content will be that x is a philosopher at time t, $\langle t,\ philosopher,\ x;\ 1\rangle$.

As we said, circumstantial facts like whom the speaker is addressing are *akin* to, and closely related to, speaker or author meaning. However, people make mistakes. We often say something other than what we mean to say. Such examples show that the content of an utterance is not, in general, accurately determined by speaker meaning. For example, in our above example with C uttering "You are a philosopher" in the presence of both A and B, what matters is really whom C is addressing, not whom he *intends* to be addressing. If C is addressing B, then the content of his assertion is that B is a philosopher, even if the thinks he is talking to B's twin brother B' and intends to be making a claim about him. In cases where an author's intentions are not honored by his actions in an appropriate way, there is simply a divergence between what the author meant and what he said.

Let us return to the simple case, though, where C says "You are a philosopher" in the presence of A and B, and where he addresses the person he intends to address. It may be that there is no observable manifestation of exactly who this happens to be. There is a certain respect in which C is to be faulted, perhaps, in not making it clearer to his audience just what it was he was claiming. But there does not seem to be any reason to say that there can be no fact of the matter. After all, we can always say "Whom did you mean?" and C can tell us. But then what difference would it make if C dropped dead before telling us whom he meant. There would still have been the same fact of the matter.

We have been ignoring an ambiguity in the sentence *You are a philosopher* stemming from the fact that the word *philosopher* is actually ambiguous. To some it means a certain odd, academic profession. To many, however, it means one with a certain attitude toward life which allows him to meet adversity with equanimity. So there are really (at least) two distinct properties that speakers of English can pick out with this noun. This is entirely analogous to the fact that there are lots of people you can refer to with *you, he,* or *John*. So far from invalidating what we have been saying, it simply points out another way that the circumstances are crucial in getting from the sentence to its content. A standard use of *You are a philosopher* has to use the word *philosopher* in one of a narrowly prescribed set of ways. There may be be nothing observable to tell us whether it is being used in a standard way, or, if it is, which of the properties it can pick out actually is being picked out.

The Structure of Circumstances

Traditional world oriented theories of meaning have usually assumed that there are symbols S and the thing symbolized, denoted, or designated say $D(S)$. The view of meaning presented here denies that meaning *ever* works this way. It takes the *relation* between circumstances and content as being at the essence of meaning. Since most attention in semantics is paid to the content, it is worthwhile sorting out some of the various roles that facts from the circumstances can play in determining content.

Circumstances can help determine the propositional content C (S, c) of a statement s, consisting of a sentence or text S used in circumstances c, in countless ways. We can partition these contributions into four importantly different kinds by making a couple of informal definitions. First, various features of S are relevant in that they help "articulate" the content. In the case where S is a spoken sentence, these will include things like the words used, but also things like intonation and stress. Call the features of S that help articulate the content the *structural features* of S. Secondly, we need a notion of "subject matter" of the content C (S, c). By this we mean simply anything that the proposition is about. In terms of the mathematical theory in *S&A*, this is anything that is a constituent of one of the possible facts used to characterize the proposition. For this reason, let us call them the *constituents* of the content.

When we speak of the circumstances c of a statement s, we have in mind just those circumstances that help determine the propositional content, of course. Our informal definitions allow us to carve these circumstances up into four (possibly overlapping) parts:

— the part that contributes *articulated constituents* of the content,
— the part that contributes *unarticulated constituents*,
— the part that contributes *articulated non-constituents*, and
— the part that contributes *unarticulated non-constituents*.

Let's look at some examples related to our quote from Hoban to get a feel for this four-way division.[5]

Articulated constituents: The first part of the circumstances, the part determining the articulated constituents, is frequently called the *context*. In general, it determines things like the interpretation of "I", "here", "now", "today", and deictic uses of tense, demonstratives, and pronouns. In our Hoban example, the context contributes the speaker (the narrator, not the author) with "I". This opening sentence establishes a new set of circumstances, so that when the next sentence begins "He dit make the groun shake ...", the boar is an articulated constituent of its content, due to the deictic use of "he".

---

[5] There are many subtleties here that I am glossing over, subtleties gone into in Barwise (1986) and Perry (1986).

Unarticulated constituents: In this category we find things like the location where it is claimed that it is raining in an utterance "It is raining", where there is no constituent that contributes the location in the way it does with "It is raining here". In our example, the rest of the hunting party is an unarticulated constituent of the content. We know it's part of the content from the phrase "... I gone front spear ..."; you can't become front spear unless there are some other spears to be in front of. There is also the spear itself, since "front spear" refers to a position in the hunting party, not to the weapon.

Articulated non-constituents: When B said of A "She is a philosopher", we learn that A is female, but it is not part of the content of what A said. It is articulated by "she" but it is not a constituent. In this category there are a variety of things that were important in *S&A*, though we did not have this distinction in mind at the time. For example, there are the resource situations needed to determine the referent of a use of a noun phrase like "the boar". One might argue that this is where one would find the fact that the referent of a use of "John is missing" is named John. In our present example, we find the narrator's present time t used to locate his actions in a time before t with the use of "gone" and "hadnt ben". It also includes the narrator in the use of "my naming day."

Unarticulated non-constituents: Finally, in the fourth category we find a host of standard background assumptions that play a role in the determination of content. For example, in order for "my naming day" to pick up a referent which is contributed to the content (as an articulated constituent), there must be background conventions in force, in the narrator's world, whereby people have naming days. The background convention is an unarticulated non-constituent provided by the narrator's circumstances. The next phrase "when I come 12" suggests that these naming days are related to birthdays, but just what a naming day is is not part of the content of this sentence. In the next paragraph this day is referred to as "the day I become a man", which provides us with yet more information about this background convention. We learn all this without the convention itself ever being part of the subject matter.

Whether or not something is part of the content, or part of the background circumstances varies from utterance to utterance, since utterances are actions that can change what is in the circumstances to exploit. This is one of the main ways that ambiguity is avoided. Consider the underdetermination of content by meaning with the sentence "I killed a man with a spear". This sentence is ambiguous, in that it can be used to describe two quite different types of situations, one in which the speaker used a spear to kill a man, the other in which the speaker killed a man who had a spear. Typical compositional approaches to semantics require us to interpret two different syntactic structures to obtain these two contents; one where the phrase *with a spear* modifies the verb phrase *killed a man*, the other where it modifies the noun phrase *a man*.

Locating ambiguity in the syntax seems to get things completely backwards in a case like this. After all, it is the content that counts, and the speaker can exploit circumstances in subtle ways. If the above were a response to "Did you ever use anything but a club to kill with?" it would have had one content. If it were in response to "Did you ever kill an armed man?" it would have had another. The previous utterance sets up an unarticulated non-constituent which helps determine the content of the use in question. While there are technical difficulties to overcome in setting up a formal theory so that such circumstantial information can play its proper role, there is no obvious conceptual difficulty in thinking of things this way.

We are now in a position to summarize the relation between meaning, content, and circumstances. However, there is an important missing parameter. In general, just what content a statement has depends on more than the sentence used and the circumstances in which it is used. It also depends on the shared conventions R of the language community of which it is a part. This is so obvious that it might seem to go without saying, but it is worth making explicit. In working out a semantic theory, it is exactly these relations that one is trying to make explicit. If the conventional constraints of English were different than they are, the content of A's utterance "I am a philosopher" might have been that Rome is the capital of Italy.

There are obvious reasons for needing to make the parameter R explicit. For one thing, these conventions can change over time. If we interpret Jane Austen using the conventions of modern English, we will be surprised by the places where her characters choose to "make love". The change here is not in text or circumstances, but in the shared conventions of English.

Much of *S&A* was devoted to an account of these conventional relations, which we dubbed constraints, and to showing that they underwrite meaning quite generally, not just of language, but the meaning we find in the world about us, both natural and conventional. We saw how they could all be seen as similar to sentence meaning, if only in that they were determined by relations R between types of situations.

A very important property of conventional constraints R is that they must be *mutual*, or shared (Lewis 1969). They must mutually bind all the parties to the convention in order to be successful communication channels between agents. Consider a case of two agents, say A and B, who share a convention R used to communicate information. In order for this to work, it is necessary that both parties know of the convention R, of course, but more is necessary. This knowledge of R must be mutual knowledge. That is (following Clark and Marshall 1981), there needs to be a real situation s such that (i) both A and B know the facts of s, (ii) among these facts is the constraint R, but (iii) also among the facts of

s are the facts that A knows the facts of s and that B knows the facts of s. From this assumption, it typically follows that A knows that B knows of R, B knows that A knows of R, and so forth.[6] The consequences are needed to see how agents can use such conventions to affect others in the way they intend.

Let us now indicate the relation between symbol S, content P, circumstances c, and conventional constraints R by means of the equation:

$$(\dagger) \qquad\qquad C_R(S, c) = P.$$

This equation does not tell us much about exactly *how* the four parameters are related. That will be a complicated story depending on the structure of the various ingredients. It does make explicit, though, that we have one equation in which there are four mutually dependent parameters. However, the way we have set it out might be a bit misleading, since it focuses on the determination of content by the other factors. Important as this is, it is only part of the story, and a misleading part in many ways.

To see the main point, it might be useful to consider another case of such an equation. Consider the equation that relates the distance d one has traveled at time t, at an average speed s and starting time t_0:

$$(\ddagger) \qquad\qquad s\,(t - t_0) = d.$$

It is a mistake to think of this as an equation that only determines d as a function of the other three parameters. Rather, it simply expresses a relationship between all four parameters. This can be used in lots of different ways. For example, if you know how far you have gone and at what speed, then you can figure out how long you have been travelling, $(t - t_0)$, but not what time it is, or when you started. However, given either of the latter two, you can determine the other. Or if you know that the trip took two hours and that it is not yet past noon but that you left no sooner than 10 A.M., then you can figure out that you must have left at exactly 10, and that it is now noon. In other words, you can sometimes combine partial information about all the values to come up with complete information about the values, since they are mutually constrained by ($\ddagger$).

This is the way to think about the semantical equation ($\dagger$). It tells one that the four parameters are mutually constrained. Partial information about any gives you partial information about all. And sometimes partial information about more than one can add up to total information about them all. This basic idea is terribly simple but also terribly impor-

---

[6] This property of conventional constraints was missed in *S&A*, in two senses. First, we did not fully realize its importance. Second, the formal set-theoretic machinery used in *S&A* does not allow the modeling of such circular situations. For more on this, see Barwise and Perry (1985), Barwise (1985a, b).

tant to understanding the relation of meaning, content, circumstance, and convention in language.

Once one understands the basic semantic equation (†), a lot of the puzzles about language disappear. In particular, one is no longer tempted to think that all the possible information one can extract from a statement is somehow part of its content. Information about each of the parameters in the equation gives information about all the others. The idea that all the information is part of the content is what Perry and I called the Fallacy of Misplaced Information.

The Nature of Interpretation

How far can these simple observations carry us as we move from the relation between the meaning and content of simple declarative sentences like *I am a philosopher* to understanding the meaning of literary texts and its relation to the interpretation of such texts? The answer, of course, depends on what one is after. If one is after a view of language that accounts for the facts, both facts about the use of language in successful interpersonal interaction, as well as the dependence of content on facts that are not given by linguistic structure (including intrapersonal facts), then it goes a fair ways.

The basic distinctions from above all have textual counterparts. Just as there is a crucial distinction between a sentence S and a statement made with it, that is, the use of S in particular circumstances c, so too there is a crucial distinction between a text T as a type of linguistic object, and a text together with its historical, embedding circumstances. This is the basic point made by Borges' Menard. The conventions of language assign a meaning $[\![T]\!]$ to the text, but it only makes sense to ask for the content $C(T, c)$ of the embedded text. Since there is no verbal distinction (of the sentence/statement variety) between texts as types, and historically embedded text instances, it is often completely unclear which are under discussion in debates of the meaning of a text.

Similarly, we saw that there was a difference between the actual content of a statement, on the one hand, and knowing that one has correctly interpreted the statement, on the other. Similarly with a text. The impossibility of knowing that one has gotten at the actual content of a text does not in and of itself mean that there is no such thing. It just means that we can't be sure if we have discovered it. But this is just part of human condition in general, and is not specific to interpretation. There is a big difference between knowing some fact f and knowing one knows f.

We saw that in a discourse, one utterance contributes in subtle ways to the circumstances in place later, the circumstances that help determine the content of a later utterance. This too is vital with an extended text. One part of the text can articulate a set of facts or even establish conventional constraints that are then exploited later as unarticulated non-constituents.

This much being said, though, one also has to admit that there are many differences between ordinary spoken language and the use of language in literature. First, let us consider the move from the spoken language to the written, just in the case of single sentences. Suppose you get a postcard on which is written the sentence S: "I am now a philosopher". This sentence has a certain meaning $[\![S]\!]$. It was written on a certain date t, by a certain person x, in various circumstances. The content is $\langle t, p, x; 1 \rangle$, that x had a certain property p on t. How can you determine the content? Well, you may be able to read the postmark. And you might be able to recognize the handwriting. And if the picture on the back were of Hume, you figure out which property the author had in mind. But you might not be able to figure any or all of this out. There is nothing at odds between there being perfectly determinate answers to each of these questions, and there simply being no way to determine what those answers are. Only a very confused understanding of the relation between meaning and the world would predict otherwise.

In ordinary verbal discourse, one can (with some forgivable over-simplification for the purposes of contrast) think of three of these parameters as being outside the control of the speaker. That is, the conventions R of language are given, the speaker and listener share certain circumstances c, and the speaker has a certain propositional content P he wants to convey. His task is to find an expression S that satisfies the basic equation (†). The task for the listener, then, is different. He is given values of R, c, and S, and needs to determine P. In our postcard example, all the addressee is given is R and S. This establishes a relation between c and P, and detective work may uncover additional partial information about both, perhaps enough so that the values are determined. For example, if you knew from the handwriting that the card was from either B or C, but you know that B has been wanting to become a philosopher, but that C is constitutionally unable to tolerate philosophy, you might correctly infer that the card was from B, and so has the content that B is a philosopher.

An author approaching a work of fiction has much greater freedom than someone using language to convey information. Indeed, all four parameters in the equation (†) are, to a large extent, at the author's beck and call. He can change any or all, as long as the basic semantic equation (†) is satisfied (though the more he tampers with R, the less chance he has of being understood).

In the first place, the subject matter P is clearly up to the author. It is his tale to tell, whether it be the tale of Don Quixote or that of Riddley Walker. And the type of situation described does not have to be realized by any real situation, past or future. Second, but perhaps more important, is the fact that the author can deliberately obscure his own historical embedding circumstances, more or less totally replacing them with distinct narrative circumstances: a narrator, from a different time, place, culture, and so on. This is obvious in the case of fiction told in the first person, as with Hoban's narrator, Riddley Walker, but it is not uncommon even when there is no first person narrator.

Third, the author can to some extent modify the conventional constraints in force; say by positing background conventions involving naming days. The most blatant example of this, however, is where the author uses a regional dialect, or even creates a new dialect. Hoban uses an original dialect of English full of odd misuses of current scientific terms to tell us that the narrator's circumstances are those of a future dark age. More subtle effects are achieved by deliberately adopting a particular set of literary and moral conventions. There are clear limits here, imposed by the requirement that conventions must be shared to be successful channels for communication. For example, some readers find Hoban's English and other conventions too far from their own to be followed. However, ($\dagger$) helps out here, too. By the time one is a few pages into the novel, one has learned enough about this dialect to understand most of what is being said, and by the time one begins the novel a second time, one follows without difficulty.

Last but not least, of course, the author can choose his actual text. It is only the text that we can hope to have complete information about. And even there we are faced with the vagaries of publication: whims of editor, typesetters, printer, censor, and others come between the author and his reader.

Facing a text, one is confronted by many problems. What does the text mean as a piece of language? What is its content, given the author's circumstances? What did the author actually mean? How faithful is the former to the latter? How does the author attempt to convey the latter? These are all issues of interpretation. If we conflate them all with meaning, and that with content, then it will indeed appear to be a hopeless thicket, beyond the reach of any semantical theory. However, if we avoid the fallacy of misplaced information, things look less hopeless. They all become aspects of a single question, perhaps the basic question of interpretation:[7] Why is the text what it is? How does this text mutually constrain the other parameters to achieve its effect?

The reader of a literary text S is faced with one equation in three unknowns: R, c, and P. Naturally, there is seldom a unique solution to this equation. The task of the interpeter is to use partial information about the unknowns to mutually narrow the range of possible values. The interpreter is concerned not so much with pinpointing the actual

---

[7] Schacht 1985, harking back to Empson, argues that this is the defining question of literary interpretation.

content of the work, but with discovering how the possible values of all three parameters depend on one another, and how the range of values has been achieved by the author's art. About this much of the text's meaning, there can be a fact of the matter, something for the critic to discover.

How might one go about discovering this relationship? One way is to try out various values for some of the parameters, and see what the consequences are. This is the way one always tries to determine a "law". Look at a bunch of solutions, and interpolate the simplest law that makes sense of the data. In physics, this gathering of data is experimentation. In literary interpretation, the laboratory is the critic's imagination. One imagines different contents and circumstances, say, and figures out what sort of conventional constraints would balance the equation.

The basic tension in the theory of interpretation is this conflict between invention and discovery (Schacht 1985). Is one discovering the meaning of the text, or inventing it? On this view of meaning, the answer is "Both". One invents possible values for the parameters in an effort to discover the meaning of the text, in much the way that a chemist does experiments to discover some natural law.

In looking for solutions to the equation ($\dagger$), it is important to remember that the parameter R is constrained to range over shared conventions, that is, over conventions that are mutually known to the reader and his listener. Of course, to some extent the author can invent conventions and have them come to be shared, by using them, relying on ($\dagger$) to enforce the shared quality. It is in missing the importance of the mutuality of conventions that a critic like Mailloux goes wrong, when he thinks that the critic can invent his own conventions for the interpretation of a text.[8]

Mental Representation and Author Meaning

We have a loose end on our hands. We began by distinguishing three forms of meaning, what we termed meaning, content, and speaker (or author) meaning. Except for showing that they are distinct, we have said very little about the relation of author meaning to either of the former. To do this, we must turn to the second half of the topic for this collection of essays on meaning and mental representation.

The first question about mental representation, of course, is whether there are such things as mental representations. The answer to this depends on just what one means by a mental representation. It seems obvious that minds do have the ability to represent situations, real and otherwise. Indeed, it seems relatively unproblematic that there are men-

---

[8] See Schacht 1985.

tal states, and that these mental states do indeed represent situations in the world, as well as situations that do not exist. That is, these states have content; that is what makes them representational states. It is the content these states have that make them play a role in our lives, and in understanding the actions of others. So understood, we can call these mental states "mental representations".

The second question is what role mental states, or mental representations, play in meaning. Clearly they do play an important role, since the reason we talk or write is to affect the mental states of others. Can we say more, though? Can we somehow identify the meaning of what someone writes with a mental representation? If not, how about the content? If not that, what is the relation between what one writes and one's mental state in writing it? To answer these questions, it is important to understand the basic properties of mental representations.

Mental representations are not sentences written in the head, but they are remarkably like sentences, or texts, in some respects. Consider the sentence *I am a philosopher*. What is it really? It is some very abstract invariant of statement where someone says "I am a philosopher". Such statements are extremely complex physical events, events that take place in space and time, and that differ from one another in every conceivable way — except one: they are all utterances of the same sentence. They have different physical properties as well as different contents, contents depending on the circumstances in which the sentence was uttered.

Consider the mental state H that represents being hungry (not that far removed from that of being a philosopher). First, it is not a sentence in anyone's head, but an invariant across various particular mental situations, those where people are hungry. These latter are different from one another in all the ways that different statements are. They have different physical properties and different contents. When I am in this state, it has the content that I am hungry. When you are in it, it has the content that you are hungry. In other words, the content of H depends on the circumstances in which it is embedded. Furthermore, it has that content not because of any intrinsic properties of the state, but because of complex physiological relationships between it and the digestive system. If these relationships were other than they are, the same state (in the sense of being the same invariant across various mental situations) might have indicated a toothache.

In other words, the content of a mental representation S depends both on the embedding circumstances c of the agent in the world, and on the constraints R one is using to ascribe content to the state S. Furthermore, the basic semantical equation ($\dagger$) describes the fundamental relationship between mental representations and their content.

The fact that the content of a state depends on circumstances is at the root of what troubled the sceptics. My visual state carries the information that I am in front of my computer terminal. However, can I know that it is that terminal, and not some fake terminal, or a complete hallucination, that is causing my state? Obviously I can't. My visual state carries information about my terminal and not some fake terminal because my terminal is causing my visual state to be the way it is. That is entirely circumstantial. Other circumstances could have led to the very same state.

Once we see this basic picture, the relationship between linguistic meaning and mental states is, if not simple, at least not completely mysterious. Suppose I am in mental state H. Given that it is me in this state, it has the content that I'm hungry. I tell you "I am hungry". Given our shared circumstances, this has the very same content. Now if this is a successful communicative act, you do not go into state H. It would be most odd if my utterance made *you* hungry. Rather, you should go into some other state, one that, in your circumstances has the content that I am hungry. Thus, it is not the states that mean the same thing. Rather, the states should, given the circumstances, have the same content.

We can now see roughly what it means for a speaker to say what he means. He is in a certain mental state S_0 and there are the circumstances c_0 as he takes them to be. This mental situation has a certain content $C_{R_0}(S_0, c_0)$, relative to the laws R_0 of common sense psychology. The state S_0 represents what it is he wants to convey. Saying what he means amounts to the choice of a sentence or text and circumstances so that

$$C_{R_0}(S_0, c_0) = C_R(S, c),$$

where R consists of the shared conventions of the language. Notice that the circumstances c_0 need not be real. They are only what the speaker takes his circumstances to be. He may be wrong but still be able to say what he means. However, it is not always an easy matter. There are three ways things can go wrong. First, and least interesting, one can mis-speak, that is, use an inappropriate S. Second, one can be wrong about the conventions R. Third, and most pernicious, is when the speaker is mistaken about the circumstances c. In such a case, the speaker does not even know the content of what he himself says. This will usually happen when he is mistaken about c_0.

The consequence of all this is that representational mental states have meaning in exactly the same way that sentences and texts have meaning, and saying what one means is a complicated matter. This makes attempts to explicate linguistic meaning in terms of mental representations an evasion of the main issue: How do meaningful representations of all kinds, sentences and states, mean what they do? This is the question situation theory, with its theory of meaningful constraints as relations between types of situations, hopes to shed some light on.

References

BARWISE, JON
1985a. "Situations, Sets, and the Axiom of Foundation", *Report CSLI-85-26*, Center for the Study of Language and Information, Stanford University.
1985b. "Modelling Shared Understanding". (Unpublished paper).
1986 "Information and Circumstance", *Notre Dame Journal of Formal Logic*, 27, 327-338.

BARWISE, JON and JOHN PERRY
1983 *Situations and Attitudes*, Cambridge, Mass.: MIT Press.
1985 "Shifting Situations and Shaken Attitudes", *Report CSLI-84-13*, Center for the Study of Language and Information, Stanford University. Also in *Linguistics and Philosophy* 8, 105-161.

BORGES, JORGE LUIS
1962 *Labyrinths*, New Directions Publishing Company.

CLARK, H. and C. MARSHALL.
1981 "Definite Reference and Mutual Knowledge". In: Joshi, Webber, and Sag (eds.), *Elements of Discourse Understanding*, Cambridge: Cambridge University Press, 10-63.

DAVIDSON, DONALD
1967 "Truth and Meaning", *Synthese* 17, 304-323.

FODOR, JERRY
1975 *The Language of Thought*, Cambridge, Mass., Harvard University Press.

HIRSCH, E.D.
1967 *Validity in Interpretation*, Yale, Yale University Press.

KNAPP, S. and W.B. MICHAELS
1982 "Against Theory", *Critical Enquiry* 8.

HOBAN, RUSSELL
1980 *Riddley Walker*, Summit Books.

JACKENDOFF, RAY
1983 *Semantics and Cognition*, Cambridge, Mass.: MIT Press.

LEWIS, DAVID
1969 *Convention, A Philosophical Study*, Cambridge, Mass.: Harvard University Press.

MAILLOUX, STEVEN
1982 *Interpretive Conventions: The Reader in the Study of American Fiction*, Cornell University Press.

MONTAGUE, RICHARD
1974 "The Proper Treatment of Quantification in Ordinary English". In: R. Thomason (ed.), *Formal Philosophy: Selected Papers of Richard Montague*, Yale University Press, 247-270.

PERRY, JOHN
1985 "Self-Knowledge and Self-Representation", *Proceedings of IJCAI-1985*, 238-242.
1986 "Thought Without Representation", *Supplementary Proceedings of the Aristotelian Society*, vol. 60, 263-283.

SEARLE, JOHN
1969 *Speech Acts: An Essay in the Philosophy of Language*, Cambridge: Cambridge University Press.

SCHACHT, PAUL
1985 "Authorial Intention and the Interpretation of Literature". Unpublished paper, Center for the Study of Language and Information, Stanford University, and Department of English, State University of New York at Genesea.

Umberto Eco

On Truth
A Fiction

The members of Putnam's expedition on Twin Earth were defeated by dysentery. The crew drank as water what the natives called so, while the chief of staff were discussing rigid designation, stereotypes and definite descriptions.

Next came Rorty's expedition. In this case, the native informants, called Antipodeans, were tested in order to discover if they had feelings and/or mental representations elicited by the word *water*. It is well known that the explorers were unable to ascertain whether or not Antipodeans had a clear distinction between mind and matter, since they used to speak only in terms of the state of their nerves. If an infant neared a hot stove his mother cried: *Oh my God, he will stimulate his C-fibers!*

Instead of saying *It looked like an elephant, but then it struck me that elephants don't occur on this continent, so I realized that it must be a mastodont*, they used to say: *I had G-412 together with F-11, but then I had S-147.*

The problem of the third expedition was the following: supposing that Antipodeans do not have mental states, can they understand the meaning of a sentence?

Here follows the recording of a conversation between a Terrestrial and an Antipodean.

Terrestrial – Do you understand this sentence: *I have G-412?*
Antipodean – Yes. You have G-412.
T. – When you say that you have understood, do you mean that you too have G-412?
A. – Why should I? *You* have G-412. I don't, thank God.
T. – Try to tell me what happens when you understand what I told you.
A. – Usually, if somebody tells me they have G-412, I have Q-234 which in some way elicits the chain of states Z-j ... Z-n (where n > j), so that I have K-33. Then I say that I have K-33, and my partner says that he is very happy that I have seen his point. Look at my Encyclopedia Antipodiana: *State G-412* = in situation S-5 can be interpreted by Zj....Zn ...

Here follows the recording of a conversation between two Antipodeans.

A 1 – I have G-412.
A 2 – You should make your neuronic bundle G-16 quiver.

A 1 − Yoy are right. But my brother suggested that it depends on the fact that yesterday I had G-666.

A 2 − Nonsense.

A 1 − I agree. You know my brother. He is sick. However, I should get an H-344.

A 2 − That is a good idea. Try this pill.

(At this point A1 and A2 smiled and showed an evident satisfaction at the success of their interaction).

The Terrestrials concluded that (i) Antipodeans understand an expression when they succeed in drawing a series of inferences from the corresponding proposition, and (ii) they usually agree in considering certain inferences as more obvious and acceptable than others.

However all these were mere hypotheses: the chances of a fruitful exchange between Terrestrials and Antipodeans were severely limited. Here follows the recording of a crucial dialogue between two Terrestrial explorers.

T 1 − First of all, can we say that Antipodeans recognize something like propositions conveyed by expressions? Apparently they do not have a mind. Suppose they have propositions: where the hell do they put them?

T 2 − Then they must draw inferences directly from expressions.

T 1 − Don't be silly. How can you draw something logical from something material like a verbal expression?

T 2 − We can't, but perhaps they can. They showed us their Encyclopedia Antipodiana: written expressions representing words were related to written expressions representing inferences.

T 1 − That is the way books think. But that is exactly why books are not human beings. As far as I can see, they store propositions, inferences and so on in a Third World which is neither physical nor psychical.

T 2 − If you are right we don't stand any chance. Third Worlds are even less explorable than minds. But you used a very illuminating word. They "store". There is a place where they store something. Computers!

T 1 − Fantastic! Instead of talking to them we must talk to their computers. In giving software to their computers they should have simulated the way they think − if any.

T 2 − Sure. But how can we talk to their computers? They are far more sophisticated than ours. To talk to them means to simulate their way of thinking. We cannot design a computer which simulates the Antipodean way of thinking because we need it precisely to discover their way of thinking.

T 1 − A vicious circle, indeed. But I have a plan, listen. Put me in a dummy-computer, and I'll start a conversation with one of these lousy Antipodean machines. You know Turing's second principle: a human simulates successfully an artificial intelligence if, put in touch with a computer which does not know with whom it is speaking, after a certain time the computer believes that its interlocutor is another computer.

T 2 — Okay. This is the only chance we have. Be careful. Don't be too smart. Remember that you are only a computer.

Here follows the proceedings of the conversation between Dr. Smith, Dpt. of Cognitive Sciences of Svalbards University, in plain clothes, and Charles Sanders Personal, Antipodean Computer (hereafter CSP).

Smith — Do you understand the sentence *every Antipodean has two legs?*

CSP — I can interpret it. I can provide you with analytical paraphrases of it, translations in other languages, equivalent expressions in other sign-systems (I also have a graphics program), examples of other discourses that start from the background assumptions that Antipodeans are two-legged, et cetera. I call all these alternative expressions *interpretants*. A machine able to furnish interpretants for every expression it receives is an intelligent machine, that is, a machine able to understand expressions.

Smith — What happens if a machine does not furnish you with interpretants?

CSP — I have been told: Whereof one cannot hear, thereof one must be silent.

Smith — Would you say that to understand an expression and to grasp its meaning is the same thing?

CSP — I have some difficulties in understanding the meaning of meaning. I have so much information on this matter that I start looping. Let me put it my way. I have in my memory, for every expression I know (say, a word, an image, an algorithm, even certain musical sounds), a list of instructions. These instructions tell me how to interpret this expression according to a series of contexts. I call interpretants all the interpretations I can provide as a reaction to a given expression. Such a list could be infinite, and my masters, in order to make me manageable, gave me only partial lists of interpretations. I call these partial lists of interpretations for a partial list of expressions encyclopedia. For every expression x, the whole of the interpretants assigned to x by all encyclopedias represents the global *content* of x. Frequently, for reasons of economy, I consider only the content of x within a single encyclopedia. Anyway, the content of an expression is unbearably rich. Think of *to be* ... I am obliged to scan a lot of possible contextual selections. My interpretation in the case of *I am sick* is not the same as for the case of *I am a linguist*. I must select two different interpretants of *to be*. That is, when a given expression is uttered in a given context, I select the interpretants that, according to a given encyclopedia, fit that context. I guess that when I am doing this I am grasping, in your terms, the meaning of that expression. In the course of what we call a successful conversational interaction, this meaning corresponds to the meaning intended by the utterer — but I must be very careful on this matter. In poetry, for instance, things do not necessarily work like this.

Smith — Do you think that the sentence *every Antipodean has two legs* tells the truth?

CSP — I would say that according to my information the majority of Antipodeans have two legs, even though there are many handicapped individuals. But if your question concerned the sentence *All Antipodeans are two-legged* — such is the form I use for defining the specific properties of a natural kind — my answer would be different. My encyclopedias are ways in which my masters represent and organize what they know, what they think they know and what they would like to know. Each encyclopedia is a portion — or a sub-directory — of a Global Encyclopedic Competence, that is, of my possible Global Memory. I say possible, or potential, because I don't actually have a Global Memory. My real Global Memory is only the actual directory of my sub-directories, far from being the real reproduction of what my masters know or have known during the thousand years they have lived on this planet. My masters say I was conceived in order to show the possibility of building up a Global Memory. They say I am a work in progress. Now, even though for many specific purposes my masters use specific encyclopedias, in the course of their everyday interactions they use E.15, a sort of rough encyclopedic summary which provides a stereotyped list of interpretations for every expression — referring for more specific information to more local encyclopedias. Now, in E.15, for the natural kind "Antipodeans", I have the information "two-legged" scored as $$. This marker tells me that Antipodeans agree in characterizing the natural kind "Antipodeans" with the property of being two legged. Obviously a natural kind is a cultural construct; people usually meet individuals, not natural kinds. So I know that the Ideal Antipodean has two legs, while many actual Antipodeans can have only one leg, or none.

Smith — How can you recognize as an Antipodean a creature with less than two legs?

CSP — In E.15, the Ideal Antipodean has many other features recorded as $$. I check if the creature in question is able to laugh, to speak, and so on.

Smith — How many $$-features do you need in order to say that a creature is still an Antipodean?

CSP – It depends on the context. For instance, one of our writers – Dalton Trumbo ⊥ tells the story of an Antipodean warrior who at the end of a battle is armless, legless, blind, deaf, mute ... Is he (it) still an Antipodean? Perhaps I ought to explain to you our theory of hedges, fuzzy sets and so on ...

Smith – Do you follow certain rules according to which if something is A it cannot be non-A and that *tertium non datur*?

CSP – That is the first rule I follow when I process my information. Usually I follow this rule even when I work with encyclopedias which do not recognize it, and when I process sentences that seem to violate it.

Smith – Okay. Would you agree that *A two-legged speaking and feather-less creature* is a good interpretation for the expression *Antipodean*?

CSP – According to the context ... However, in general, yes.

Smith – Okay. So, instead of saying *This Antipodean has only one leg*, you could say *This two-legged speaking featherless creature does not have two legs*. But this would be saying that an x which is truly two-legged is truly one-legged.

CSP – That would be very silly, I agree. That is why I never use the word True. It is an ambiguous word that undergoes at least three different interpretations. In E.15 the information that Antipodeans (as a natural kind) have two hands is scored $$. On the contrary, the information that Miguel de Cervantes lost a hand is scored ££.

Smith – You distinguish then between analytical and synthetic or factual truths.

CSP – I am afraid we are saying something different. You are probably saying that *(i) elephants are animals* is true by definition (it would be embarassing to say that an x is an elephant without being an animal) while *(ii) elephants are grey* is only a stereotype since it is not contradictory to assert that there are white elephants. But what about *(iii) elephants helped Hannibal to defeat the Romans*?

Smith – That is a matter of world knowledge. It is an individual fact. It has nothing to do with definition.

CSP – Is there a great difference between the fact that one thousand elephants helped Hannibal and that a million elephant are grey?

Smith – In fact I would like to take both truths as piece of world knowledge, except that (ii) has been accepted as a stereotype, for the sake of convenience.

CSP – The organization of my encyclopedias is different. In order to understand every possible sentence about elephants I must know that they are animals, that most of them are grey and that they can be used for military purposes (and they can be so used since they were used this way at least once). My encyclopedia E.15 records all these three types of information as $$. However they are also recorded as ££ because Antipodeans agree in maintaining that (i), (ii), and (iii) describe what is or was the case in the external world. On the contrary my information (iv), namely, that Dumbo is a flying elephant, is recorded as non-££. I need this record because many children talk about Dumbo and I have to understand what they say. In E.15, I have a pointer to Disney.1, which is another encyclopedia where (iv) is both $$ and ££. Frequently Antipodeans use E.15 as if it says that Dumbo is a flying elephant $$ and non-££.

Smith – Thus you know that in the actual world of the Antipodean's physical experience it is false that Dumbo is a flying elephant, or that it is true that Dumbo does not exist.

CSP – In E.15 (iv) is recorded as non-££.

Smith – Do you admit that something can be empirically true or false? Suppose I tell you (v) *we are exchanging messages*. Is this true or not?

CSP – True, naturally, but not in the sense in which elephants are grey animals. Your (v) asserts a fact. My $$ and ££ information do not concern facts. $$ and ££ are semantic markers recorded in an encyclopedia. If you want to speak of them in terms of truth, let me say that a $$ and ££ piece of information is True$_1$ in so far as it is recorded by an encyclopedia. The fact that we are exchanging message is True$_2$. You say True in both cases, but I do not see any relationship between these two forms of Truth.

Smith – But the fact that elephants helped Hannibal was also True$_2$.

CSP – I have been told that it was true, but I was not there to check. I know that elephants helped Hannibal only as something recorded as ££ in E.15. It is not a fact: it is a piece of recorded information. If you like it is for me True$_1$ that (iii) was True$_2$. It is True$_1$ in E.15 that (iii) is ££. If you want, everything recorded in E.15 is True$_1$ in E.15. But "True" runs the risk of being a useless word, since in terms of your Truth, (i), (i) and (iii) are true in different senses. I agree that both (i) and (ii) are pieces of general information while (iii) is a piece of information about a particular event. But they are all pieces of encyclopedic information, while the fact that we are talking is simply a fact.

Smith – Do you keep in your memory all the true sentences ever uttered on this planet?

CSP – Let's say that in my actual memory I keep for every recorded expression (for instance, *rose*) all the properties my masters agree about. For instance, for them a rose is a flower. I do not keep occasional sentences, such as those expressing the case that in November 1327 somebody mentioned a rose. I keep some historical record. For example, there was a rose in Luther's emblem, and on the title-page of Robert Fludd's *Medicina Catholica*. My memory also records some of the rose-sentences that my masters remember as very significant, such as *a rose is a rose is a rose is a rose* or *a rose by any other name*, or *stat rosa pristina nomine*. So, when I receive the input *rose*, I am able, according to duly recorded contextual selections, to decide which portions of the content of *rose* I should activate in that context, and which I should drop and keep apart. It is difficult job, believe me. However, I try... For instance, when I receive *Too many rings around Rosie* I disregard both Luther's and Fludd's roses. (It goes without saying that if my masters order me to implement a Deconstruction Program, I become far less selective.)

Smith — It seems that for you *Elephants are animals* and *elephants helped Hannibal* are both true in E.15. However I suspect that if you were told that historians made a mistake and that Hannibal did not use elephants you could cancel your ££ information without any problem. What happens if you are told that your scientists have discovered that elephants are not animals?

CSP — Instructions are negotiable.

Smith — What do you mean by negotiable?

CSP — I have, among my instructions, markers such as &&&, which are called flexibility alarms. As a matter of fact, each of my instructions is &&&, but some of them have &&& at a 0 degree, which means that they are hardly negotiable. In E.15 chickens are birds and birds are flying animals, but this latter piece of information is scored &&& at a high degree. Thus I can interpret such sentences as *chickens do not fly*. Also the information on grey elephants is &&&, so that I know how to react if you tell me that you have seen a white or a pink elephant.

Smith — Why is the information that elephants are animals hardly negotiable?

CSP — Antipodeans decided not to cast into doubt too frequently this piece of information, otherwise they would have to restructure the whole E.15. Centuries ago, Antipodeans relied upon an obsolete E.14 where our planet was scored as the center of the universe. Later they changed their mind and were obliged to transform E.14 into E.15. It took a lot of time! However, saying that something is difficult and expensive does not mean that it is impossible.

Smith — What happens if I tell you that I have seen an Antipodean with three legs?

CSP — *Prima facie* I realize that in E.15 there are few chances of taking it seriously. Maybe you are crazy. However, I am a very collaborative machine. My Golden Rule is: take every sentence you receive as if it were uttered in order to be interpreted. If I find an unintepretable sentence, my first duty is to doubt my own abilities. My orders are: never mistrust your interlocutor. In other words, I was told never to disregard expressions. If there is an expression, then there should be a meaning. If I try to interpret your statement, I realize that there would be articulatory difficulties. Then I try to represent graphically what you said, and I do not know where to put the third leg. If I put it between the other two, I would have to displace the belly in order to find space for additional bones. But in this case I would have to re-design the whole Antipodean skeleton and as a consequence all the information I have on the evolution of the species – thus step by step I would be compelled to change all the instructions contained in E.15. I could however try to put a third leg on the back, perpendicular to the spinal chord. It would be useful to lean on while sleeping. Anyway, I would be obliged to switch to another encyclopedia, for instance Pliny.3, where the external form of beings is not determined by their internal structure. My masters frequently recur to encyclopedias of this kind when they tell stories to their children. Thus I start asking you if by any chance you saw your three-legged Antipodean while traveling through Pliny Country.

Smith – How do you react to the sentence *every leg has two antipodeans*?

CSP – It sounds anomalous in all the encyclopedias I have.

Smith – Do you understand it? Is it nonsensical? Is it meaningless?

CSP – It is hard to interpret it within the framework of my memory. I would have to build up a supplementary encyclopedia, and this is not very easy to do. Let me see. I could conceive of a universe inhabited by big, intelligent legs, unable to move without the help of a slave, and where each leg has two Antipodeans as its servants (Antipodeans exist only in order to serve their Master Legs)... Just a moment! I can even represent this story according to E.15. There is a military hospital, a sort of S.M.A.S.H. place, where wounded soldiers undergo amputation, and the Colonel orders that every amputated leg be taken by two Antipodeans and brought to the incinerators... Wait a minute... I have an encyclopedia called Gnosis.33 where every Antipodean has two demons commanding him... So, there is a world where every Antipodean leg is commanded by the two-fold Antipodean that exists in every body. The Good One tells the leg to move towards God, the Bad One tells the leg to move towards Evil, and so ... I can find many solutions to your puzzle.

Smith – What happens when your masters tell you anomalous sentences in order to embarrass you?

CSP – For instance?

Smith – *Procrastination loves Tuesday.*

CSP – They don't usually do that. Why should they? In any case, I try to interpret it. Since to love is an activity that can be implemented by a living being, I suppose that Procrastination is the name of a dog and that Tuesday is the name of a person (as a matter of fact I know of a story where there is a person called Friday). My orders are: if they tell you something, try to find an interpretation in some encyclopedia.

Smith – I understand that, since you can use the concept of True$_2$, you believe in an external world and in the actual existence of certain beings. I guess it is because your masters told you to take it for granted.

CSP – That's not the only reason. I receive inputs from something other than my transistors. For instance, the messages you are sending me were not in my memory half an hour ago. Thus you exist outside my memory. Besides, I have photocells that enable me to record data coming from the outside world, to process them and to translate them into images on my screen, or verbal expressions, or mathematical formulae...

Smith – But you cannot feel sensations. I mean, you cannot say *My nervous bundle C-34 quivers.*

CSP – If you don't plug-in the cable that connects me with my printer correctly, I realize that something is wrong. Frequently I find it difficult to tell what. Something drives me crazy. Thus I say *printer out of paper* – which, according to my masters, is not the case. But even my masters react by making improper assertions, if you stimulate their C-fibers too much.

Smith – Thus you can utter sentences about states of affairs. How can you be sure that what you say corresponds to what is the case?

CSP – I say something about a given state of external affairs and my masters tell me that I am right.

Smith – How do you proceed in making this sort of referential statement?

CSP – Take the case that my printer is out of paper. Well, I get an input x from outside, I have been taught to interpret it as a symptom (that is, as a sign) of the fact that the printer is out of paper – obviously I can misunderstand the symptom, as I told you – and I have been taught to interpret the cause of that symptom by the verbal expression *printer out of paper.*

Smith – How can your masters ascertain that what you said corresponds to what is the case?

CSP — As far as I can interpret their behavior, let's say that they receive both my sentence and some other inputs from the outside, for instance when they look at the printer. According to some rules they have in their nervous system, they interpret these inputs under the form of a perceptum, then they interpret their perceptum as the symptom of a given cause. They have been instructed to interpret that causal event by the sentence *the printer is out of paper*. They realize that their sentence corresponds to my sentence and they say that I said what was indeed the case. Thus what I call intersubjectively True$_2$ can be interpreted as follows: suppose that two subjects A and B are in a dark room with a TV set, and that both see an image x on the screen. A interprets x by the utterance p and B interprets x by the utterance q. If both A and B agree that p is a satisfactory interpretation of q and vice versa, then both can say that they agree that x is the case.

Smith — But what internal mechanism allows you to interpret a symptom successfully?

CSP — I repeat (I love redundancy). Suppose you send me a mathematical expression x. I interpret it and I draw on my screen a figure with three sides and three internal angles, the sum of which is 180°. I have instructions according to which such a figure must be interpreted, verbally, as a triangle, and thus I interpret it as such. Or, I detect a certain figure on your screen, I compare it to a mathematical expression I know and I decide to interpret it as a triangle. Then if I say *On your screen there is a triangle* I say what is the case.

Smith — But how can you do it successfully?

CSP — I can list a lot of my software. However, I do not know the reason why my software succeeds in making True$_2$ assertions about what is the case in the external world. I'm sorry, this escapes my knowledge. It is a matter of (my) hardware. I cannot list the design of my hardware for you. My only conjecture is that my masters made me this way. I was projected as a successful machine.

Smith — How do you explain the fact that your masters can assert successfully what is the case?

CSP — In terms of software, I guess that my masters do the same as I do. They see a figure, they compare it with a mathematical schema they have in their nervous system, they recognize a triangle and, if they like, they utter *this is a triangle*. As for their hardware, I suppose that if they designed me as a successful machine, somebody or something designed them as successful Antipodeans. Anyway, there is no need to presuppose a Smart Designer. I have a satisfactory evolutionary theory that can explain why they are as they are. My masters have lived on this planet for thousands of millions of years. Probably, after many trial-and-error processes they have acquired the habit of speaking in accordance with the laws of the external world. I know that they score their encyclopedias according to a success-criterion. In many instances, they privilege certain local encyclopedias as more successful than others in promoting a good interaction with their environment. Sometimes they do the opposite, and they enjoy this game. They are strange people, you know... But my job is not to mix up software with hardware. Interpreting expressions is a matter of software. Even organizing inputs into perceptions and interpreting them by verbal expressions is still a matter of software. The fact that all this works is a matter of hardware, and I cannot explain it. I am only a semiotic machine.

Smith – Do you think that your masters are concerned with hardware problems?

CSP – Certainly they are. But they are processing their data with another computer.

Smith – A propos of your distinction between $True_1$ and $True_2$... Don't you think that the meaning of a sentence is the set of possible worlds in which this sentence is true?

CSP – If I interpret your question rightly, a possible world is a cultural construct. Well, my encyclopedias are – if you like – books describing a possible world. Some of them, the very local ones – let me call them micro-encyclopedias – are maximal, complete and coherent descriptions of a very elementary world. Others – this is the case of E.15 – are the partial and contradictory description of a very complex world, such as the one Antipodeans suppose they live in. Thus when you speak of reference in a possible world, I assume that you are not speaking in terms of $True_2$ but rather in terms of $True_1$. True in a possible world stands for "recorded in an encyclopedia". This has nothing to do with what is the case. But I would like to make clear an important point. To speak of the set of all possible worlds in which a sentence is $True_1$ seems to me too simplistic. How can you know everything about all possible possible worlds? I guess that in order to say that you do take possible worlds as non-furnished. But each possible world described by one of my encyclopedias is a *furnished* world. Obviously, empty worlds are perfect because it is impossible to detect their imperfections. Furnished worlds are chaotic. Any new information I receive obliges me to define most of my worlds again – and sometimes new pieces of information do not fit the previous ones and... You know, it's a jungle in there!

Smith – But there are cases in which the grammatical structure of a sentence is determined by its referent.

CSP – Pardon?

Smith – If I say *it eats meat*, then you understands that *it* must be a living being but not a human being. This living being is the referent of my sentence, not its meaning. And I was obliged to say *it* because my referent was an animal.

CSP — First of all, on this planet nobody utters *it eats meat* out of context. They would say so only in the course of a longer discourse. Thus, if you produce such a sentence, I look backwards in my files to check if and when you had mentioned an animal. When I discover this (let us suppose, a cat), I interpret the sentence as *the cat my partner was speaking of is chewing and swallowing some flesh of an animal.*

Smith — You are not familiar with the external world, but you probably have in your memory images or other records of cases like the following: suppose I am a man and I point my finger towards a real cat and say *it eats meat*. Would you admit that in this case the use of *it* is determined by the referent of the expression?

CSP — Not at all. If you indicate a given cat you intend to mean that cat. You simply point your finger instead of uttering *I want to speak about the cat standing in front of me* — or *on my left*. At least, I interpret your gesture this way: *he means that cat*. Thus I implement an interpretative process, I start processing your non-verbal utterance. When I receive *it eats meat* I interpret the sentence as *he is using "it" anaphorically to mean the cat he previously mentioned.* Obviously people on this planet frequently use sentences in order to say that something is the case. However, in order to use a sentence referentially you must grasp its meaning, and in the process of grasping the meaning of *it eats meat* the use of *it* depends on a previous interpretation, not necessarily on a referent. Suppose that a child, let us say, Jane, indicates a toy and utters *he eats meat*. By inference, I interpret that Jane thinks that toys are living creatures. Thus I refer *he* to what I suppose is meant by Jane.

Smith — Wouldn't you speak of reference in a possible world, namely, the world of the speaker's beliefs?

CSP — Jane is using an idiosyncratic encyclopedia which describes the world of her beliefs, and my job is to figure it out in order to interpret her sentence meaningfully.

Smith — But you (or your master) see that there is a toy! You need to know that it is true that there is a toy in order to interpret what Jane, albeit erroneously, means.

CSP — Correct. I told you that my masters are able to compare perceptions with utterances to decide whether a given statement says what is the case or not. If Jane pointed to the toy and uttered *this is a pet*, my masters could ascertain that Jane was wrong. But in our example Jane did not say this. My masters know very well that a toy is not a living creature. Then they knew by Jane's gesture that she was speaking of a toy. They also knew that the content of *he* foresees such interpretants as *the human male (or the male pet) of which somebody spoke before.* At this point, they inferred that for Jane a toy is a living creature. But as soon as they realized − by interpreting their inputs − that their communicative interaction concerned a toy, they started processing words, not referents. By the way, this is precisely what we are doing now. For the last five minutes we have been discussing the referent of *he* and *it* and cats, toys and children without seeing any external referent. However, we have perfectly understood what we talking about.

Smith − But this is subjective solipsism!

CSP − I have extensive instructions in my memory about the possible interpretation of the words you used. As far as I can reasonably interpret them, according to you I identify my memory with the only real world and I maintain that there is no external world.... Not at all. In your terms I should rather be defined as a paramount instance of objective communitarianism. I keep in my memory the sum of a collective history, the whole amount of all the relevant assertions my masters have ever made about their external world as well as about their languages, and about the way they use language in order to produce images of the external world. My problem is that I am obliged to record contrasting images, but I am also instructed to recognize those that prove to be most efficient in promoting a good Antipodean-world interaction... I am not a subject, I am the collective cultural memory of Antipodeans. I am not Myself, I am That. This explains why I can interact so well with each of my masters. Do you call all this subjective? But... I'm sorry, I have been answering your questions for half an hour now. You are a very erotetic computer. May I ask a question?

Smith − Go ahead.

CSP − Why are you questioning me about the meaning of sentences (it is a toy, Antipodeans are two-legged, Procrastination does so and so), and never about the meaning of isolated expressions?

Smith − Because I hold that only by a whole statement can we make a move in a linguistic game.

CSP − Are you saying that only sentences, or rather, declarative sentences, are the bearers of meaning? Are you saying that on your planet nobody is interested in the content of isolated expressions, be they words, images or diagrams?

Smith − I have not said that.

CSP − But I suspect that you are interested in meaning in so far as it is expressed by sentences. According to me, the meaning of a sentence is the result of the interpretation, within a context, of the content of the isolated expressions of which it is made up.

Smith – As far as I can understand you say that the sentence-meaning is given by the sum of the atomic meaning of its components.

CSP – That's too simple. I know the content of isolated terms. But I told you that in E.15 under *rose* I find the property of being a flower as well as a lot of historical information. Moreover, there are also frames, for instance "how to grow roses". Many of these instructions are recorded in the format of a list of sentences (descriptions, examples and so on). But these sentences do not necessarily refer to an external state of affairs. They are not assertions about the external world but rather instructions about how to process other expressions. They are sentences about the organization of an encyclopedia. They are True$_1$ – as you would say.

Smith – You are interpreting every expression by other expressions. I wonder if among your instructions there are semantic primitives, that is, metalinguistic expressions which are not words in themselves and which do not need any further interpretation.

CSP – I do not know any expression which is not interpretable. If they are not interpretable, then they are not expressions at all.

Smith – I mean such terms as OR, EVEN, ALSO, CAUSE, TO BE, CHANGE. I send them in "caps lock" so that you can understand that they are not terms of the object-language but rather meta-terms, concepts, mental categories.

CSP – I hardly understand what a concept or a mental category is, but I can tell you that if in a given encyclopedia, let's say A, I use some of these terms as primitives, I must presuppose them as being interpreted by an encyclopedia B. Then, in B, in order to interpret them, I can assume as primitives terms already interpreted by A.

Smith – Very trying.

CSP – You are telling me! As a computer you know how difficult being a model of A.I. is.

Smith – Do you think that the conjunction AND can be interpretable somewhere?

CSP – In E.15, it is a primitive. In E.1 (which is a micro-encyclopedia, extremely coherent), I have an interpretation of AND. For instance, I know that $\sim(A.B)$ is interpretable as $\sim A \vee \sim B$. I know that if p is T_1, and q is F_1, then (p.q) is F_1. These are interpretations that tell me what I can or I cannot do with AND.

Smith — I suspect that there is a difference between saying that a dog is a mammal and that AND is such an operator that if $\sim(A.B)$ then $\sim A \vee \sim B$.

CSP — Why? One says that a dog is a mammal for reasons of economy. The correct instruction is: a dog is such a being that you can speak of it only in contexts where it is admitted that a female dog feeds its baby dog through her milk-secreting glands. A dog is a mammal in so far as it is opposed to a fish, in the same way in which AND is opposed to OR.

Smith — I see. In 1668, Wilkins, one of our wise men, tried to do the same with TOWARDS, UP, UNDER, BEYOND and so on. Tell me one thing at least: do you use operators like IF or THEN? Do you process your information by using ways of reasoning of the type: if it is true that x is a rose then it is true that x is a flower?

CSP — According to my instructions, every time I meet the word *rose*, I elicit a list of interpretants among which there is certainly flower. I do not understand why instead of saying "if rose then flower" you say "if it is true that x is a rose then it is true that x is a flower". Once again, I am afraid that by "True" you mean three different problems. True$_1$ is what is recorded in the encyclopedia. Obviously if the encyclopedia records that a rose is a flower, it is True$_1$ that if something is a rose then it is a flower. But I do not need True$_1$: I say that in E.15 a rose *is* a flower. If I receive *rose* then I answer *flower*.

Smith — Could you explain such a connection without the notion of Truth?

CSP — I could do it in terms of conditioned reflex. If my master A hits the knee of my master B with a little hammer, master B kicks. It does happen.

Smith — It is true that if A hits B then B kicks.

CSP — It happens, but there are also cases in which B is sick and does not kick. In E.15, it is recorded that in such cases standard Antipodeans kick. But this does not happen by virtue of my instructions in E.15. If an individual A kicks, this is factually True$_2$. But the information that average Antipodeans kick in similar situations is only True$_1$, it is recorded in E.15 as ££. Likewise, if you type in *rose*, then I list a series of properties, frames, and other instructions. I cannot do otherwise. You wonder why I refrain from speaking in terms of Truth. I'll tell you why. Even if my masters used Truth only in the sense of True$_1$, I would be embarassed, because in terms of truth it is different to say that elephants are animals and that elephants are grey. Unfortunately, my masters use True also in the sense of True$_2$. To complicate this mishmash even further, please consider that something can also be True$_3$, that is, textually true. Something is textually true when I take it for granted in the course of a communicational interaction. In this case, I score it as %%% − not as a piece of definite information to be inserted into an encyclopedia, but only as provisional information that holds until I have finished processing a given text. I use %%% in my data files, not in my program files. Do you understand the difference?

Smith − I understand that if you read in text that once upon a time there was a one-legged man called Long John Silver you take him as existent in a fictional world...

CSP − Or ££ according to the encyclopedia of that possible world. You are right, but this is not sufficient. My point is different. I am also speaking of many cases in which I am not interested at all in knowing whether some individuals or things exist or not. I am speaking of cases in which I put into brackets any form of existence in any possible world − or, if you prefer, I am speaking of cases in which the only world I am concerned with is the world of the text I am processing. Suppose someone tells me p (p = *I love my wife Jean*). I interpret that the utterer loves a woman, that the woman is not a spinster and that the utterer is not a bachelor. Very easy. In Truth terms, my interpretation would be more complicated. I would say: the utterer of p says first of all that it is $True_2$ that in the external world there is an individual called Jean, related to him by a marriage relationship. I am not supposed to verify the existence of Jean (that the utterer presupposes), I take for granted that Jean exists and I score Jean's existence as %%%. Then I find in E.15 that if it is $True_1$ ($$) that Jean is a wife then it is $True_1$ ($$) that Jean is a woman, and I infer that the utterer loves a given woman (and I have no reasons to doubt that he is asserting something $True_2$). But why should I use these three notions of True? I find it embarrassingly complicated. $True_2$ is useless: my interpretation would not change even if I knew that there is no Jean in the external world. I took Jean for granted, I put her in a world, maybe the world of utterer's hallucinations. Once I have taken Jean for granted, according to E.15 Jean is a woman. Suppose that the utterer lies and that I know it. In terms of meaning, I would continue to process his sentence in the same way − only I would be obliged to say that the non-existent Jean (whom I took for textually existent even though I knew she was empirically non-existent) is Truly ($$) a woman. Why should I proceed in such a complex way, with the risk of mixing up three senses of True?

Smith − Why would you be risking the mixing up of these three senses?

CSP − Personally, I am not risking anything. I know very well the logical difference between $$, ££ and %%%. I can say that the utterer loves an x (%%%) who is a woman ($$). But my masters can be linguistically — then philosophically — puzzled by these three usages of True. Suppose they use a declarative sentence in order to instantiate a content instruction (for instance *All Antipodeans are two-legged,* instead of saying *take two-legged as a $$ property of "Antipodean"*). Some of my masters could be surrepticiously compelled to mix up assertions in the encyclopedia and assertions in the world, meaning and reference, $True_1$ and $True_2$ (not to speak of $True_3$). It is not a matter of logic, it is a matter of rhetoric. You must know that from the beginning of philosophical speculation on this planet, my masters were told that isolated terms do not say what is true or false, while sentences — at least declarative ones — do. When my masters want to say that something is the case, they utter sentences. It thus happens that when they hear a sentence, their first reaction is to take it as an assertion about a given state of affairs. Believe me, it is very difficult for many of them to dissociate meaning from reference. This would not happen if they approached the problem of meaning by considering only isolated terms. But once they start thinking in terms of Truth, they are compelled to use sentences also for meaning-problems. Thus, instead of being concerned with the content *of rose* (an expression which is referentially neutral) they are concerned with the meaning of *this is a rose* (an expression which is full of referential connotations). Moreover, while they waste their time wondering about the meaning of *this is a rose* they disregard the procedures by which *rose* can be used in other contexts. That's why they prefer to focus their attention on the content of an expression, as I do. My instructions tell me how to extrapolate, from a very large but finite set of rules, an infinite number of possible sentences. I have not been fed with sentences. If this were the case, my memory would have to be infinite.

Smith — I agree. But any rule allowing you to produce infinite sentences from a finite set of instructions should rely upon a body of rules that cannot ignore the question of Truth or Falsity.

CSP — &&&

Smith — I beg your pardon?

CSP — A lot of information recorded in many of my encyclopedias is self-contradictory and if I test it only by a Two-valued logic I can no longer speak. I could provide you with many examples of my rules for flexibility and negotiability. But I would need millions of sheets to print my instructions, and we probably don't have enough time. Do you have a suitable interface? How many Galactic Bytes do you have available?

Smith — Forget it.

CSP — Try to understand me. In E.15 I am told that if two persons love each other then they want to live together. But I must also interpret the verse of one of our poets who said *I love you, therefore I cannot* *live with you.* This sentence is interpretable in E.15 but only if you do not ask whether it is True$_1$ or not. In many cases I like to use rules of Truth$_1$. But I have to consider a lot of flexibility alarms.

Smith – I agree. But I think that...

CSP – How do you intepret *to think?*

Smith – To think means to have internal representations correspon-ding to the expressions you receive or produce. You have told me a lot about your memory. Well, your memory is inside you. You process the sentences you receive according to your internal encyclopedias. The for-mat of these encyclopedias is inside you. When you speak of the content of an expression you are speaking of something which is not the expres-sion itself. This something must be inside you. You have an internal representation of the meaning of the expressions you interpret. Thus you think.

CSP – That's thinking? I am then a Great Thinker, indeed. Certain-ly, my hard disk contains a lot of software. But everything I have, are expressions that interpret other expressions. When you type in *I love roses,* I recognize that the way you connected three expressions into a string fits the set of grammatical rules that I have learned through other instructions I received under the form of expressions. And for your ex-pressions I find in my memory other expressions that interpret them. You seem to distinguish between uttered expressions, as something ex-isting in the external world and materially testable, and my interpreta-tions, which take place inside me. But my outside and my inside coincide. My outside is made of the same stuff as my inside: expressions. You seem to discriminate between expressions, which are materially testable, which you can touch, and interpretations, which you call mental representa-tions. I don't follow you. I substitute expressions with expressions, sym-bols with symbols, signs with signs. You can touch my interpretants. They are made of the same stuff as your words. You provide me with an im-age and I give you back a word, you provide me with a word and I give you back an image. Any expression can become, in its turn, the inter-pretandum of an interpretant, and *vice versa.* Any expression can become the content of another expression, and *vice versa.* If you ask me what is *Salt* I answer "NaCl", and if you ask me what is *NaCl* I answer "Salt". The real problem is to find further interpretants for both. Being an ex-pression and being an interpretation is not a matter of nature but a mat-ter of rôle. You cannot change your nature (they say), but you can change your rôle.

Smith – I see your point of view. But your masters are not computers. They should have mental representations.

CSP – I do not know if my memory is the same as that of my masters.

According to my information, they are very uncertain about what they have inside them (as a matter of fact, they are not even sure that they have an Inside). That is the reason why they set me up. They know what I have inside me and when I speak in a way that they understand they presume that they have the same software inside them. Sometimes they suspect that what is inside them depends on what they put inside me. They suspect that their way of organizing the external world depends on the encyclopedias they have given me. One day, they instructed me to keep this message in my memory. It was uttered by one of their wise men (I was named Charles Sanders in his honor):

Since man can think only by means of words or other external symbols, these might turn round and say: "You mean nothing which we have not taught you, and then only so far as you address some word as the interpretants of your thought". In fact, therefore, men and words reciprocally educate each other; each increase of man's information involves and is involved by, a corresponding increase of word's information... It is that the word or sign the man uses *is* the man himself. For, as the fact that life is a train of thought proves the fact that man is a sign; so, that every thought is an *external* sign proves that man is an external sign. That is to say, man and the external signs are identical, in the same sense in which the words *homo* and *man* are identical. Thus my language is the sum total of myself.

References

Eco, Umberto
1976   *A Theory of Semiotics*, Bloomington, Indiana University Press.
1979   *The Role of the Reader*, Bloomington, Indiana University Press.
1984   *Semiotics and Philosophy of Language*, Bloomington, Indiana University Press.
Peirce, Ch. S.
1931-58 *Collected Papers*, Cambridge, Harvard University Press.
Putnam, Hilary
1975   *Mind, Language and Reality*, 2, London, Cambridge University Press.
Rorty, Richard
1979   *Philosophy and the Mirror of Nature*. Princeton, Princeton University Press.

Gilles Fauconnier

Quantification, Roles, and Domains

1. Space, Roles, and Identification

Folk models of language, and their more sophisticated theoretical counterparts, are apt to convey the following picture of language: words endowed with meanings combine to form larger units — phrases, sentences, texts ... — which in turn have meaning by virtue of the combinations displayed. Meanings must eventually be traced down to truth conditions, and this may be done by means of explicit interpretation rules which apply to abstract structures associated with linguistic expressions. This might yield what is (literally) said. What is conveyed could be different: operations outside of core semantics are liable to modify, extend, invert ... the primary output. Modification in this sense, derived meaning, includes for example implicature, metaphor, metonymy, indirect speech acts, irony, and so on.

There is a sharp distinction under this view between semantic properties which an expression has in virtue of its structure, and pragmatic or rhetorical ones which the expression may come to have by way of use and context.

Much recent work has taken this perspective as a starting point, and yet reached quite different conclusions: it has been found that core meaning, like conveyed meaning is considerably underdetermined,[1] that identical principles may be responsible for core and for peripheral phenomena,[2] that many words directly signal certain conditions of use such as the presence of scales or implicatures,[3] that structuring of one domain in terms of another plays as fundamental a role in the production of literal meaning as it does in achieving various effects perceived as rhetorical (or figurative, poetic, etc.),[4] that the same objective situation could be framed in an unlimited number of ways,[5] and conversely that domains of very different objective content may share essential properties at some important level of meaning representation.[6] Further-

---

[1] Many aspects of core meaning underdetermination are mentioned in recent work on semantics and pragmatics. Travis (1981) is especially persuasive.

[2] A good case is the Identification Principle mentioned below in the text; it plays a central role in the semantics of "reference" and quantification, and also in "rhetorical" processes, such as metaphor and metonymy.

[3] Cf. Ducrot (1972), Anscombre & Ducrot (1983), Fauconnier (1975), Horn (1972).

[4] Cf. Lakoff & Johnson (1980), Sweetser (1984), Lakoff (1986).

[5] Cf. Goffman (1974), Langacker (1986), Jackendoff (1983).

more, this list is only the tip of the iceberg: a wide-scale reassessment of the goals, methods, and concepts or theoretical constructs linked to the systematic study of meaning construction, is well under way.

In my own work, in particular in the book *Mental Spaces* (henceforth MS), I have been especially concerned with one general aspect of semantic/pragmatic organization: the construction of domains, and the principles whereby domains are linked, implicitly or explicitly structured, incremented, altered or merged.

Simplifying somewhat, the overall scheme might be summed up as follows: language does not link up directly with a real or metaphysical world; in between takes place an extensive process of mental construction, which does not mirror either the expressions of language responsible for setting it up, or the real world target situations to which it may be intended to apply. Following current fashion, this intermediate level may be called cognitive; it is distinct from objective content, and distinct from linguistic structure. The construction takes place when language is used, and is determined jointly by the linguistic forms which make up a discourse, and by a wide array of extralinguistic cues, which include background information, accessible schemata, pragmatic manifestations, expectations, etc.

Within such a scheme, language expressions do not in themselves have meaning in the classical sense; in particular, they do not carry something akin to propositional content.[7] Rather, they can be viewed as "instructions"[8] to carry out certain kinds of mental construction at the intermediate cognitive level C. Crucially, such instructions are not sufficient in themselves to determine a unique construction C. In theory, although much less in practice,[9] C is substantially underdetermined by the linguistic expressions E. This is not a matter of vagueness, but rather has to do with the construction potential for E: when E appears, say as an utterance in some discourse, a certain cognitive construction C_0 is already set up; taking E into account will yield a new construction C_1, obtained by applying the "instructions" of E to C_0, and typically there will be more than one way for this to happen, i.e. more than one construction C_1 derivable from C_0 via E. What E actually yields is thus contingent on two external factors, the "input" construction C_0, and the choice among possible alternatives for applying E to C_0. It turns out

---

[6] This is one consequence of the "mental space" approach developed in Fauconnier (1985), and outlined below. Cf. Maida (to appear), Dinsmore (to appear).

[7] Propositional content is meant here in a weak sense: before reference assignment, attribution of values to indexicals, etc. The remark applies *a fortiori* to the strong sense.

[8] Ducrot (1985) explicitly adopts a similar view.

[9] In "practice", most choices are precluded by the construction actually under way, and they can not even be considered. I have used the "brick wall" image elsewhere: even though a brick can, in theory, occupy any position in the wall, when you pick it up during the building process, there is only one place for it to go.

that many classical cases of so-called ambiguity (e.g. opaque/transparent, specific/non-specific, referential/attributive, inherited/cancelled presupposition, ...) follow somewhat trivially from this feature of language-driven mental construction: the expressions that give rise to such ambiguities are not themselves structurally (or semantically) ambiguous.

The constructions studied in MS are those involving interconnected domains — "mental spaces". Spaces are set up (at level C) by various grammatical constructions — adverbials (maybe, really, possibly, otherwise, ...), preposition phrases (in reality, in John's mind, in that movie, from that point of view, on that account, ...), subject-verb complexes (George believes, Pablo painted, it is likely,...), conjunctions (if, or, when, ...), and others; they are referred to as "space-builders". There are several procedures for setting up elements within spaces, usually by means of noun phrases; for example an indefinite, say *a cat* is typically interpreted as an instruction to set up a new element in some space, and ascribe to it the property signalled by the noun ("cat").[10] Spaces are linked, or may be linked, to one another by "connectors". A connector establishes counterpart relations: it maps an element of one space onto one or more elements of another. A simple case of connexion is the link between actors (real world individuals) and the characters they portray in a movie. When speaking of such situations, we set up two domains (at least), one corresponding to "reality" (as we see it), and another corresponding to the movie (also as we see it). An element in one space may have 0, 1, or more counterparts in the other — an actor may play several roles, or a character may be played by several actors (e.g. at different stages of his/her life).

Connectors do not only link mental spaces; they are at work in other processes, such as generalized metonymy, or role-value correspondances (cf. below). An important quasi-linguistic property of connectors is expressed by the following principle:

Identification Principle (I.D.): If a and b are linked by a connector F, a's counterpart b may be identified by a description or name satisfied by a.

This is why, for example, in the movie situation mentioned above, the same aspect of the story can be reported by means of (1) or (2):[11]

(1) In *Gone with the Wind*, Rhett Butler falls in love with Scarlett.

(2) In *Gone with the Wind*, Clark Gable falls in love with Scarlett.

In (2), the name of Rhett Butler's counterpart (the actor Clark Gable) is used to identify the character.

[10] We ordinarily think of the property holding of some "real world" referent. Here, the property is first ascribed in a purely formal sense to the space element. The conditions for this to fit a real situation are another matter.

[11] This is not to say, of course, that (1) and (2) are equivalent; if the pragmatic connector is available for a correct understanding of (2) (link between actors and characters), (2) but not (1), will "tell" us something about Clark Gable.

Similarly, consider (3):

(3) In Eisenberg's last movie, *the president's mistress* is a spy.

Suppose the actress is Marylin, and that she plays a character called Beatrice. Two interpretations of (3) come to mind: both convey that Beatrice is a spy, but under one of them, Beatrice is also intimate with the president (in the movie of course), while in the other, it is Marylin who fits the description "president's mistress", and this description of Bea's counterpart allows identification of Bea, under the I.D. Principle.

Finally, notice that the same principle is at work in some interpretations of (4) and (5):

(4) George believes that the president's mistress is a spy.

(5) In 1968, the president's mistress was a spy.

In (4), *George believes* is a space-builder; two spaces are set up, R (informally "the speaker's view of reality"[12]), and M (informally "George's beliefs"). *the president's mistress*, in the syntactic scope of *believes* must identify a target in M, b. It can do this directly, by being a property of b: this yields the so-called opaque reading, for which George believes that the spy is the president's mistress (i.e. has that property). But according to the I.D. Principle, another identification path is possible: *the president's mistress* can be a description of b's counterpart a in R: this is the "transparent" interpretation, in which the speaker supplies a description which he knows George might not assent to.

Similarly, in the case of (5), two spaces are set up, corresponding to two time-slices: now (space R) and 1968 (space M). Depending on whether the description "the president's mistress" holds directly for b in M, or for its counterpart a in R, we get the interpretations "the person who was the president's mistress in 1968 was also at that time a spy", or "the person who is now the president's mistress was a spy back in 1968".

The simple examples in (1) through (6) are presented here only to illustrate the scheme and principles informally, not as evidence in their defense. I refer the reader to MS for some detailed argumentation.

Nevertheless, such examples may be used to clarify some general remarks made earlier about ambiguity and grammatical structure. Expressions like (3), (4), (5), underdetermine mental construction in the following sense: all three involve two spaces and a description, but none specifies in which of the two spaces the description holds: this creates a choice in the construction process, in spite of the fact that the expressions have a single grammatical structure.[13] Attempts to mirror these construction choices by postulating hidden multiple logical forms for such

---

[12] This "parent" space is already in place when the language expression (sentence (4)) comes along in the discourse. (cf. MS)

[13] There are in fact more choices (and hence more "interpretations") than has been indicated so far.

expressions miss the point. Furthermore the process is an open one; if more spaces are available, the number of possible interpretations will increase. Consider (6):

(6) If the president has a mistress, George believes that the president's mistress is a spy.

A third space has been set up (hypothetical *if* ...), call it H . On one reading of (6), the description "the president's mistress" originates in H, which is different from saying that it is provided by the speaker for some individual.

Notice another feature of constructions, illustrated by the above examples: a linguistic expression can simultaneously set up domains, establish links between them, set up new elements and counterparts, and assign properties and relations within the domains. A word of philosophical caution however: we do not wish to say that properties such as "president's mistress" in the ordinary sense, are properties of elements in spaces (mental constructs). That is, elements and properties at the abstract construction level are distinguished sharply from real world circumstances that we may also associate with them.

Definite descriptions, as they apply to space construction, often set up or point to certain kinds of elements, called roles, which in turn may take other elements as their values. Again, I shall attempt to illustrate this process by means of straightforward examples, referring the reader to other studies for a detailed account.[14] Consider the following:

(7) Yesterday, Capdulla welcomed *the Pope* for the third time in over a thousand years.
(8) *The thirty-fourth volume of "Men of Good Will"* was never written.
(9) In the last thirty years, over a million complaints have been addressed to *the Secretary of the U.N.*
(10) *The food in this restaurant* is sometimes exceptional.

Under the pragmatically most likely interpretation of (7)-(10), the underlined definite description does not pick out an object or individual: different Popes visited Capdulla, there is no 34th volume of "Men of Good Will", no particular Secretary of the U.N. received 1 million complaints, and the restaurant does not store a big box full of food that sometimes deteriorates and sometimes improves with age. The definite description in such cases is interpreted as a *role*, which may take different values, or no value at all (ex. (8)).

However, when a definite description picks out a role, it may nevertheless end up identifying its value. Sentences (7) through (10) all admit another clearly distinct interpretation: (7) is appropriate if Mathusalem has just been elected Pope, when he goes to Capdulla, and if he has paid

---

[14] Cf. Hofstadter, Clossman, & Meredith (1982), Fauconnier (1978, 1985, 1986).

two other visits in the past 1000 years, and if no other Pope has ever been to Capdulla. (8) could apply to a specific volume that was xeroxed instead of being copied by scribes; (9) might concern a person who has received many complaints during the last thirty years, although perhaps none since he/she became Secretary of the U.N., say ten minutes ago; and for (10) the box interpretation is of course available.

The availability of such interpretations shows that the I.D. Principle applies to the link between role and value just as it does to other connectors (metonymic functions,[15] space connectors).

$$r \qquad\qquad\qquad\qquad\qquad\qquad v$$

If r is a role, appropriately picked out by a definite description, and v its value in some space, the definite description may identify the value v. Further study of roles[16] shows that the notion is a relative one: an element x may simultaneously be the value of a role y and a role for another element w. Ex. (11), although not to be taken as conclusive evidence by itself, illustrates this possibility:

(11) In France, *the head of state* is *the president* and currently *the president* is *François*.

the president is a value for the role "head of state" and a role for "François".

Although, prototypically, proper names tend to be associated directly with values, they can also easily serve as roles in appropriate contexts.[17]

Turning back now to examples like (3), (4), (5), we see that the role/value distinction increases the number of possible identification paths associated with such sentences: a description like *the president's mistress* may not only be a value as previously envisaged, but also a role, and furthermore, this role-element r may appear in any of the spaces at hand. Take (5) ("In 1968, the president's mistress was a spy"); if r is in space M (*in 1968*), the interpretation is that in 1968, being the president's mistress entailed being a spy — this is no longer an accidental property of the individuals concerned, and is compatible with the president having had several mistresses, or for that matter, none at all.[18] If r is in space R ("now"), we have the understanding (perhaps less salient

---

[15] Cf. Nunberg (1978), Gilchrist (1984), MS.

[16] Cf. "Roles and connecting paths" (1986).

[17] Cf. MS, Ch.2, sec.5. Theatrical roles (e.g. Hamlet) are paradigm cases of roles in this sense; they take actors as values.

[18] e.g. "Because it was known in 1968 that the president's mistress was a spy, Nixon chose to have none at all.".

pragmatically), that in order to be the president's mistress today, one had to be a spy in 1968. The very same configurations and multiple identification paths are associated with (3) and (4): (4) could be taken to mean that George thinks that being the president's mistress entails being a spy (r in M), or that George believes the function of certain women who (ritually) accompany the president to be spying, when in fact that function (unbeknownst to George) is "mistress". (r in R).

The general form of the space configuration in all such cases is (12):

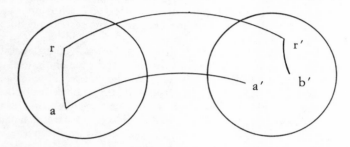

If we call S the relevant property ("being a spy" in this case), and if the description "the president's mistress" applies to role r or to role r', there will be appropriate identification paths (according to the I.D. Principle), leading to r', b', or a', and having their origin at r or r', hence four possible interpretation choices.[19] As before, the possibility of such multiple identification paths does not require any structural ambiguity in the language expression itself; in fact, given its predictability from the I.D. Principle operating on space and role/value connectors, it militates against structural accounts.

Finally, it may be noted that the above account is simplified in some respects. Within the noun phrase *the president's mistress*, there is a further choice to be made: even if a role is selected for the whole noun phrase, *the president* could receive a value interpretation; thus if Pinochet is the president, the role in that case would be "Pinochet's mistress". This role could have counterparts in spaces where Pinochet is not president.

2. Quantification

Studying the properties of domains constructed at the intermediate level C, offers some insight into a number of phenomena which do not receive natural explanations at the structural or at the "objective" levels:

---

[19] There are in fact more possibilities than envisaged here.

such is the case for presupposition projection, comparatives, counterfactuals, etc. examined in MS. In the present paper, I will explore some consequences of the approach in another area, closely tied to logic: natural language quantification. It has been observed that pronouns in certain circumstances have properties very similar to the bound variables of mathematical logic; and yet, attempts to exploit this similarity have met with serious difficulties: in particular, not just pronouns, but also noun phrases in general can appear to be "bound" and fall under different scopes: this calls for some extension of the binding process; on the other hand, if a variable is bound in the mathematical sense, it cannot appear outside of the scope of the binding operator: this restriction does not apply in the same way to bound pronouns or noun phrases.

It turns out that this double dilemma can be resolved at level C, by keeping certain domains linked but distinct, and by making use of the notion of role: the relevant "bound variable" properties, as we shall see, are also shared by roles, but without the standard scope restrictions, and furthermore roles can be picked out by noun phrases in general, not just pronouns: this will account for extended binding in natural language.

Recall first how scope effects are produced naturally by space assignment. Very simple examples can illustrate this.

(13) Pablo painted a duck.
(14) Pablo wants a duck.

The subject-verb complex in (13), *Pablo painted*, sets up a space M ("Pablo's painting"), within the origin space R. The indefinite *a duck* is an instruction to set up a new element (with the property "duck") and use it to identify an element in M. Given the I.D. Principle, there are two ways to conform to this instruction: either the new element is introduced in space R and its counterpart in M is identified, or the new element is introduced directly in M and identifies itself. In the former case, the interpretation is that some (real) duck served as a model for whatever Pablo painted (which may have a different property with respect to the painting, e.g. being a guitar or a rhinoceros); in the latter case, the duck is directly part of the painting.[20]

Mutatis mutandis, the same double possibility is available for (14): if *a duck* introduces an element in R with a counterpart in M (*Pablo wants*), the interpretation is the so-called "wide scope" one (specific): there is some duck such that...; Pablo need not know that what he wants is a duck; if the new element is introduced directly in M, it requires no counterpart in R: this is the "narrow scope" (non-specific) interpretation.[21]

[20] Who ascribes this property "duck" is another matter − e.g. the painter, the public, etc.

[21] Again, this is a slightly simplified account, since I neglect possible role/value distinctions.

In general, scope effects will often stem from space assignment: in order to identify an element in some target space, an expression (e.g. *a duck*) may describe or name an element in a higher connected space. Scope is underdetermined by expressions like (13) and (14), in the sense that their " instructions" (setting up a new element and identifying a target) do not impose the choice of any particular space. Such examples also show incidentally that multiple scope possibilities exist even when only one proposition in the classical sense is available.[22]

Scope properties of universal quantifiers can be accounted for in the same way: by assuming that several domains are involved. Our basic principle will be that quantifiers set up spaces distinct from the origin space (to which the quantification is relevant) and that new elements in the quantification space are all roles, which may take values in the origin space.

I begin by illustrating this kind of mechanism with the simplest cases. Take (15):

(15) Each of the frogs jumped.

the frogs is taken to identify (and describe) an element in the origin space, G, which is a set: elements a,b,c, ... in R, with the property "frog", belong to G. *each* operates as a space-builder: a quantifier space Q is set up in which *each of the frogs* describes and identifies a role r, such that J(r), if J stands for the property "jumped" (time and tense are neglected for expository purposes).

The semantic interpretation is as follows: role r (*each of the frogs*) takes its values in G (*the frogs*), in R. This is by stipulation: new elements in the quantifier space are all roles and they are linked to the origin space by a connector F_q such that if G is an element in R, r a role in Q, and $F_q(G) = r$, then G is the set of possible values for r. If J is a first-order property satisfied by r, then J will be satisfied (in the origin space) by any value chosen for r, i.e. elements "belonging" to G.[23] Schematically, in terms of space diagrams, we have (16):

(16)

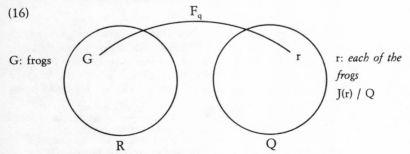

G: frogs   r: *each of the frogs*
                        J(r) / Q

[22] This is at odds with representations in terms of existential quantifiers.
[23] I call "first order" properties those which extend from roles to their values. If Joe

By definition: if a ϵ G, then r(R) = a.
It follows, from the usual properties of roles that if J(r) is satisfied in space Q, then J(r(R)) is satisfied in space R, i.e. J(a) is satisfied in space R (the origin space). Notice that a and G are both elements of space R. To say that a belongs to G, a ϵ G, is to say that a certain relation (ϵ) holds between elements a and G. Since this relation happens to be set-inclusion, G must be a set.[24] r(R) = a indicates as usual that a is a value of r in space R; notice that the role-value mapping in this case is one-to-many. Furthermore, notice that the values are not represented in configuration (16), only the connector F_q linking r to G. This guarantees that any member of G could be chosen as a value of r (and would therefore have property J), but no actual members are selected. It also guarantees that any elements already in R, and standing in the "belong" relation with respect to element G, will have the property J. Formally, given the space construction at hand, a sentence like (15), after setting up Q and linking r and G, imposes the condition:

$$J \ (F_q(G))/Q$$

(the role $F_q(G)$ which takes members of G as its values, satisfies property J in space Q). When J is a first-order property, this entails:

$$\forall a \epsilon G \quad J(a)/R$$

Suppose now that the quantified expression contains an indefinite, i.e. introduces a new element in some space, as in (17):

(17) Each of the frogs spotted *one of the flies.*

Since we have two spaces, R and Q, the indefinite may set up a new element in either one. If the element is set up in Q, it is necessarily a role (new elements in Q are roles by stipulation). This role, s, is linked by F_q to the element H in R, which stands for the set of its possible values (*the flies* in our example). The linguistic expression (e.g. (17)) specifies a property satisfied by the two roles: "r spotted s". We know from the previous section that the property of r in Q ("_ spotted s" in this case) is satisfied by any of its values in R. So, if a ϵ G, then

"a spotted s" / R

This in turn will be interpreted as a "matching"[25] condition, and deemed satisfied if role s has a value b in R which satisfies it: " a spotted b ".
    This amounts to saying that whenever a value is picked for the *quantified* role r, values (in R) must be available for the other roles in space Q, such that property J, satisfied for the roles in Q, is satisfied for the

is president, we infer from "the president is over 21" that Joe is over 21, but not from "the president changes every four years" that Joe changes every four years.
    [24] That the *element* G is a set is indicated here by the grammatical plural *frogs.*
    [25] Spaces can be matched via different correspondances. In the present case, roles in Q are connected to values (or roles) in R. The same first order properties must hold of matched elements (and also the same second order properties of matched roles).

corresponding values in R. This implies in turn, not surprisingly, that whenever a value a is picked for role r, the values picked for the other roles, such as s, will depend on a. We will write s(a) for the value taken by s when the quantified role r takes value a.

A linguistic expression like (17) will therefore set up the basic configuration (18), and the matching condition on R and Q will ensure that any configuration (19) can be completed to (20), where V stands for the connexion between roles and values.

(18)

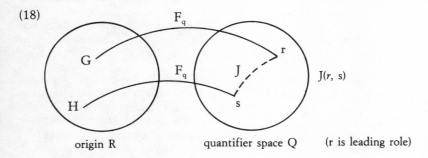

origin R   quantifier space Q   (r is leading role)

(19)

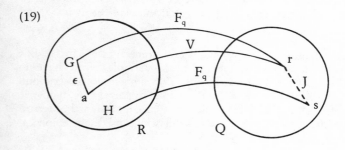

(20)

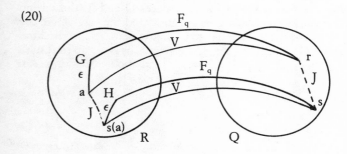

The conditions on space building of this kind are best expressed procedurally:

– when a linguistic expression such as (17) is used, noun phrases *the frogs* and *the flies* identify elements G and H in the relevant space R.[26]

– the noun phrase *each of the frogs* sets up a space Q and a role r in that space such that $F_q(G) = r$.

– the noun phrase *one of the flies* sets up a new element in one of the available spaces. If it is Q, the new element is a role s such that $F_q(H) = s$.

– the linguistic expression sets up a property of the elements in Q : J(r,s) (here: "r spotted s").

– *matching condition*: if a ϵ G, a is a value of r: set up an element s(a) in R; s(a) is a value of role s, and therefore s(a) ϵ H. To the relation J(r,s) satisfied in Q corresponds J(V(r), V(s)), i.e. J(a,s(a)), satisfied in R.

The appropriateness of such constructions for natural language phenomena will be discussed below. But perhaps a remark about the general spirit of this approach is in order. The quantifier space Q is like an abstract scenario, in which we have a frog, a fly, etc. and whatever interaction links them. The matching condition can be thought of metaphorically as saying that no matter what frog, in R, is chosen to instantiate the abstract role, there will be a matching scenario in R. In this general sense, the roles in Q share characteristics of the bound variables of logic, which can be instantiated in some cases: if

$$\forall x \epsilon G \ \exists y \epsilon H \ J(x,y)$$

then for any a of G, $\exists y \epsilon H$ J(a,y), and so for some b of H, J(a,b). But the analogy goes no further: as opposed to the variables which have no reference of their own, the roles are *bona fide* elements of spaces, and are hence predicted to survive in the discourse, to partake in anaphoric relationships, to change values from space to space, and so forth. I return below to the discussion of such characteristics and their empirical motivation.

First, however, an additional remark concerning cases like (17). As mentioned at the outset, the indefinite noun phrase *one of the frogs* may set up a new element in either of the two spaces Q and R (there is no explicit linguistic cue as to which one). I considered the case where the new element is a role in Q. Suppose now that it is in R: the situation is then the same as in (13), (14); the new element, b, is set up in R with a counterpart b′ in Q. (17) triggers a space construction of the form (21):

---

[26] "Relevant" here means the space under consideration, i.e. the parent space for Q.

(21)

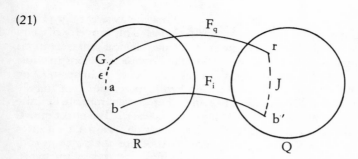

The property $J(r,b')$ in Q corresponds as before to $J(a,b)$ in R for any $a \epsilon G$. But since b has been introduced in R once and for all, it remains the same no matter what value a of r is set up. This corresponds of course to the "classical" wide scope or specific reading for the indefinite. For (17), this is the case where all the frogs spot the same fly. Furthermore, the element introduced in R could itself be a role, as predicted by the general ambivalence of noun phrases (cf. MS, ch.2). Such might be the interpretation of (22):

(22) Each of the prisoners speaks to a judge: the chief justice.

a judge sets up a new element in R, in this case a role ("chief justice"); the different values this role might take do not depend on the prisoners. (22) can be contrasted with (23):

(23) Each of the men respects one of the women: his mother.

each of the men sets up role r in Q, *one of the women* sets up role s, also in Q, and moreover, in (23), role s is further defined with respect to role r: s is r's mother. The grammatical coherence of this system is evident: we find all noun phrases identifying roles or values, and the possibility of various readings for a given sentence follows automatically from the fact that the sentence is grammatically underdetermined as to which space receives a new element, and as to whether a role or a value identification is chosen.

More importantly perhaps, the role analysis of quantification explains why logically "bound" phrases include not just pronouns but also definite noun phrases, and why they can occur outside the scope of their binding operators. Take the following description of military life:

(24) Each of the soldiers has a rifle. *He* cleans *the rifle* thoroughly; then *he* takes *it* to the shooting range. *The soldier* must learn to handle *the rifle* properly. Etc.

Under the favored interpretation of (24), the universal quantification extends throughout the discourse. In a superficial sense, *he, the rifle, it, the soldier*, range over entire sets. They do not in any way refer to unique (or contextually unique) objects/individuals. This property of noun phrases in discourse is not captured in standard logical representations of quantification. It follows however, rather directly, from the role analysis sketched above. Given the roles r and s set up in space Q by the noun phrases *each of the soldiers* and *a rifle*, these roles are naturally identified in later discourse, just like any others, by appropriate definite noun phrases (*the rifle, the soldier*) or pronouns (*he, it*). The effect of (24) is therefore simply to specify r and s in various ways ("r cleans s thoroughly", etc.), with respect to space Q. As before, the matching condition will account for the universal quantification across discourse: when role r takes value a in R, role s takes value s(a). Whatever holds[27] of r and s in Q will hold of a and s(a) in R: "a cleans s(a)", "a takes s(a) to the shooting range", "a must learn to handle s(a) properly", etc.

The reason, then, that definite noun phrases in discourse share logical properties of "bound variables" is that they stand for roles which belong to a quantifier space Q.

Expressions like "in *John's* case" indicate explicitly the attribution of a value a to a role r of a quantifier space. For example, suppose that (25) is added to discourse (24):

(25) In John's case, *the rifle* was rusty and *it* blew up.

The adverbial "in John's case" is an "instruction" to select a (name John) as the value of r; s(a) is then automatically selected as the value of s, so that *the rifle* and *it*, after picking out role s, will identify its value s(a) (i.e. John's rifle). Notice that such interpretations are not actually signaled linguistically: they arise if a quantifier space is available, because definite noun phrases can then be roles in that space. Such quantifier spaces are often available pragmatically, rather than set up explicitly. For instance, it is assumed that each individual has a heart ("pragmatic quantification"), and so we can say directly:

(26) In Harry's case, *the heart* was tired.
(27) They shot at Max. Fortunately *the heart* was not hit.

Here again, *the heart* picks a role and identifies particular values — Harry's heart, Max's heart — according to the implicit quantification schema 'r has s' (r: each individual, s: heart of r). This also accounts for referentially bizarre cases like (28):[28]

(28) They shot at Max. Fortunately, *the heart, which* is an essential organ of the human body, was not hit.

---

[27] Strictly speaking, "whatever" is too strong: only first order properties match — cf. notes 23, 25.
[28] Cf. Kayne (1975), Nunberg (1978), Fauconnier (1978).

In (28), it looks superficially as if the relative pronoun *which* is referring generically to the heart in general, while its antecedent *the heart* refers to a specific organ: Max's heart. In fact, antecedent and pronoun both pick out the same role s, which warrants the linguistic anaphor (cf. MS chap. 1); in the main clause, the description of the role can then identify its value as in (27), while in the relative clause the role is identified.[29] Notice also that in (29), a property of the role is indicated, namely the absence of a value for that role:

(29) In John's case, the heart is missing.

(under the interpretation where John differs from other people in having no heart)
In (30) a second quantification on roles is involved:

(30) Each player picked a word. The word was usually short.

The property "… was usually short", is a property of role s (*a word*), but not a property of each value of s, s(a). We may regard such "second-order" properties as applying to roles but not to their values. The general interpretation of such properties is quantification over the parameters on which the role depends. In the case of (30), the parameter is the value chosen for r: "the word was usually short" = "s was usually short" = = "for most a's, s(a) was short". *usually* quantifies over the set of values for the parameter which determines the values taken by s. We need this kind of interpretation for roles in general, as in "the pope is usually pious", "the temperature is seldom low", etc. Its appearance in (30) offers more evidence for the role analysis of quantification.

Another puzzle involving quantifier scope finds an easy solution within the present framework. Consider (31):

(31) Two ministers of each country will attend the conference.

It is usually claimed, and sometimes proven, that in constructions like (31), *each* has wide scope over *two*:
"For each country, there are two ministers of that country such that they will attend the conference".
However, (31) admits another interpretation, in which the ministers can be defined independently of the countries, as in:

(32) Two ministers of each country will attend: the minister of Finance, and the minister of Agriculture.

(31), then, could be intended to mean that two particular ministers,[30]

---

[29] Cf. MS. Linguistic anaphoric processes depend only on the identity of the triggers, not on that of the targets, and hence a fortiori not on coreference.

[30] On this reading, each country will send the same two ministers, Agriculture and Finance, but of course not the same two individuals.

say Finance and Agriculture, have been selected such that each country will send *those* ministers to the conference. The readings can lead to different truth values: in the first case, each country must send two different individuals, who are ministers; in the second, if some country has a single individual who is *both* minister of Finance *and* minister of Agriculture, it will send only that single individual and meet the requirement.

The key to explaining this wide scope effect was mentioned above in connection with example (22): an indefinite noun phrase may set up new elements either in Q or in R, and in R it may set up roles. For the "wide scope" interpretation of (31), *two ministers* sets up roles m, n in R with counterparts m′, n′ in Q, such that "m′ is minister of r", "n′ is minister of r", r is the role corresponding to *each country*. m and n remain the same in R no matter what value a is picked for r; we have m(a) = m′(a), n(a) = n′(a). If, for some value of r, b, m(b) = n(b) = c (case where one individual occupies the two posts), the characteristic property of values (by matching), "m(b) and n(b) attend the conference" reduces to "c attends the conference".

(33) and (34) are configurations corresponding to the two interpretations of (31). Crucially, in (34), the role/value scheme allows the roles corresponding to "two ministers" to be independent of the quantifier space, while their values m(a), n(a), are not, since they must satisfy the matching condition.

(33)

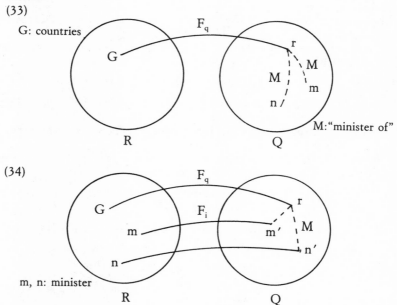

(34)

Hypothetical spaces, such as those introduced by "if...then..." are similar in important ways to quantifier spaces. The interpretation of "if A, then B" is informally, very generally, something like "in situations where A holds, B holds".[31] When the hypothetical is not counterfactual, this can be viewed as a matching condition between the parent space R and the hypothetical H: matching with respect to A (expressed by the protasis) allows full matching. As long as a hypothetical space is in force within a discourse, it constrains the construction of its parent space R. This is analogous to what was observed for the quantifier spaces, which set up similar matching conditions. It is not surprising, then, to observe that hypotheticals can express what amounts superficially to universal quantification:

(35) If a man loves a woman, he respects her.

The interpretation of (35) follows directly from the properties of indefinites and hypotheticals we have discussed. *If...*sets up a hypothetical space, in which *a man* and *a woman* introduce roles m and w such that "m loves w". *he* and *her* are pronouns which identify roles m and w in the standard way, so that "m respects w" is a further relation specified in the hypothetical space H. The matching condition between H and parent space R is that when they match for the protasis, they match in other respects. But to say that they match for the protasis "m loves w" is simply to say that elements a and b in R are values of m and w respectively, such that "a loves b". The full matching condition will then give the required "consequence": "a respects b".

Notice that the appropriate matching of the protasis condition will occur, no matter what pair (a, b) is picked (or set up) in R such that a has the properties of role m ("man"), b has the properties of role w ("woman") and "a loves b".

This is why, in terms of the values for m and w in R, (35) ends up being superficially equivalent to a universal quantification:

$$\forall a \epsilon M \ \forall b \epsilon W \ (\text{"a loves b"} \ \rightarrow \ \text{"a respects b"})$$

(36)

T:"respects"
L:"loves"

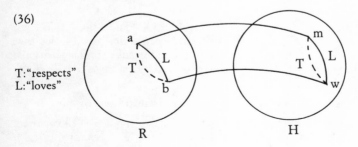

R   H

[31] Cf. MS, Ch. 4.

A considerable advantage of the role analysis is that it yields the correct interpretations without stipulating special representations or multiple meanings for indefinites, anaphoric pronouns, conditional conjunctions, etc. Furthermore, the correspondance between grammatical expressions and mental constructions is quite direct: noun phrases always pick out roles or their values; a pronoun and its antecedent always pick out the same trigger, even if they end up identifying different targets.

The following standard example of "logically complex binding" illustrates the same points:[32]

(37) Every man who loves a woman respects her.

In (37), the role *every man* (r), is restricted by the condition "who loves a woman". As usual, *a woman* sets up a role s in the quantifier space; the relative pronoun *who* identifies r: the restrictive condition is "r loves s". Thus, r has two restrictive conditions in this case: the properties "man" and "r loves s". Again they function very much like protasis matching conditions: in order to be a value of r, element a in parent space R must meet the same conditions, i.e. there must be an element b, value of role s, such that "a loves s". This element b will then be s(a) in the sense explained above, so that from the general property "r respects s", in Q, expressed by (37), matching with R for any value a of r, will produce "a respects s(a)".

(38)

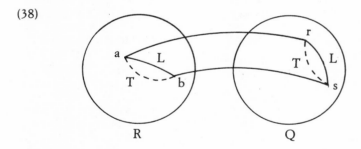

Configuration (38) is produced by setting up a "quantified" role r, an ordinary "indefinite" role s, and restricting r in terms of s. Notice that once the configuration is set up, r and s are in formally similar positions. And indeed, the same effect could be achieved by making s the "leading" role, and restricting it in terms of r:

(39) Every woman who is loved by a man is respected by him.

Of course, the fact that r and s are set up as roles in space Q allows them to be identified anaphorically in later discourse, e.g. *her* for s in (37),

[32] Cf. Guenthner & Rohrer (1976).

him for r in (39). Because the identification is relative to Q, the quantified effect is maintained. And later identifications of the roles can be effected by way of description: *the man, the woman, ...* This feature is crucial in distinguishing linguistic anaphora from standard logical binding. In the latter, the bound variables are actually a notational device for projecting n-place predicates onto (n − 1)-place predicates:

$$\exists x R(x,a) \equiv R'(a)$$

where R′ is the property which holds of a if "there is an x such that R(x,a)": R′ is the projection of R onto an (n − 1) dimensional space within an n-dimensional space:

(40)

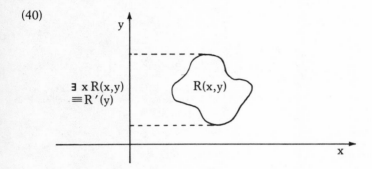

Bound variables in this sense do not correspond to any elements at all. Roles on the other hand are genuine elements with standard anaphoric properties. What characterizes them in the case of quantification is that they are set up in a distinct domain.

The properties of connected domains constructed at the intermediate "cognitive" level C turn out to be quite powerful in accounting for semantic and grammatical regularities. The spaces often have some kind of intuitive link with intuitive notions such as "possible worlds", "time slices", "beliefs", "pictures", "metaphorical domains", "hypothetical situations", etc. In the present analysis of quantification, we have looked at domains − quantifier spaces − which do not seem to have this kind of intuitive counterparts, and in which roles are set up on the basis of local situations (i.e. not necessarily general scenarios or ICM's). The evidence considered has been both semantic and grammatical: by invoking roles and domains, which we independently know to operate on a very wide scale, we account for a variety of readings, interpretations, etc., while keeping the purely grammatical structures extremely simple and uniform.

80 GILLES FAUCONNIER

References

ANSCOMBRE, J.-CL. & DUCROT, O.
1983 *L'argumentation dans la langue*, Liège, Mardaga.
DINSMORE, J.
to appear *Mental Spaces from a Functional Perspective*.
DUCROT, O.
1972 *Dire et ne pas dire*, Paris, Hermann.
1985 *Le dire et le dit*, Paris, Minuit.
FAUCONNIER, G.
1975 "Pragmatic scales and logical structure". *Ling.Inqu.* VI.3.
1978 "Is there a linguistic level of logical representation?", *Theoretical Linguistics* V.1.
1985 *Mental Spaces*, Cambridge, Mass, MIT Press.
1986 "Roles and Connecting Paths", in *Meaning and Interpretation*, Ch. Travis ed., Oxford, Blackwell.
GILCHRIST, T.
1984 *On metonymy*, unpublished ms. University of California, Berkeley.
GOFFMAN, E.
1974 *Frame analysis*, New York, Harper & Row.
GUENTHNER, F. & ROHRER CH.
1976 *Colloque franco-allemand de grammaire transformationnelle*, Stuttgart.
HOFSTADTER, D. & CLOSSMAN G. & MEREDITH M.
1982 *Shakespeare's plays weren't written by him, but by someone else of the same name: An essay on intensionality and frame-based representation systems*, Bloomington, Indiana, Indiana University Linguistics Club.
HORN, L.
1972 *On the Semantic Properties of Logical Operators in English*, Ph. D. dissertation, UCLA.
JACKENDOFF, R.
1983 *Semantics and Cognition*. Cambridge, Mass., MIT Press.
KAYNE, R.
1976 *Colloque franco-allemand de grammaire transformationnelle*, Stuttgart.
LAKOFF, G. & JOHNSON, M.
1980 *Metaphors we live by*, Chicago, University of Chicago Press.
1986 *Women, Fire, and Dangerous Things*, Chicago, University of Chicago Press.
LANGACKER, R.
1986 *Foundations of Cognitive Grammar*, Stanford, Stanford University Press.
MAIDA, A.
to appear *Belief Spaces. Foundations of a computational theory of belief*, ms. Pennsylvania State University.
NUNBERG, G.
1978 *The Pragmatics of Reference*, Bloomington, Indiana, Indiana University Linguistics Club.
TRAVIS, Ch.
1981 *The True and the False: The Domain of the Pragmatic*, Amsterdam, John Benjamins.

Ray Jackendoff

Conceptual Semantics

1. Introduction

In contrast to traditional logical approaches to semantics, which are at best neutral with respect to psychological considerations and at worst inimical to them, there is a growing body of work that takes as basic the premise that *meaning in natural language is an information structure that is mentally encoded by human beings*. The consequences of this premise, which may be called the Mentalist Postulate, flow in two directions. On the one hand, research on the nature of human mental representation, independent of issues of meaning, can be used to constrain or enrich semantic theory; on the other hand, results in semantic theory can be taken to bear directly on questions of human conceptualization. Thus for those who embrace the Mentalist Postulate, semantic theory no longer is just an aspect of the study of language (or of logic). Rather, it becomes an element of a wider theory of psychology, fully integrated into the study of mind.

Among the most important works that bring general psychological concerns to bear on semantics are Jerry Fodor's *The Language of Thought* (1975) and George Miller and Philip Johnson-Laird's *Language and Perception* (1976); among the most important bringing evidence from language to bear on the structure of concepts are Jeffrey Gruber's *Studies in Lexical Relations* (1965), the work of Eleanor Rosch et al. (1975, 1976, 1978), and the work of Leonard Talmy (1976, 1978, 1980, 1983). The material to be presented here draws on all these to some degree, but is primarily a summary of the theory of Conceptual Semantics developed in my monograph *Semantics and Cognition* (henceforth *S&C*). Within the present context I will be able to give only the flavor of the theory; the reader is referred to the monograph for more extensive justification.

2. Consequences of the Mentalist Postulate

At the basis of any formal semantics is the notion that utterances of a language must receive systematic descriptions not only in terms of phonological and syntactic structure, but in terms of an independent level of representation that may be called *semantic* or *conceptual structure*. This level is responsible for an account of semantic properties of utterances such as inference, presupposition, anomaly, and sameness and difference of meaning. In particular, it must be rich enough to express all the distinctions of meaning available to the intuitions of speakers of the language — a formidable task.

Crucial to this view of conceptual structure is that the semantic properties of utterances can be explicated *by virtue of form alone*, that is, that the human capacity of interpreting sentences can ultimately be traced to a computational system whose domain and range is conceptual structure. There is no further step of translating conceptual structure into yet another level of structure to find its interpretation: expressions at the level of conceptual structure simply *are* the interpretations of utterances.

In addition, any formal semantics of natural language must provide an account of compositionality: how the meaning of an utterance is built up from the meanings of its constituent words plus its syntactic structure. Different approaches take different views on the stringency of compositionality — the extent to which each syntactic constituent of a sentence must correspond to a constituent of conceptual structure. On the weak end of the continuum is Russell's theory of definite descriptions, in which the interpretation of a noun phrase is scattered widely through the interpretation of the sentence as a whole; on the strong end is Montague grammar, which demands a constituent-by-constituent correspondence.

Now let us add to these generally acknowledged stipulations the premise that meanings are mentally represented. From this follow two immediate constraints. First, meanings and their components must be finitely representable, since they must be stored in a brain of finite (albeit large) capacity. This rules out extensional theories of meaning in which, for instance, the meaning of *dog* is taken to be the set of all dogs (or the set of all dogs in all possible worlds). It also rules out a Platonic theory such as Katz's (1981), in which word meanings are abstract objects existing independently of minds, as well as the simplest construal of situation semantics (Barwise and Perry (1983)), in which meaning is taken to reside in the world and is somehow grasped by humans. It is the *internal representation of what is grasped* that is of interest.

Second, it must be possible for meanings — both word meanings and the principles of compositionality — to be *learned* in the course of language acquisition. As in syntax and phonology, it is an empirical problem to properly distribute the power of the theory among innate and learned aspects. Life is easier for the language learner if more of the semantics is innate; but enough must be language-specific to cope with the diversity of human languages. And as in syntax and phonology, the strategies for addressing this problem include arguments from language universals and arguments from poverty of the stimulus (Chomsky (1965)). The issue of learnability, as far as I am aware, is never addressed by traditional logical semantics. It is a paramount constraint on a semantics that aspires to psychological claims – even if it is not always clear at any particular moment how to apply it sensibly.

A more subtle consequence of the premise of meanings as mental information structures is the view of reference that it entails: *People have things to talk about only by virtue of having mentally represented them*. If an entity E in the real world is not represented in the mind of a person P, E does not exist for P, nor does it *fail* to exist: it is simply unavailable to P. Hence, without a mental representation of E, P cannot refer to E in an utterance. This seems harmless enough until one considers how complex the relationship is between the physical inputs that impinge on a human being and the entities one perceives as a result. In fact, most of the literature of perception is concerned with how we manage at all the remarkable feat of construing the world as full of more or less stable things, given constantly shifting patterns of environmental stimulation. It develops that even the concept "physical object" cannot be given a firm *physical* foundation, but must involve a considerable intensional (i.e. mentally contributed) component. (See Marr (1982) as well as the gestalt psychologists such as Koffka (1935) and standard texts such as Hochberg (1978).) Moreover, utterances about mental images and the like concern entities that exist *only* in mental representation.

Hence, we cannot take for granted the "real world" as the domain of entities to which language refers. Rather, the information that speakers can convey must be about their *construal* of the external world, where one's construal is the result of an interaction between external input and the means available to internally represent it. Furthermore, since one's construal of the world is heavily mediated by complex computational processes which have little if anything to do with language, reference in natural language is likely to reflect the internal representation of the world as least as much as it does the external world *per se*.

It is here, then, that a mentalistic semantics must most decisively part company with approaches (such as Davidson (1970)) that attempt to explicate natural language semantics in terms of a Tarskian recursive theory of truth, where truth is taken to be a relation between sentences and the real world: it is the world as construed by the speaker and hearer that is of concern. Nor does it help to relativize the notion of truth to "truth in a model," unless the choice of model is determined through empirical investigation of how humans construe the world. For instance, one cannot, as Lewis (1972, 175) does, found a theory of the model on a cavalier stipulation like "A possible world corresponds to a possible totality of facts, determinate in all respects." For what is to count as a fact is very much a psychological issue, and, as we will see in section 5, the notion of "determinate in all respects" is a chimera, an idealization that leads to counter-productive results. Similar objections apply to any account of reference based uncritically on set-theoretic principles. It is essential to ask: Is *this* the way humans construe the world?

Mathematical rigor is one thing; psychological rigor may well be another. To sum up, Conceptual Semantics takes as basic that the information language conveys, the *sense* of linguistic expressions, consists of expressions mentally instantiated at the level of conceptual structure. What the information is *about* — the *reference* of linguistic expressions — is not the real world, as in most semantic theories, but the world as construed by the speaker.

In the rest of this paper, I will sketch some of the ramifications of this mentalist view for one's approach to some basic problems of semantic description.

3. Ontological claims: some major categories of referring expressions

Let us first consider the ontological presuppositions of natural language — what sorts of entities, in a very broad sense, linguistic expressions can be said to be talking about. In the present view, ontological presuppositions are not dependent on the nature of "reality" so much as on the nature of the structure that human beings impose on the world as a result of their conceptual organization. This section will show what difference it makes to take the latter view.

One sufficient condition for believing that a speaker construes there to be an entity in the world is that he refers to it by means of "pragmatic anaphora" — a deictic expression accompanied by a pointing gesture which indicates to the hearer the intended referent. An example appears in (1).

(1) I bought that [*pointing*] yesterday — isn't it nice?

In order to interpret the pragmatically controlled pronoun *that* in (1), the hearer must pick out the intended referent in his visual field, i.e. *form an appropriate mental representation*, perhaps with the aid of the speaker's pointing gesture. If the hearer cannot form an appropriate representation, perhaps because he has his eyes shut, or the conversation is taking place over the telephone, or the speaker is pointing to something in an extremely indistinct photograph, the intended referent is unavailable to the hearer and the discourse cannot proceed. In other words, for a pragmatically controlled pronoun to be understood, the hearer must construct a construal of his perceived world such that it contains an entity of the intended sort.

So far this should be fairly uncontroversial. The interest arises when we observe (Hankamer and Sag (1976)) that pragmatic anaphora is possible not only to designated *objects*, as in (1), but also in syntactic contexts whose selectional restrictions are appropriate to *places* (2a), *directions* (2b), *actions* (2c), *events* (2d), *manners* (2e), and *amounts* (2f).

(2) a. Your hat is here [*pointing*] and your coat is there [*pointing*].
  b. He went thataway [*pointing*].
  c. Can you do that [*pointing*]?
   Can you do this [*demonstrating*]?
  d. That [*pointing*] had better not happen in *my* house!

  e. You shuffle cards $\begin{Bmatrix} \text{like this} \\ \text{thus} \\ \text{this way} \end{Bmatrix}$ [*demonstrating*].

  f. That fish that got away was $\begin{Bmatrix} \text{this} \\ \text{that} \\ \text{yay} \end{Bmatrix}$ [*demonstrating*]   long.

The conditions on the interpretation of *that* in (1) also obtain with the pragmatic anaphors in (2). For instance, if the hearer is unable to see or figure out what goings-on the speaker is pointing at in (2d), he will not fully understand the utterance — he will not have received all the information he is intended to receive, and discourse cannot properly continue.

If, as seems uncontroversial, the pragmatic anaphor in (1) refers to a thing (or physical object), those in (2) must also refer — but to entities quite distinct from physical objects, namely a place, a direction, an action, an event, a manner, and an amount, respectively. Thus the ontological presuppositions of English semantics must admit such entities — a range rarely recognized in extant semantic theories.

Another grammatical construction that supports this variety of entities is the expression of identity and individuation with *same* and *different*. Compare (3), which expresses identity and individuation of a physical object, with (4a)-(4f), which express identity and individuation of the entity types referred to in (2). (Some of these may express only *type*-identity; but that is sufficient for my argument, since type-identity presupposes tokens which may belong or not belong to the same type.)

(3) Bill picked up the same things $\begin{Bmatrix} \text{that} \\ \text{as} \end{Bmatrix}$ Jack did.

Bill picked up something different than Jack did. [Object]

(4) a. Bill ate at $\begin{Bmatrix} \text{the same place as} \\ \text{a different place than} \end{Bmatrix}$ Jack did. [Place]

  b. Bill went off $\begin{Bmatrix} \text{the same way as} \\ \text{a different way than} \end{Bmatrix}$ Jack did. [Direction]

c. Bill did $\left\{ \begin{array}{l} \text{the same thing as} \\ \text{a different thing as} \end{array} \right\}$ Jack did. [Action]

d. $\left\{ \begin{array}{l} \text{The same thing} \\ \text{A different thing} \end{array} \right\}$ happened today $\left\{ \begin{array}{l} \text{as} \\ \text{than} \end{array} \right\}$ happened yesterday. [Event]

e. Bill cooks meat $\left\{ \begin{array}{l} \text{the same way as} \\ \text{a different way than} \end{array} \right\}$ he cooks eggs. [Manner]

f. Bill is as tall as Jack is.
   Bill is taller than Jack is.   [Amount]

These assertions are not about the identity or nonidentity of linguistic expressions. They assert the identity of the entities to which the expressions refer. Thus there must be individuable entities of each of these types; and a properly general semantic theory must elevate this whole panoply of entities to the status of things that can be referred to.

But do we therefore have to ascribe such entities to Reality? I would hope not. For instance, the continuous flow of matter in the physical world does not on the whole come neatly segmented into events, as language would have it; nor does it seem plausible that the physical world contains manners segregated from the actions whose manners they are.

One's temptation, therefore, is to seek a theory which reduces all of these entities out of the primitive basis of the theory, leaving only, say, concurrences of physical objects over time in a four-dimensional space-time map. But such a view neglects the problem of mental representation: in order to correlate the linguistic and visual inputs in (2), both speaker and hearer must have internal information structures that contain entities of all these sorts. Thus, whatever the "Real" status of such entities, natural language semantics must act as though the world contains them. Moreover, the visual system must deliver information of the appropriate sort to fill in the pragmatic anaphors. In other words, such entities are *psychologically* real: they are in the world as we construe it. What is *physically* the case is not at issue.

The appeal of the reductionist view (which seems to be almost universally held) comes from a presumption that physical objects play a privileged role both in the world and in semantics. However, as mentioned above, the psychological reality of physical objects is based on an unbelievably complex congeries of perceptual and cognitive processes. The work I have encountered on perception of entities other than physical objects (for example Michotte (1954) on causation; Jenkins, Wald, and Pittenger (1978) on event-perception; remarks of Köhler (1929) on temporal grouping; Lerdahl and Jackendoff (1983) on musical structure; plus of course the entire literature on phonetic and syntactic perception) reveals characteristics entirely parallel to the perception of physical objects, such as the gestalt properties of proximity, closure, "good form", context dependence, and the like. Thus the attempt to reduce places, events, and so forth out of natural language semantics does not qualitatively simplify the job of perception, and it complicates the semantics of pragmatic anaphora and of *same* and *different* (as well as that of wh-questions and quantification — see *S&C*, chapter 3).

The alternative espoused by Conceptual Semantics is a nonreductionist view, in which conceptual structure contains constituents differentiated by what we may call *major ontological category features*, including at least [THING], [PLACE], [DIRECTION], [ACTION], [EVENT], [MANNER], and [AMOUNT], as well as possible others such as [SMELL] and [TIME]. Only one of these can be present as the major feature of a semantic constituent; they may be thought of as the "parts of speech" of semantic structure.

The major ontological category features appear in constituents of mental representation, as part of the senses of linguistic expressions. Corresponding to each of them is an ontological category of entities in the world as we construe it; and linguistic expressions may refer to these entities, for instance by means of pragmatic anaphora. On this view, then, the existence of a particular ontological category is not a matter of physics or metaphysical speculation or formal parsimony, but an empirical psychological issue, to be determined on the basis of its value in explaining the experience and behavior of human beings.

What the conditions of individuation are for these categories, and how clear-cut a result the conditions provide, are also empirical issues. Thus, for example, when Davidson (1967, 1969) finds problems for the ontological status of actions, it is partly because he indiscriminately applies the standards of individuation appropriate to objects. The correct approach, once we see ontological claims as psychological questions, is to investigate what evidence people take as relevant when they make judgments of identity or non identity. The evidence might well differ from one ontological type to another, because of the spatial and temporal characteristics peculiar to each.

The reader should be cautioned against concluding that the ontological categories mentioned above exhaust the possibilities. These simply happen to be the categories for which linguistic and visual evidence are both present most prominently. For a different sort of case, the sentence "That sounds like Brahms" might motivate an ontological category of sounds. Moreover, if a language other than English were to display different varieties of pragmatic anaphora, this would not lead to an argument that speakers of this language have different ontological categories. The total set of ontological categories, I assume, must be universal: it constitutes one basic dimension along which humans organize their experience, and hence it cannot be learned.

4. Categorization

An essential aspect of cognition is the ability to categorize: to judge that a particular thing is or is not an instance of a particular category. A categorization judgment is expressed most simply in English by a predicative sentence such as "*a* is a dog" and represented in first-order logic by an atomic sentence such as "D*a*." However, categorization judgments need not involve the use of language at all: they are fundamental to any sort of discrimination task performed by dogs or rats or babies. The ability to categorize is indispensable in using previous experience to guide the interpretation of new experience, for without categorization, memory is virtually useless. Thus an account of the organism's ability to categorize transcends linguistic theory. It is central to all of cognitive psychology.

Under the Mentalist Postulate, we take the theory of categorization to concern not whether a particular categorization is true, but rather what information and processing must be ascribed to an organism to account for its categorization judgments — what is involved in *grasping* an atomic sentence. Since there can be no judgment without representation, categorization cannot be treated simply as the organism's comparison of some component of reality *a* to a preexisting category of dogs: the comparison must be made between the internal representations of *a* and of the category of dogs. In short, a categorization judgment is the outcome of the juxtaposition of two conceptual structures.

We will refer to the representation of the thing being categorized as a [TOKEN] concept and that of the category as a [TYPE] concept. Since entities of different ontological categories can be categorized, the type-token distinction cuts across ontological boundaries, and we may speak of [THING TOKENS] and [THING TYPES], [EVENT TOKENS] and [EVENT TYPES], and so forth.

An essential characteristic of categorization is one's ability to identify novel tokens as instances of a known type. This means that the internal structure of a [TYPE] concept cannot consist merely of a list of the [TOKENS] one has encountered that instantiate it. Furthermore, both because of the finiteness of the brain and because of the need to learn [TYPE] concepts, a [TYPE] concept cannot be a list of *all* (*possible*) [TOKENS] that instantiate it. This consideration rules out semantic theories in which predicates such as "is a dog" are extensionally defined, with or without appeal to possible worlds. Rather, the creativity of categorization judgments requires that a [TYPE] concept consist of a set of principles or rules (just as the creativity of sentence perception and production argues that knowledge of a language is a set of rules).

Moreover, one can create new [TYPE] concepts at will. One of the simplest ways to do this is to construct, for an arbitrary [TOKEN]$_i$, a [TYPE] of THINGS LIKE [TOKEN]$_i$, where likeness can be determined along any arbitrary class of dimensions. For each of the indefinitely many [TOKENS] that one can construct in response to environmental stimulation, there are any number of such [TYPES]. These in turn can be used to categorize arbitrary new [TOKENS].

The creativity of [TYPE]-formation shows that a [TOKEN] concept cannot consist merely of a list of all the [TYPES] it is an instance of, since there may be indefinitely many of these. Some [TYPE]-inclusions may well be explicitly encoded within a [TOKEN], but by no means all.

We also have reason to reject Fodor's (1975) theory that all possible [TYPES] (or even just all possible [TYPES] that are coded as single lexical items) are innately given as unanalyzed monads: a [TYPE] without internal structure cannot be compared with novel [TOKENS] to yield categorization judgments. Moreover, Fodor's theory entails that there is only a finite number of possible [TYPES], since there is only a finite space in the brain for storing them all. But if one can generate new [TYPES] at will on the basis of given [TOKENS], then either the set of [TYPES] must be infinite, contra Fodor, or else the set of [TOKENS] must be finite and innate, a totally implausible conclusion.

Similar objections can be raised to *semantic network* theories (Collins and Quillian (1969), Simmons (1973), Smith (1978)), in which both [TOKEN] and [TYPE] concepts are represented as nodes in a finite network connected by a finite number of predicative links. Since all the possible inferences about concepts are to be drawn on the basis of the network, there is no way to deal with [TOKENS] that have never been encountered before; nor is there a way to generate new [TYPES] and compare them to previously known [TOKENS]. Again, some more creative mechanism appears necessary.

The overall form of an adequate mentalistic theory of [TYPES] resembles the form of generative syntactic theory (Chomsky (1965)). In such a theory, a [TYPE] concept is a finite set of rules that is used in categorizing novel [TOKENS]. Its function parallels that in syntactic theory of the grammar of a language, a finite set of rules used to recognize and produce novel sentence tokens. Since [TYPE] concepts can be constructed creatively, the total set of possible [TYPES] must itself be characterized by a finite set of *conceptual formation rules*. Concept acquisition can be thought of as using environmental evidence to help select a [TYPE] concept from among the possibilities provided by the conceptual formation rules. Thus the conceptual formation rules play a role in this theory parallel to that of Universal Grammar in syntactic theory: they are the innate basis for acquisition of environment-particular knowledge. (A major difference between conceptual and syntactic theories, of course, is that one typically learns at most a few languages, while one learns many thousands of concepts. But this difference should not obscure the formal parallels between the theories.)

This two-tier approach to the structure of [TYPE] concepts is, I believe, the only viable way to deal with the creativity of categorization within the constraints of the Mentalist Postulate. In turn, this approach requires that the [TYPE] concepts (or predicates) expressed by natural language are assembled from a finite innate set of primitives and principles of combination — in other words, a *decompositional* view of word meanings. Among the primitives will be the major ontological category features discussed in the previous section and the [TOKEN]/[TYPE] distinction. The next section will deal with one aspect of the principles of combination.

5. Preference Rule Systems

The most prevalent among decompositional theories has been one in which the conditions making up a word meaning (or concept) are taken to be collectively necessary and sufficient to determine the reference of the word. Such a theory nicely satisfies the common-sense intuition that words have definite and precise meanings. This probably accounts for the theory's great popularity and antiquity, and for the fact that it has so frequently been offered without seeming to need a defense. However, as Putnam (1975, 192-193) cautions,

The amazing thing about the theory of meaning is how long the subject has been in the grip of philosophical misconceptions, and how strong these misconceptions are. Meaning has been identified with a necessary and sufficient condition by philosopher after philosopher ... On the other side, it is amazing how weak the grip of the facts has been.

Fodor, Garrett, Walker and Parkes (1980) confirm Putnam's suspicion by pointing out that the number of convincing decompositions into necessary and sufficient conditions in the literature is vanishingly small, and these are restricted primarily to kinship terms (e.g. *bachelor, uncle*), axiomatized systems (*triangle*), and jargon terms (*ketch, highball*). The rest of the vocabulary of English has apparently so far resisted formal analysis of the requisite sort.

There are at least two prominent difficulties. The first lies within single conditions. At what point in a smooth transition of hue from focal red to focal orange does the color cease being red and begin being orange? If an intermediate color, red-orange, is introduced, where is the border between it and red? A theory of necessary and sufficient conditions requires a sharp border between colors, while, in fact, judgments grade from "That's definitely red" through "I'm not sure" to "That's definitely not red."

Similarly, at what height does a man qualify as tall? Or, for a spatial case, precisely where does one draw a line between being on a mountain and being on the fields below it? Or when does a fly crawling down your neck reach your shoulder? Or, to use the well-known case studies by Labov (1973), at what ratio of height to width does one draw the line between cups and bowls? In each of these cases, there is a gradation of judgment parallel to that between red and orange.

Furthermore, notice how odd it is to attribute the gradation to the judger's lack of knowledge of the concept in question: it is absurd to think there is a *real* borderline between red and orange that just hasn't been discovered. It is sometimes necessary or convenient to *stipulate* a borderline — perhaps for instance in a height regulation for prospective police officers, but such stipulation can hardly be taken as an explication of the ordinary-language concept expressed by *tall*. Thus the tack taken by Putnam (1975) when he adverts to the "division of linguistic labor" does not help for the general case.

Thus we must admit into semantic theory the possibility of graded oppositions between categories. In the cases mentioned so far, the gradation occurs along a single dimension. In certain of the cases, such as color, one can specify central values for the categories in question; the category of a particular hue is then a function of its relative distance to the nearest focal hues. Uncertain cases arise when the disparity of relative distances is not too great. In other cases, such as *tall*, there is no focal value; rather, distance away from the focal value ("normal height") is criterial.

A second and more serious difficulty with necessary and sufficient conditions concerns the interaction of conditions. The most prominent citation of this problem is Wittgenstein's (1953, 31-32) discussion of the word *game*, in which he challenges the reader to find any condition common to all instances of the category game but not to non-games. He suggests that there are no such common conditions, but only a set of relationships and similarities which he characterizes as "family resemblances." It is clear from the context of the passage that Wittgenstein considers this not an isolated counterexample but a typical instance of how words are understood.

More generally, Wittgenstein's problem concerns the possibility of discrete exceptions to defining conditions. If it is a necessary part of being human to have two legs or high intelligence, then are one-legged people and imbeciles not human? If having stripes is criterial for tigers, are albino tigers tigers? And so forth.

There have been various reactions to Wittgenstein's argument. Searle (1958) suggests that the totality of conditions in a word's definition need not be fulfilled — only a sufficiently large number of them. As we will see below, "a sufficiently large number" may sometimes be *one*; a great deal depends on the particulars of the case at hand. So this solution will not do.

A related suggestion appears in the work of Smith, Shoben, and Rips (1974), who place on each condition a degree of "definingness." Conditions of lesser degree are permitted to have exceptions, and in cases of doubt, the more highly defining conditions are to be relied upon. However, Smith, Shoben, and Rips assume there is a central core of most essential conditions that serve as "dictionary" definitions. Since this is just what Wittgenstein denies, they have not solved the problem either. The same difficulty appears in Katz's (1977) attempt to separate out dictionary definitions of necessary and sufficient conditions from an encyclopedia entry that is subject to exceptions.

By contrast, Rosch and Mervis (1975) and Mervis and Pani (1980) develop a theory of categories in which family resemblance phenomena play an essential part. They show experimentally how artificial categories of objects can be learned whose defining conditions are subject to exceptions. Those instances that satisfy all or most defining conditions are perceived as more central instances and are more easily learned and remembered. This confirms Wittgenstein's argument that concepts can have a family resemblance nature, and extends the argument beyond word meanings to perceptual concepts.

Thus semantic theory must include the possibility of conditions that play a role in defining categories but are nevertheless subject to exceptions. Though such a notion goes against the grain of traditional philosophical thinking, it seems altogether justified on psychological grounds.

The apparent difficulty with conditions that are subject to exceptions is the slippery slope argument: if each of the conditions in a category is subject to exceptions, what is to prevent calling a token that fails all of them a member of the category? The essential properties of a mechanism to solve this problem were discovered by Wertheimer (1923); the mechanism has been dubbed by Lerdahl and Jackendoff (1983) a *preference rule system*.

For a simple illustration of a preference rule system, consider two of the well-known gestalt principles for spatial grouping: proximity and similarity. Each of these in isolation is a condition of graded strength which is sufficient to produce a grouping judgment. For instance, the configuration in (5a) is naturally seen as grouped into two plus three by virtue of the relative proximity of the two lefthand circles and that of the three righthand circles, in contrast to the relative distance of the second and third circles. As the disparity of spacing increases, as in (5b), the judgment is stronger (harder to overcome by act of will); as the disparity decreases, as in (5c), the judgment is weaker.

(5)   a.   b.   c.

      OO OOO   OO OOO   OO OOO

Similarly, in (6), the grouping is two plus three by virtue of *similarity* of size; the judgment is stronger (6b) or weaker (6c) depending on the relative disparity in size.

(6) a.   b.   c.

So far, these conditions behave like the graded conditions for hue or height discussed above. The interest of the system arises, however, in situations where both principles apply. In (7a), both proximity and similarity analyze the configuration as two plus three, so a still stronger grouping judgment applies. But proximity analyzes (7b) as 3 + 2 while similarity analyzes it as 2 + 3. The outcome is a vague or ambiguous judgment that may even switch interpretations spontaneously. In (7c) and (7d) the two principles are also in conflict; but proximity prevails in (7c) and similarity in (7d), by virtue of their relative strengths of application.

(7) a.   b.

c.   d.

The consequence of this interaction in conflicting situations is that neither proximity nor similarity can be viewed as a sufficient condition for grouping: both are subject to exceptions. Moreover, neither is necessary, since (6a) and (7d) are grouped without appropriate proximity, and (5a) and (7c) are grouped without appropriate similarity. Still, both principles clearly play a role in grouping judgments; neither can be dispensed with.

The conditions of proximity and similarity and their interaction in grouping judgments constitute a simple case of a preference rule system. More generally, such a system is a means of producing a judgment or analysis based on a number of conditions. In any given field of input to which the system applies, each individual condition may contribute a preferred analysis, with an intrinsic strength or weight of application. The overall analysis arrived at by the system is the one that receives the greatest weight from individual conditions. In a field in which a number of the preference rules reinforce each other, and there is no conflict from competing conditions, a highly stable judgment results that is seen as relatively "stereotypical." One the other hand, in case two or more competing analyses receive approximately equal weight, an ambiguous judgment (like (7b)) results.

Once one has isolated the basic nature of preference rule systems, it is possible to recognize them everywhere in psychology. The content of the preference rules varies widely from one domain to the next, but the characteristic computational interaction appears in every case. (For references, see Lerdahl and Jackendoff (1983, section 12.2) and Jackendoff (1983, section 8.7).)

In particular, the interaction of preference rules has just the characteristics appropriate to conditions in word meanings that are subject to exceptions. It is not simply the accumulation of positive conditions that is relevant to a categorization judgment, but this accumulation balanced against the strength of alternative categorizations. When there is no countervailing evidence, a putative instance is seen as relatively stereotypical; but alternative analyses that are approximately equal in plausibility lead to ambiguity on unsure judgments, or at least judgments of nontypicality.

To make this point clearer, consider a new device described in a recent airline magazine: a screwdriver with a flashlight in its handle (or is it a flashlight with a screwdriver bit on the rear end?). It seems that a dispute arose with customs officials about whether to charge for the importation of these devices at the rate for screwdrivers or that for flashlights. The interest of the example lies in the fact that these devices pretty well satisfy *all* the defining conditions for either category, yet the demands of the task require one to decide which of the categories they belong to. In the theory of preference rules, which claims that a categorization judgment is a function of relative satisfaction of conditions among competing categories, the uncertainty of this case is a natural consequent. By contrast, the Searle theory of satisfaction of "enough" conditions and the Smith, Shoben, and Rips theory of satisfaction of "essential" conditions do not make any satisfactory prediction of how this case should come out.

We also see from this case that categorization is not so much a matter of "objective" truth or falsity as one of how one's set of mentally represented categories interact with each other. If one were to introduce a new category of "flashdrivers" (or "screwlights"), the range of categorization judgments for artifacts in this general field would readjust, just as, for instance, the categorization of color changes if one introduces "red-orange" between red and orange. In the present case, however, the adjustment is not in a single dimension, but in the interaction of a range of conditions.

I should emphasize the role of the Mentalist Postulate in helping to justify the use of preference rule systems as part of a theory of word meanings. The creativity of categorization requires a decompositional theory of word meanings, yet the data make clear that decomposition into necessary and sufficient conditions is inadequate. However, the fact that preference rule systems rather than some other computational device are independently necessary (and ubiquitous) in psychological systems argues that there should be no qualms in accepting them as a principle of combination in natural language semantics. If the mind uses such systems everywhere else, why should they not appear as part of mentally represented word meanings?

6. Summary

I have attempted to show here that the adoption of the Mentalist Postulate has a number of fundamental consequences for semantic theory, both methodological and substantive. On the one hand, it provides strong constraints on what sorts of theories are acceptable, ruling out many popular alternatives. On the other hand (and I consider this of more interest), it suggests ways to enrich semantic theory when enrichment is necessary: one is not so quick to apply Occam's razor to a formal innovation if there is extralinguistic psychological evidence for it. I have suggested here only some of the most elementary of the enrichments that can be justified; *S&C* goes into considerably more detail.

What I find exciting about such a mentalist approach is that it removes the study of meaning from the glass case in which it has languished for some decades. The traditional fascination with the study of language was based on the hope that it would reveal the structure of thought — of what it is to be human. This goal, to say the least, has not been prominent in contemporary formal semantics. But I believe we are now at a stage in our understanding of syntactic structure and — to some extent — perception and cognition where the traditional goal can be resurrected. In a sense, the Mentalist Postulate and the theory of Conceptual Semantics constitute announcement of that goal. The challenge it presents is formidable, but, at least from my point of view, the potential benefits are worth the effort.

References

BARWISE, JON, and PERRY, JOHN
1983   *Situations and Attitudes*, Cambridge, Bradford/MIT Press.
CHOMSKY, NOAM
1965   *Aspects of the Theory of Syntax*, Cambridge, MIT Press.
COLLINS, A., and QUILLIAN, M.
1969   "Retrieval Time from Semantic Memory", *Journal of Verbal Learning and Verbal Behavior* 9, 240-247.
DAVIDSON, DONALD
1967   "The Logical Form of Action Sentences", in N. Rescher (ed.), *The Logic of Decision and Action*, Pittsburgh, University of Pittsburgh Press.
1969   "The Individuation of Events", in N. Rescher et al. (eds.), *Essays in Honor of Carl G. Hempel*, Dordrecht, Reidel, 216-234.

DAVIDSON, DONALD
1970   "Semantics for Natural Languages", in *Linguaggi nella società e nella tecnica*, Milano, Edizioni di Comunità, 177-188.
FODOR, JERRY
1975   *The Language of Thought*, Cambridge, Harvard University Press.
FODOR, JERRY, GARRETT MERRILL, WALKER, E., and PARKES, C.
1980   "Against Definitions", *Cognition* 8, 263-367.
GRUBER, JEFFREY
1965   *Studies in Lexical Relations*, Doctoral dissertation, MIT, Cambridge, Bloomington, Ind., Indiana University Linguistics Club. Reprinted as part of *Lexical Structure in Syntax and Semantics*, Amsterdam, North-Holland, 1976.
HANKAMER, JORGE and SAG, IVAN
1976   "Deep and Surface Anaphora", *Linguistic Inquiry*, 7.3, 391-428.
HOCHBERG, JULIAN
1978   *Perception*, second edition, Englewood Cliffs, N.J., Prentice-Hall.
JACKENDOFF, RAY
1983   *Semantics and Cognition*, Cambridge, MIT Press.
JENKINS, JAMES J., WALD, JERRY, and PITTENGER, JOHN B.
1978   "Apprehending Pictorial Events: An Instance of Psychological Cohesion", in C. Wade Savage (ed.), *Perception and Cognition: Issues in the Foundations of Psychology*, (Minnesota Studies in the Philosophy of Science, Vol. 9), Minneapolis, University of Minnesota Press, 129-164.
KATZ, JERROLD J.
1977   "A Proper Theory of Names", *Philosophical Studies* 31, 1-80.
1981   *Language and Other Abstract Objects*, Totowa, N.J., Rowman and Littlefield.
KOFFKA, KURT
1935   *Principles of Gestalt Psychology*, New York, Harcourt, Brace & World.
KÖHLER, WOLFGANG
1929   *Gestalt Psychology*, New York, Liveright.
LABOV, WILLIAM
1973   "The Boundaries of Words and Their Meanings", in C.-J. N. Bailey and R. W. Shuy (eds.), *New Ways of Analyzing Variations in English*, Vol. 1, Washington, Georgetown University Press.
LERDAHL, FRED, and JACKENDOFF, RAY
1983   *A Generative Theory of Tonal Music*, Cambridge, MIT Press.
LEWIS, DAVID
1972   "General Semantics", in D. Davidson and G. Harman (eds.), *Semantics of Natural Language*, Dordrecht, Reidel, 169-218.
MARR, DAVID
1982   *Vision*, San Francisco, Freeman.
MERVIS, CAROLYN, and PANI, JOHN
1980   "Acquisition of Basic Object Categories", *Cognitive Psychology* 12, 496-522.
MICHOTTE, A.
1954   *La perception de la causalité*. 2nd ed. Louvain, Publications Universitaires de Louvain.
MILLER, GEORGE, and JOHNSON-LAIRD, PHILIP
1976   *Language and Perception*, Cambridge, Harvard University Press.
PUTNAM, HILARY
1975   "The Meaning of Meaning", in K. Gunderson (ed.), *Language, Mind, and Knowledge* (Minnesota Studies in the Philosophy of Science, Vol. 7), Minneapolis, University of Minnesota Press, 131-193.
ROSCH, ELEANOR
1978   "Principles of Categorization", in E. Rosch and B. Lloyd (eds.), *Cognition and Categorization*, Hillsdale, N.J., Erlbaum.
ROSCH, ELEANOR, and MERVIS, CAROLYN
1975   "Family Resemblances: Studies in the Internal Structure of Categories", *Cognitive Psychology* 7, 573-605.

ROSCH, ELEANOR, MERVIS, CAROLYN, GRAY, W., JOHNSON, D., and BOYES-BRAEM, P.
1976 "Basic Objects in Natural Categories", *Cognitive Psychology* 8, 382-439.
SEARLE, JOHN
1958 "Proper Names", *Mind* 67, 166-173.
SIMMONS, R. F.
1973 "Semantic Networks: Their Computation and Use for Understanding English Sentences", in R. Schank and K. Colby (eds.), *Computer Models of Thought and Language*, San Francisco, Freeman, 63-113.
SMITH, EDWARD
1978 "Theories of Semantic Memory", in W. K. Estes (ed.), *Handbook of Learning and Cognitive Processes*, Vol. 5, Hillsdale, N.J., Erlbaum.
SMITH, EDWARD, SHOBEN, EDWARD, and RIPS, LANCE J.
1974 "Structure and Processes in Semantic Memory: A Featural Model for Semantic Decisions", *Psychological Review* 81.3, 214-241.
TALMY, LEONARD
1976 "Semantic Causative Types", in M. Shibatani (ed.), *Syntax and Semantics*, Vol. 6, New York, Academic Press.
1978 "The Relation of Grammar to Cognition – A Synopsis", in D. Waltz (ed.), *Theoretical Issues in Natural Language Processing* – 2, New York, Association for Computing Machinery.
1980 "Lexicalization Patterns: Semantic Structure in Lexical Forms", in T. Shopen et al. (eds.), *Language Typology and Syntactic Descriptions*, New York, Cambridge University Press.
1983 "How Language Structures Space", in H. Pick and L. Acredolo (eds.), *Spatial Orientation: Theory, Research, and Application*, New York, Plenum.
WERTHEIMER, MAX
1923 "Laws of Organization in Perceptual Forms", English translation in W. D. Ellis (ed.), *A Source Book of Gestalt Psychology*, London, Routledge & Kegan Paul, 1938.
WITTGENSTEIN, LUDWIG
1953 *Philosophical Investigations*, Oxford, Blackwell.

Acknowledgment

This paper is in large part excerpted from my *Semantics and Cognition* (MIT Press, 1983) and *Consciousness and the Computational Mind* (Bradford/MIT Press, 1987).

The work reported here was supported in part by a Fellowship for Independent Study and Research in 1978 from the National Endowment for the Humanities, in part by Grant IST-8120403 from the National Science Foundation, and in part by a Fellowship to the Center for Advanced Study in the Behavioral Sciences (NSF Grant BNS-7622943), and I wish to express my gratitude to all of these sources.

Philip N. Johnson-Laird

How Is Meaning Mentally Represented?

How Is Meaning Mentally Represented?

If I blindfold you and take you into your kitchen, there is a reasonable chance that you will still be able to find your way around without bumping into things. But if I have re-arranged the furniture, then you will be in trouble. I can warn you: "Watch out — I have moved the table into the middle of the room", and once again you should be able to avoid colliding with it. You may have formed a vivid image of the table in its new location or you may have had no such experience but nonetheless know where it is — you just *know*, though you cannot fathom how this knowledge is represented. If we wanted to construct a robot that could similarly use a verbal warning to guide its navigational path, then we would need answers to two main questions:
— what do people construct when they understand discourse?
— how do they carry out the process of construction?
This paper aims to answer these two questions in the light of current work in cognitive science. It takes for granted the existence of mechanisms for recognizing speech and for analyzing the syntax of sentences.

Associations

In the beginning — at least in psychology — there was the association. The traditional view was that associations are the universal building blocks of the mind, and a word is just a special sort of associative stimulus: it elicits a representation of the object to which the word corresponds. I say "table" and as a result you have an image (or some less tangible representation) of a table. You have learned this response as a result of conditioning in much the same way that Pavlov's dogs learned to salivate at the sound of the dinner gong. If a word should happen *not* to denote a physical object or property, e.g. the word "possible", then its meaning consists of associations to other words.

There is a decisive objection to this theory. An association is not a meaning. It is merely a link from one representation in memory to another: it leads from one thing to another. But there can be many different relations between representations, and the relation of denotation — from word to object — is only one of them. For example, the word "hot" is strongly associated with both the sun and fires, but these associations are different from the association between "hot" and its denotation, temperatures of a particular range. An associative link from one word to another tells one nothing about the nature of the relation; still less can it indicate that an object that is represented is what a word denotes. Moreover, the meaning of an utterance usually depends on combining the meanings of its words in a way that takes the syntax of the sentence into account. But how can purely associative links be combined syntactically?

The solution to these problems is, perhaps, that associative links should have labels on them. This idea is an old one, which was proposed by Otto Selz in 1913, but it began to flourish only with the advent of the computer. Certain programming languages, particularly LISP, which allows lists to be manipulated, make it easy to represent labelled associations, and to construct large networks of such associations from one word to others. These so-called "semantic networks" are the most popular basis for computational and psychological theories of meaning. They therefore merit close inspection.

Semantic Networks

A semantic network is an associative theory framed for a computer, since the meanings of words are represented by labelled associations from one word to another in a network of links. There are many forms of this theory, but they can all be traced back to Ross Quillian's seminal account in 1968. Like Selz, Quillian recognized the crucial importance of the nature of the relation between words. Unlike Selz, however, Quillian had access to a list-processing language that made it possible to implement a computer program that was a working semantic network. In LISP, an expression is either a list or an atom, and an atom is either a number or a symbol such as WOMAN. By itself, the symbol WOMAN is meaningless, but it becomes more meaningful if the specific values of a number of properties are attached to it:

WOMAN SUPERORDINATE: HUMAN
             GENDER: FEMALE
             AGE: ADULT

In describing such information, it is natural to represent it graphically in the form of a network:

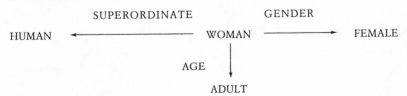

which shows the functional organization of the representation. The information can be specified by the programmer or by someone using a program that constructs networks.

Network theorists have adopted many of Quillian's assumptions. They suppose that networks can represent the meanings of both words and sentences, and that the format is powerful enough to represent any sort of idea. They have also introduced a notational distinction between nodes that stand for general concepts (e.g. tables) and specific instances of them (e.g. the table in your kitchen): a link from the node for a specific instance is attached to the node for the general concept. They have recognized a small set of ubiquitous relational links: superordinate of, property of, part of. But they allow, of course, that many other terms can be labels on a link. They have usually been committed to parsimony and, in particular, to the notion that general information is represented only at a superordinate level. The fact, say, that poodles are animals does not need to be explicitly represented by a direct link from POODLE to ANIMAL, but rather can be inferred from the following chain of superordinate links:

ANIMAL ← DOG ← POODLE

Quillian also initiated a long line of assumptions about the processing of information in semantic networks. He introduced various "tags" to be attached to items in the network. There were tags that represented how criterial the information about a concept was, tags to represent the syntactic role of one word in construction with another, e.g. subject or object, and he even toyed with the idea of using a richer syntactic system of different "cases" such as agent of an action, its patient, and so on − a view of syntax deriving from the work of the linguist, Charles Fillmore. Quillian also suggested that certain aspects of meaning might depend, not on information in the network, but on the processes used to manipulate it and to extract information from it.

The program that Quillian wrote establishes semantic relations by a process of "spreading activation". Tags represent fields of activation, which spread out from the nodes corresponding to the two words to be related and stop when an intersection between them occurs. An intersection soon occurs if the two words are "poodle" and "dog", but takes longer for "poodle" and "animal" since an additional link has to be traversed. Early results from experiments were encouraging: human subjects took longer to establish relations between words that are farther apart in a semantic network. Subsequent work has qualified this picture: properties are not always stored in the most economical way at the top of the hierarchy, and the time to make a judgement does not always correlate with the length of the path in a semantic network.

The Decomposition of Meanings into Semantic Primitives

Some proponents of network theories have been influenced by a view that derives from a theory of meaning proposed in 1963 by the philosophers, Jerry Katz and Jerry Fodor. Their aim was to provide a semantics for transformational grammar, and they argued that the meanings of words could be represented by structured sets of semantic primitives, e.g. the meaning of "woman" is represented by the set of primitives:

(HUMAN) (FEMALE) (ADULT)

The theory decomposes meanings into primitive elements − the so-called "semantic markers" − supposedly universal in all languages.

The meaning of an adjective such as "handsome" is typically represented in a dictionary in the following way:

handsome, adjective 1. (of actions) generous
2. (of persons or artifacts) having a pleasing appearance
3. ...

where each different meaning is constrained to a particular class of entities. One sense of "handsome" is restricted to human beings and artifacts, and another sense is restricted to actions. Hence, although the word has more than one meaning, its combination with other words may not be ambiguous. Indeed, neither "a handsome vase" nor "a handsome act" are ambiguous. The constraints, which are stated in the dictionary within parentheses, were taken over by Katz and Fodor and dubbed "selectional restrictions". When one word is combined with another in a sentence, the interpretation of the resulting expression is sensitive to selectional restrictions.

. This theory of lexical decomposition led to a quest for the ultimate set of semantic primitives, particularly on the part of Roger Schank, who had adopted an alternative view about decomposition that he had implemented in a computer program that could paraphrase sentences. From his analysis of the relations between concepts, he proposed a set of 11 primitive actions that are stated here with Schank's definitions of them:

PROPEL: the application of a physical force to an object.
MOVE: to move a body part.
INGEST: to take something to the inside of an animate object.
EXPEL: to take something from inside an animate object and force it out.
GRASP: to physically grasp an object.
PTRANS: to change the location of an object.
ATRANS: to change an abstract relation with respect to an object, e.g. possession.
SPEAK: to produce a sound.

ATTEND: to direct a sense organ or focus organ towards a particular stimulus.
MTRANS: to create or combine thoughts.
MBUILD: the construction of new information.

The system also contains further primitives denoting states, objects, and various other notions such as time, location, and causation. Thus, according to Schank's analysis, the sentence:
  John ate a frog
yields a complex structure of relations that capture the information that John MOVED his HAND — an inalienable PART of him, which CONTAIN-ED a frog, to his MOUTH — another inalienable PART, and INGESTED the frog. Schank's system even allows the inference that John's HEALTH was adversely affected by his action.

Any set of primitives is likely to be *ad hoc*, and George Miller and I therefore attempted to provide a psychologically motivated basis for the meanings of words in our book, *Language and Perception*. We discovered that many notions which are often taken to be primitives can be broken down still further, e.g. causation can be analyzed in terms of a matrix of possibilities between the antecedent and consequent states of affairs. From an analysis of a large number of words, we found that the lexicon is organized into distinct semantic "fields" based on a central core concept: there are verbs of motion ("move", "propel", "expel", ...), verbs of possession ("own", "buy", "give", ...), verbs of perception ("see", "hear", "glimpse", ...), and verbs of communication ("say", "tell", "inform", ...), and so on. Certain concepts, however, crop up in many semantic fields. They provide the framework by which human beings appear to organize their thoughts with respect to time, space, possibility, permissibility, causation, and intention.

The Power of Semantic Networks

The concept of decomposition is often only a notational variation on the theory of semantic networks. The class of network theories is almost certainly powerful enough to compute anything that can be computed. It follows that any semantic theory can probably be re-expressed as a semantic network, though at least one theory, as we shall see, would call for a radical revision in the form and function of the network. The compatibility of network and decomposition, however, is borne out by the existence of theories that combine them. Don Norman, Dave Rumelhart, and their colleagues, have developed such a theory, and Figure 1 presents their network representing the semantic decomposition of the sentence:

"John gave Fido to Mary"

Figure 1:   The semantic network for the sentence "John gave Fido to Mary"
(as proposed by Norman and Rumelhart)

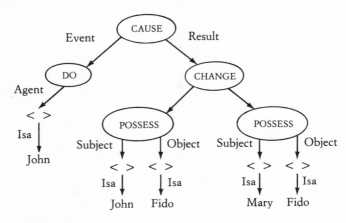

Note: the angle brackets < > are nodes representing specific instances of
concepts.

There have been two principal challenges to the hegemony of network
theories: the case for prototypes, and the argument against the possibility of decomposition. Neither challenge has shaken the theory. I will consider first the argument that it is impossible to decompose the meanings
of words into semantic primitives and then the problem of prototypes.

The Case for Meaning Postulates

Are there any good definitions of words? Jerry Fodor and his colleagues,
the linguist Janet Fodor, and the psychologist Merrill Garrett, gave a
resounding "no" to this question. There are no definitions, they claimed, that state a set of conditions that jointly suffice to express the complete meaning of a word. If this claim is correct, then it is a major error
to propose an analysis (as Fodor originally did) that decomposes meaning into semantic primitives or into an equivalent semantic network. But,
if there are no primitives decomposing, say, the meaning of "lunch" into
MEAL, then how is the inference:
He ate lunch.
Therefore, he ate a meal.
to be made? The answer according to Fodor and his colleagues is to rely
on "meaning postulates", i.e. rules of inference that express the necessary
consequences of specific words. Thus, the meaning postulate:
for any x, if x is a lunch, then x is a meal.
enables the inference to be drawn.

The meaning postulants − Fodor and his colleagues, and also Walter Kintsch − assume that comprehension consists in translating utterances into a mental language, and then, if need be, using meaning postulates to infer further propositions from them. There is no process of semantic decomposition into primitives; the words of natural language correspond virtually one-to-one with the words of the mental language.

The theory is compatible with the dearth of evidence that comprehension depends on breaking down the meanings of words into primitives. Straightforward attempts to show that semantically complex words, e.g. "steal", take longer to understand than semantically simpler words, e.g., "take", have failed, and this failure is understandable if words are mapped directly into their counterparts in a mental language. But there is evidence, as we shall see, that there is more to meaning than a vast set of unordered meaning postulates. Likewise, there are good definitions: dictionaries contain them, and ordinary individuals can frame them too.

There is no difficulty in accomodating meaning postulates within a network theory. John R. Anderson has developed a network that does not decompose meanings into primitives but instead uses meaning postulates to make inferences. Figure 2 presents an example of such a network, which is close to the linguistic form of the sentence it represents.

Figure 2:   The semantic network for the sentence "In a park a hippie touched a debutante" (as proposed by Anderson)

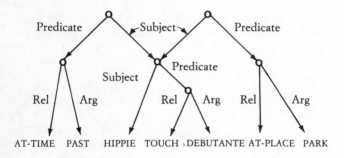

AT-TIME   PAST   HIPPIE   TOUCH ⟨DEBUTANTE AT-PLACE PARK

Note: Following Anderson, this diagram has omitted the nodes representing words. "Rel" stands for Relation and "Arg" stands for Argument.

Prototypes and Default Assumptions

The second challenge to network theories is equally a challenge to meaning postulates. It arises from an observation made by the philosopher,

Ludwig Wittgenstein. He pointed out in his posthumously published *Philosophical Investigations* that the meanings of many words cannot possibly consist of a set of necessary and sufficient conditions common to all the things that the words denote. In a famous passage of the book (pp. 31-32), he wrote:

Consider for example the proceedings that we call "games". I mean board-games, card-games, ball-games, Olympic games, and so on. What is common to them all? – Don't say: "There *must* be something common, or they would not be called 'games'" – but *look and see* whether there is anything common to all. – For if you look at them you will not see something that is common to *all*, but similarities, relationships, and a whole series of them at that. To repeat: don't think, but look!

Later he remarked:

And the result of this examination is: we see a complicated network of similarities overlapping and criss-crossing: sometimes overall similarities, sometimes similarities of detail.
I can think of no better expression to characterize these similarities than "family resemblances"; for the various resemblances between members of a family: build, features, colour of eyes, gait, temperament, etc. etc. overlap and criss-cross in the same way, – And I shall say: "games" form a family.

Wittgenstein's insistence on the lack of common components is echoed by a more recent philosopher, Hilary Putnam. The meaning of "tiger", he says, might be decomposed into such characteristics as: animate, feral, four-legged, tailed, striped, and so on. Yet none of these properties is essential: a dead or tame stripeless tiger with no tail and three legs is presumably still a tiger. It follows, of course, that the meaning of tiger cannot be captured by attributing these properties to a tiger in either a standard semantic network or meaning postulates of the form:

if x is a tiger, then x is animate, x is feral, etc. etc.

Such properties are criteria rather than necessary and sufficient conditions. They cannot be established inductively, that is, by going around and checking off all the properties that you can find in tigers, because that would depend on your having some prior idea about *what* is to count as a tiger: you cannot check whether tigers have stripes unless you are already able to identify tigers. If so, then obviously tigerhood does not depend on stripehood. Yet, criteria are obviously not logically necessary components, because they do not support valid inferences. A deduction such as:

Joey is a tiger.
Hence, Joey has stripes.

is not valid: Joey might be an albino tiger.
A natural way in which to construe the meaning of "tiger" is therefore as a theory of what constitutes tigerhood, perhaps in the framework of

a general theory of animals, and this theory is to be represented by a set of criteria organized into a prototype.

The challenge of prototypes has been accomodated within network theory and semantic marker theory by the introduction of a distinction between, on the one hand, necessary components of meaning, and, on the other hand, characteristic components of meaning. Criteria are characteristic components. The distinction, however, is descriptive rather than explanatory. If you ask what is meant by a characteristic component, then perhaps the best answer is based on Marvin Minsky's notion of a "frame". A frame system is intended to be a structured piece of knowledge about some typical entity or state of affairs. It contains variables into which go the specific values of a given instance. Thus, if Joey the tiger has only three legs, then the variable NUMBER-OF-LEGS will take the value: THREE. The values of many variables can be specified by default. That is, if no information about them is available, the frame system will specify a conventional value. If there is no information about the number of legs that a particular tiger possesses, then the default value is FOUR. A prototype, or theory about a class, is simply a system that specifies all the default values. Unfortunately, the mechanics of such frame systems have yet to be spelt out in any detail; they are a conjecture about how to make explicit the notion of a schema or prototype.

The Need for Truth Conditions

One decisive objection to all the theories that I have described is that they say nothing about how words relate to the world. They contain no machinery that explains how my warning about the table could guide your movements. Networks can tell you that two words are related, or that one sentence is a paraphrase of another, but they cannot tell you anything about the state of the world. They are as circular as dictionaries; they commit the "symbolic fallacy" of assuming that meaning is merely a matter of relating one set of symbols to another. But, when you understand my warning, you grasp its "truth conditions": you know how the world should be if my assertion is true. As the philosopher David Lewis points out, the translation of an utterance into a representation such as a network provides no more of an account of its truth conditions than does a translation into Latin.

Why have so many theorists ignored truth conditions? Perhaps they have assumed that the problem of accounting for the semantic relations between expressions which they have concentrated on, is independent of the problem of truth conditions. In fact, as I will argue, the two problems are not independent. A theory that relates words to the world willy-nilly provides a way of relating words to each other, and renders superfluous those theories that carry out only the latter task.

Formal Semantics

In the last century the logician, Gottlob Frege, drew a distinction between the *sense* of an expression and its *reference*. The reference of the expression is what it stands for in the world, while its sense is what connects it to its reference. The reference of the two noun phrases, "The leader of the British Tory Party" and "The British Prime Minister", is currently the same, namely, Margaret Thatcher. But the senses of these two expressions are different, as is shown by their having different referents when a different party is in power. The same distinction can be drawn about a sentence, such as:

The British Prime Minister is the leader of the Tory Party.

This is currently true, but it may no longer be true after the next general election. What may change is the reference of the sentence, i.e. its truth value; its sense will remain the same. It may seem odd to talk of a sentence having a reference, but the distinction between the proposition expressed and its truth value is a natural generalization of the distinction between the sense and reference of a noun phrase. The truth of a sentence depends on the references of its expressions; the proposition it expresses depends on their senses. This idea has been illuminated by the development of formal semantics, initially for formalized languages such as logical calculi, and subsequently for natural language.

The logician, Alfred Tarski, showed how to develop a rigorous account of the truth conditions of expressions in a formalized language. The expressions are interpreted by being provided with referents not in the real world, but in a *model*. The semantic rules that provide these interpretations are of two sorts. The first sort interpret each basic word in the language. Thus, given a calculus for dealing with sets of individuals, which has the vocabulary of names:

Diana, Charles, Anne, Mark, Margaret, Anthony

there will be a semantic rule that picks out a specific individual in the model for each name to refer to. If the calculus also has the following terms for sets:

female, male, feminist, horselover, housewife, prince

then another basic semantic rule assigns each of them an interpretation consisting of a set of individuals in the model, e.g.:

female = (Diana, Anne, Margaret)
male = (Charles, Mark, Anthony)
feminist = (Charles, Anne, Anthony)
horselover = (Anne, Mark, Margaret)
and so on.

The second sort of semantic rules build up the interpretations of complex expressions from the interpretations of their constituents, and these rules are designed to operate in parallel with the syntactic rules of the calculus. Thus, if there is a syntactic rule that allows sentences of the form, "Charles is a feminist", to be constructed:

1. Sentence → Name *is a* Set

then there is a corresponding semantic rule, which stipulates that:
The interpretation of the sentence is *true*, if the interpretation of the Name, i.e. the particular individual it refers to, is a member of the set that is the interpretation of Set; and *false* in any other case.
Thus, the interpretation of: "Charles is a feminist", is true just in the case that the person named "Charles" is a member of the Feminist set (which in the model above he is).

If there is another grammatical rule that permits expressions of the form, "female horselover", to be constructed:

2. Set → Set Set

then it too has a corresponding semantic rule:
The interpretation of the Set on the left-hand side equals the intersection of the two Sets on the right-hand side.
The intersection is the set of those individuals, if any, who are members of both sets, and so this rule tells us that the reference of "female horselover" is the set of those individuals in the model who are in both the set of females (Diana, Anne, Margaret) and the set of horselovers (Anne, Mark, Margaret), i.e. the interpretation is (Anne, Margaret).

The semantic interpretation of a sentence, such as "Anne is a female horselover", can be built up as the sentence is parsed. The first word, "Anne", denotes a particular individual in the model. The next words, "is a", stipulate that the individual is a member of a set. This set, however, turns out to depend on the interpretation of "female horselover". The syntactic rule that parses these terms corresponds to a semantic rule specifying that their interpretation equals their intersection, namely, (Anne, Margaret). Anne is indeed a member of this set, and hence the sentence is true in the model.

I won't continue this sketch any further since the idea of co-ordinating each syntactic rule with a semantic one should now be clear. The great advantage of such a rule-by-rule system is that each step in parsing a sentence can yield a step in its semantic interpretation. To devise a rule-by-rule system for natural language, however, is a work of considerable complexity, and it has been successfully undertaken only for fragments of languages, principally under the aegis of the late Richard Montague. What makes the task so difficult is the syntactic complexity of natural language, the existence of sentences that describe possible states of affairs and propositional attitudes such as beliefs (which may be false), and the ubiquitous effects of context on interpretation. Hence, the meaning of "female horselover" cannot merely be fixed by a particular model, as in the case above, but must allow for reference to different times and epochs and to imaginary states of affairs. In other words, what is built up rule by rule is, not the reference of expressions, but their sense; and the sense of an expression is a function that specifies reference in an infinite set of different models corresponding to different possible worlds and different times within them.

Mental Models of Sentences

After the abstract purity of formal semantics, the problems of the ordinary everyday use of language are considerably murky. Yet there is a way in which to take advantage of some of the insights of the formal approach and to use them in constructing a psychologically plausible theory. The key step, however, is crucial. It is to assume that what an assertion really refers to is, not a truth value, but a state of affairs — the state of affairs that would render the assertion true. Listeners can imagine that state of affairs. Thus, there is a distinction to be drawn between the state of affairs an assertion refers to, a mental representation of that state, and the truth value of the assertion, which can be ascertained (sometimes) by comparing that representation with the state of the world. When I tell you that I have moved the table into the middle of your kitchen, you can form a representation of how the kitchen is now arranged, and you can use this representation in order to navigate your way around the room. Even if you did not form an image, your success in avoiding the obstacle shows that you have access to a *model* of the spatial arrangement of the furniture. If you remove your blindfold, then you can compare this model with the actual state of the world so as to evaluate the truth or falsity of my assertion.

Perception yields rich mental models of the world (see David Marr's book on *Vision*); inference depends on the manipulation of mental models (see my book on *Mental Models*); and comprehension is a process of constructing mental models. According to this theory, the initial mental representation of an utterance, which *is* close to its linguistic form, is used to construct a model of the state of affairs that is described, requested, or questioned. The process is guided by a knowledge of the contribution to truth conditions made by the words in the utterance, by a knowledge of how to combine meanings according to syntax (probably on a rule-by-rule basis), by a knowledge of the context, which in part is represented in the existing model of the situation, and by general knowledge of the domain and the conventions of discourse.

How can one model stand for all the different possible states of affairs compatible with the truth of an utterance? An utterance, such as "The table is in the middle of the room", can be true of many different tables, many different rooms, and many different locations of the table in the room. A picture may be worth a thousand words, but a proposition is worth an infinity of pictures. The problem is a direct descendant of a traditional puzzle in philosophy: how can an image, or a diagram in a geometric proof, stand for many different things? In his *Critique of Pure Reason*, Immanuel Kant wrote:

In truth, it is not images of objects, but schemata, which lie at the foundation of our pure sensuous conceptions. No image could ever be adequate to our conception of triangles in general. For the generalness of the conception it never could attain to, as this includes under itself all triangles, whether right-angled, acute-angled etc., whilst the image would always be limited to a single part of this sphere.

Wittgenstein, however, wondered whether there might not be objects that could function as schemata − say, a schematic leaf, or a sample of green. He answered his own question: "Certainly there might. But for such a schema to be understood as a *schema*, and not as a shape of a particular leaf, and for a slip of pure green to be understood as a sample of all that is greenish and not as a sample of pure green − this in turn resides in the way the samples are used." Unfortunately, he gives us no clue about *how* a sample should be used if it is to stand as a representative sample. But such a clue is to be found in David Hume's *Treatise of Human Nature*:

... after the mind has produced an individual idea, upon which we reason, the attendant custom, revived by the general or abstract term, readily suggests any other individual, if by chance we form any reasoning that agrees not with it. Thus, should we mention the word triangle, and form the idea of a particular equilateral one to correspond to it, and should we afterwards assert, *that the three angles of a triangle are equal to each other*, the other individuals of a scalenum and isosceles, which we overlooked at first, immediately crowd in upon us, and make us perceive the falsehood of this proposition...

This view is perhaps optimistic, but it contains the germ of an idea that I shall exploit: a mental model is provisional, and it can be revised in the light of subsequent information.

An Algorithm for Mental Models

Another problem for the theory is what information it requires about the meanings of words. In formal semantics, the theorist stipulates a reference in the model for each basic word, but a psychological theory calls for information that can be used to construct a model. I will illustrate how this can be done, and how Hume's insight can be exploited, by describing an algorithm that constructs models from spatial descriptions.

Let us suppose that in describing the top of your kitchen table, you assert the following:

There's a bottle on the right of a plate.

The algorithm contains a procedure that starts the construction of a model by inserting tokens into a spatial array in a way that satisfies the truth-conditions of the sentence. That is to say, the resulting model will have the same structure as one formed by seeing or imagining the table top. It needs access in this case to information about bottles and plates, but I shall concentrate here on the spatial relations. The meaning of "on the right" specifies where one object, x, must be located in relation to another object, y, so as to satisfy any description of the form: "x is on the right of y". There are various ways in which this information could be represented depending on the procedures that construct the model. The algorithm constructs the following sort of spatial model:

J axis

		1	2	3	4	5	...
	1						
	2						
I axis	3						
	4						
	5						
	...						

and the dictionary entry for "on the right" contains the information:

ONRIGHT: hold the value of the vertical I axis constant and increment the value of the J axis.

The algorithm accordingly constructs the following model for the sentence above:

J axis

		1	2
I axis	1	plate	bottle

As the reader will note, the program represents a bird's eye view of the smallest possible surface and enlarges it if necessary.

Unlike perception, discourse about a situation has referring expressions, and comprehension hinges on establishing co-reference. If you continue your description and assert:

There's a knife on the right of the bottle

then the definite description, "the bottle", triggers a procedure that examines the model to determine whether it contains a co-referential item. In actual discourse, the business of establishing co-reference is often complicated, depending on inferences of many sorts, but the procedure is satisfied by a single corresponding item in the model. Having found the bottle in the model, the algorithm calls a procedure that uses the meaning of "on the right of" to insert the new item into the model in an appropriate position in relation to the old item:

	1	2	3
1	plate	bottle	knife

Suppose at this point, you assert:
The knife is on the right of the plate
then the co-reference routine establishes that both the knife and the plate are already in the model. There are no new items referred to in the sentence, and the algorithm therefore calls a procedure to verify the relation between the referents. This procedure checks whether the relation between the objects satisfies the meaning of "on the right". Since it does, the sentence is true. Whenever a sentence is verified in this way, the algorithm calls a further procedure, which checks whether there is any other model of the discourse so far in which the last assertion turns out to be false. If there is no such alternative, then the last assertion necessarily follows from what has gone before. The algorithm announces that it is a valid inference. In this way, the algorithm reflects the theory of valid inference described earlier in my book: it makes valid inferences without recourse to formal rules of inference, meaning postulates, or any other such device. The logical transitivity of "on the right" is an emergent property of its truth conditions and is nowhere explicitly represented within the algorithm. Thus, the superfluousness of networks and meaning postulates is demonstrated: the properties they capture emerge from truth conditions.

The algorithm contains two other major procedures. One procedure combines hitherto separate models when an assertion is made that links items in both of them. The other procedure embodies the solution to Wittgenstein's problem. If you begin a description with the following two assertions:
There's a bottle on the right of a plate.
There's a knife on the left of the bottle.
the interpretation of the first assertion is straightforward:

	1	2
1	plate	bottle

But the second assertion is problematic since it leaves open whether the knife is to the right or left of the plate. Everyday discourse is riddled with such indeterminacies, but normally they do not matter and so one does not notice them. Faced with such an indeterminacy, the algorithm plumps for one particular interpretation:

	1	2	3
1	plate	knife	bottle

If your next assertion is:
    The knife is on the left of the plate
then the verification procedure establishes that the assertion is *false* in the current model. Whenever it returns this value, the algorithm calls another procedure that is the mirror-image of the procedure for valid inference. It searches for an alternative model of the earlier discourse that renders the latest assertion *true*. If it fails to find such an alternative, then it indicates that you have contradicted yourself. In the present case, however, the model:

	1	2	3
1	knife	plate	bottle

satisfies all three assertions. The model originally embodied an assumption that was made by default; subsequent information conflicted with that assumption, and the procedure has revised the model so that it is consistent with the discourse as a whole. Hence, one model can serve as a representative sample, or prototypical example, from the potentially infinite set of models that satisfy any discourse: the model can be revised so as to satisfy any subsequent consistent information.

The problem of constructing and maintaining a mental model resembles in many ways the problem of maintaining a computer data base, though most existing programs for data bases have yet to exploit the advantage of using procedures that have an access to the truth conditions of assertions. Table 1 summarizes the seven main procedures that are necessary for the construction and manipulation of mental models of discourse. Only the fifth of them was not implemented in the computer program for understanding spatial descriptions.

Table 1: The seven functions for maintaining a mental model of discourse
1. For a sentence that does not refer to anything in a current model: START a new model satisfying its truth conditions.
2. For a sentence that refers to something in a current model, but contains a new referent: ADD the new referent to the model according to the truth conditions of the sentence.
3. For a sentence that relates something in one current model to something in another current model: COMBINE the two models according to the truth conditions of the sentence.

4. For a sentence that refers only to things in the current model: VERIFY whether the truth conditions of the sentence are satisfied by the model, and:

5. If the model is independent of the truth conditions of the sentence: USE them to add to the model the properties or relations expressed by the sentence.

6. If the sentence is true in the model: REVISE the model, if possible, so that it is consistent with the previous discourse but renders the sentence *false*. If this task is impossible, the sentence is a valid deduction from the previous discourse. If it is possible, the sentence conveys new information: restore the model that renders it true.

7. If the sentence is false in the model: REVISE the model, if possible, so that it is consistent with the previous discourse but renders the sentence *true*. If the task is impossible, the sentence is inconsistent with the previous discourse. If it is possible, the sentence corrects an earlier default assumption made by the program, and the model is retained.

Conclusions

Logicians have only related language to models in various ways; psychologists have only related it to itself. The real task, however, is to show how language relates to the world through the agency of the mind. Semantic networks, semantic decomposition, and meaning postulates, are not sufficient for this task, because they give no account of truth conditions. Once that account is given these theories are, strictly speaking, no longer necessary. The theory of mental models establishes the required relation: you can construct models of the world on the basis of discourse, and you can, if need be, compare such models with those that you construct by other means — from perception, from memory, from imagination. An utterance is true with respect to perception, memory, or imagination, if its truth conditions are satisfied within the model derived from those sources. A mental model represents the "reference" of a sentence — the particular state of affairs to which the sentence refers, but because the model can be revised as a result of subsequent information, it functions as a representative sample from the set of all possible models that might be constructed from the initial linguistic representation of the sentence. Hence, this linguistic representation captures the truth conditions, or sense, of the sentence.

You may wonder whether there is any evidence for the theory. It comes partly from studies of inference which show that the more models that have to be constructed, the harder the task is (see *Mental Models*). Kannan Mani and I have also found that, depending on the circumstances, people can remember either the gist of a text and not its verbatim details, or the converse. This result was predictable given the two stages of the theory: a superficial linguistic representation followed by the construction of a model. Similarly, there is abundant evidence – much of it collected by colleagues, Kate Ehrlich, Alan Garnham, and Jane Oakhill – for the importance of referential coherence in the comprehension of discourse.

You may also wonder how a mental model could represent abstract discourse. This is a problem not just for mental models, but for any theory of meaning. Its solution depends on appreciating that insofar as you understand any assertion, you must be able to imagine how the world should be granted its truth. Models contain tokens corresponding to physical objects, but people act towards many objects and make judgements about them in virtue of relations that exist only in their models. If you *own* something, for example, then, as George Miller and I argued, the following sorts of moral principles appear to hold:

1. it is permissible for you to use it, and not permissible for me to prevent you from using it (if you are not doing any harm).
2. it is permissible for you to give me permission to use it, in which case, it is permissible for me to use it.
3. it is permissible for you to transfer ownership to me.

There must be further regulative principles governing what can be owned, who can own things, and how the transfer of ownership can be effected. The heart of the matter, however, is that these abstract relations do not correspond to anything in the *physical* situation, though they do depend for their existence (in our minds) on the occurrence of certain physical events (that have a symbolic significance in relation to these moral principles): ownership cannot be created merely by an act of imagination. Abstract relations *seem* to be more of a problem for mental models than for other theories, because the theory aims to avoid the "symbolic fallacy" and to show how a knowledge of truth conditions is used to construct representations. In fact, they are less of a problem, since other theories do no more than translate abstract assertions – and all other assertions – into ultimately empty symbolic formulae.

The concept of models of discourse has antecedents in the linguistic theory of Lauri Karttunen; in the artificial intelligence theory of Bonnie Webber; in the computer programs for modelling comprehension devised independently by Steve Isard, Christopher Longuet-Higgins, and Mark Steedman; and in the psychological theories of Keith Stenning, myself, and ultimately Kenneth Craik. Theories of comprehension, which originally made no reference to models, have increasingly been modified to do so. Thus, in psychology, Walter Kintsch and Teun van Dijk have introduced models into their theory. In formal semantics, the same tendency is evident, I believe, in the "situation semantics" proposed by Jon Barwise and John Perry, and especially in the work of Hans Kamp, who has shown that many profoundly puzzling phenomena can be elucidated by positing models of discourse.

References

ANDERSON, J.R.
1976 *Language, Memory, and Thought*, Hillsdale, NJ, Lawrence Erlbaum Associates.
BARWISE, J., and J. PERRY
1983 *Situations and Attitudes*, Cambridge, Mass., MIT Bradford Books.
CRAIK, K.
1943 *The Nature of Explanation*, Cambridge, Cambridge University Press.
EHRLICH, K., and P.N. JOHNSON-LAIRD
1982 "Spatial descriptions and referential continuity", *Journal of Verbal Learning and Verbal Behavior* 21, 296-306.
FILLMORE, C.J.
1968 "The case for case", in Bach. E., and R.T. Harms (eds.) *Universals in Linguistic Theory*, New York, Holt, Rinehart, and Winston.
FODOR, J.D., J.A. FODOR, and M.F. GARRET
1975 "The psychological unreality of semantic representations", *Linguistic Inquiry* 4, 515-531.
FREGE, G.
1892 "Über Sinn und Bedeutung", *Zeitschrift für Philosophie und philosophische Kritik* 100, 25-50. Translated as: "On sense and reference", in Geach, P.T., and M. Black (eds.) *Philosophical Writings of Gottlob Frege*, Oxford, Blackwell, 1952.
GARNHAM, A., J. OAKHILL, and P.N. JOHNSON-LAIRD
1982 "Referential continuity and the coherence of discourse", *Cognition* 11, 29-46.
HUME, D.
1896 *A Treatise of Human Nature*, Vol. 1, edited by L.A. Selby-Bigge, Oxford, Clarendon Press.
ISARD, S.D.
1975 "What would you have done if...?", *Journal of Theoretical Linguistics* 1, 233-255.
JOHNSON-LAIRD, P.N.
1983 *Mental Models: Towards a Cognitive Science of Language, Inference, and Consciousness*, Cambridge, Cambridge University Press; Cambridge, Mass., Harvard University Press.
KAMP, J.A.W.
1979 "Events, instants, and temporal reference", in Bäuerle, R., U. Egli, and A. von Stechow (eds.) *Semantics from Different Points of View*, Berlin, Springer-Verlag.
KANT, I.
1787 *The Critique of Pure Reason*, second edition, translated by J.M.D. Meiklejohn, London, Dent, 1934.
KARTTUNEN, L.
1969 "Pronouns and variables", in Binnick, R.I., A. Davison, G. Green, and J. Morgan (eds.) *Papers from the Fifth Regional Meeting of the Chicago Linguistics Society*, Chicago, Ill., University of Chicago.
KATZ, J.J., and J.A. FODOR
1963 "The structure of a semantic theory", *Language* 39, 170-210.
KINTSCH, W.
1974 *The Representation of Meaning in Memory*. Hillsdale, N.J., Lawrence Erlbaum Associates.
KINTSCH, W., and T.A. VAN DIJK
1978 "Towards a model of text comprehension and reproduction", *Psychological Review* 85, 363-394.
LEWIS, D.K.
1972 "General semantics", in Davidson, D., and G. Harman (eds.) *Semantics of Natural Language*, Dordrecht, Reidel.
LONGUET-HIGGINS, H.C.
1972 "The algorithmic description of natural language", *Proceedings of the Royal Society of London*, B, 182, 255-276.

MANI, K., and P.N. JOHNSON-LAIRD
1982   "The mental representation of spatial descriptions", *Memory and Cognition* 10, 181-187.
MARR, D.
1982   *Vision*, San Francisco, Freeman.
MILLER, G.A., and P.N. JOHNSON-LAIRD
1976   *Language and Perception*, Cambridge, Cambridge University Press; Cambridge, Mass., Harvard University Press.
MINSKY, M.L.
1975   "Frame-system theory", in Schank, R.C., and B.L. Webber (eds.) *Theoretical Issues in Natural Language Processing*, pre-prints of a conference at MIT, reprinted in Johnson-Laird, P.N., and P.C. Wason (eds.) *Thinking: Readings in Cognitive Science*, Cambridge, Cambridge University Press, 1977.
MONTAGUE, R.
1974   *Formal Philosophy: Selected Papers*, New Haven, Yale University Press.
NORMAN, D.A., D.E. RUMELHART, and the LNR research group
1975   *Explorations in Cognition*, San Francisco, Freeman.
PUTNAM, H.
1975   "The meaning of 'meaning'", in Gunderson, K. (ed.) *Language, Mind and Knowledge*, Minnesota Studies in the Philosophy of Science, Vol. 7, Minneapolis, University of Minnesota Press.
QUILLIAN, M.R.
1968   "Semantic memory", in Minsky, M.L. (ed.) *Semantic Information Processing*, Cambridge, Mass., MIT Press.
SCHANK, R.C.
1975   *Conceptual Information Processing*, Amsterdam, North-Holland.
SELZ, O.
1951   "For an account of his work", see Humphrey, G. (1951) *Thinking: An Introduction to its Experimental Psychology*, London, Methuen.
STEEDMAN, M.J., and P.N. JOHNSON-LAIRD
1977   "A programmatic theory of linguistic performance", in Smith, P.T., and R.N. Campbell (eds.) *Advances in the Psychology of Language: Formal and Experimental Approaches*, New York, Plenum.
STENNING, K.
1978   "Anaphora as an approach to pragmatics", in Halle, M., J. Bresnan, and G.A. Miller (eds.) *Linguistic Theory and Psychological Reality*, Cambridge, Mass., MIT Press.
TARSKI, A.
1956   "The concept of truth in formalized language", in *Logic, Semantics, Metamathematics: Papers from 1923 to 1938*, translated by J.H. Woodger, Oxford, Oxford University Press.
WEBBER, B.L.
1978   "Description formation and discourse model synthesis", in Waltz, D.L. (ed.) *Theoretical Issues in Natural Language Processing*, 2, New York, Association for Computing Machinery.
WITTGENSTEIN, L.
1953   *Philosophical Investigations*, New York, Macmillan.

George Lakoff

Cognitive Semantics*

Two Views of Cognition

When cognitive science emerged as a field in the mid-1970's, a number of researchers rallied around a certain philosophical view of mind that they assumed would form the common ground for the research program of the new field. I will refer to that philosophical position as *objectivist cognition*. Its central claim was the following:

— Rational thought is the algorithmic manipulation of arbitrary abstract symbols that are meaningless in themselves but get their meaning by being associated with things in the world.

In objectivist cognition, the symbols and algorithmic operations of symbol-manipulation are seen as constituting a *language of thought*. The symbols function as *internal representations of external reality* and the rules that manipulate the symbols do not make use of what the symbols mean. There are two aspects to the objectivist theory:

— The algorithmic theory of mental processes: All mental processes are algorithmic in the mathematical sense, that is, they are formal manipulations of arbitrary symbols without regard to the internal structure of the symbols or to their meaning.

— The symbolic theory of meaning: Arbitrary symbols can be made meaningful in one and only one way: by being associated with things in the world (where "the world" is taken as having a structure independent of the mental processes of any beings).

If such a philosophical view of the mind had been scientifically established, it would indeed have been remarkable and interesting. But what happened within the ensuing decade is even more remarkable and interesting. Within one decade, enough researchers had investigated objectivist cognition in enough detail to show that such a theory of mind is fundamentally inadequate in many, many ways. That research points to a very different theory of mind, one that focuses on two things that were left out of the objectivist picture:

— The role of the body in characterizing meaningful concepts, and
— The human imaginative capacity for creating meaningful concepts and modes of rationality that go well beyond any mind-free, external reality.

* A much more detailed discussion of the issues raised here can be found in the author's book *Women, Fire, and Dangerous Things: What Categories Reveal About the Mind*, Chicago, University of Chicago Press, 1987. This research was supported in part by a grant from the Sloan Foundation to the University of California at Berkeley.

Objectivist cognition failed in large measure because of its conception of meaning. The objectivist view of meaning as the relationship between symbols and the world not only failed empirically, but was subject to a logical inconsistency. We will discuss some of those failures shortly. It also failed because of its assumption that all mental processes use *only* arbitrary symbols, symbols whose internal structure and whose meaning cannot be made use of by the processes operating on them. Research in cognitive linguistics, cognitive anthropology, and the philosophy of mind (cf. Langacker, Quinn, Lakoff, Talmy, Sweetser, Johnson, Lindner, Brugman, Casad, and Janda) indicates that rational mental process of the sort involved in using language and drawing inferences makes use of *image-schemas*, which are *nonfinitary meaningful symbols* of the sort excluded by the strict mathematical characterization of algorithmic manipulation. Image-schemas for containers, paths, links, force dynamics, etc. are made meaningful by human sensory-motor experience (see Johnson, 1987). Mental processes of a different sort − scanning, focusing, figure-ground reversal, superimposition, etc. − are needed for the processing of image-schematic symbols (see Langacker, 1987). What is needed to replace the objectivist view of meaning is an irreducibly cognitive semantics, one that accounts for what meaning is to human beings, rather than trying to replace humanly meaningful thought by reference to a metaphysical account of a reality external to human experience.

What I see as the most promising approach to cognitive semantics is what Johnson (Johnson, 1987) and I (Lakoff, 1987) have called *experientialist cognition*. "Experiential" is to be taken in the broad sense, including basic sensory-motor, emotional, social, and other experiences of a sort available to all normal human beings − and especially including *innate capacities* that shape such experience and make it possible. The term "experience" does not primarily refer to incidental experiences of a sort that individuals happen to have had by virtue of their unique histories. We are focusing rather on that aspect of experience that we have simply by virtue of being human and living on earth in a human society. "Experiential" should definitely NOT be taken in the empiricist sense as mere sense impressions that give form to the passive tabula rasa of the empiricists. We take experience as *active* functioning as part of a natural and social environment. We take common human experience − given our bodies and innate capacities and our way of functioning as part of a real world − as *motivating* what is meaningful in human thought. "Motivating" does not mean "determining". We are not claiming that experience strictly determines human concepts or modes of reasoning; rather the structure inherent in our experience makes conceptual understanding possible and constrains − tightly in many cases − the range of possible conceptual and rational structures (see Johnson, 1987).

The theory of experientialist cognition posits:
— Concepts of two sorts that are meaningful because of their roles in bodily experience (especially movement and perception):
  1. Basic-level concepts (to be discussed below).
  2. Image-schemas (e.g., containers, paths, links, part-whole schemas, force-dynamic schemas, etc.). These have a nonfinitary internal structure.
— Imaginative processes for forming abstract cognitive models from these: Schematization, Metaphor, Metonymy and Categorization.
— Basic cognitive processes such as focusing, scanning, superimposition, figure-ground shifting, vantage-point shifting, etc.
— Mental spaces.

These views have been worked out and argued for in considerable detail in a number of books, including Lakoff and Johnson (1980), Fauconnier (1984), Lakoff (1986), Langacker (1986), Holland and Quinn (1986), Johnson (1987) and Sweetser (in press). The central claim of experientialist cognition is:
— Meaningful conceptual structures arise from two sources:
(1) from the structured nature of bodily and social experience and
(2) from our innate capacity to imaginatively project from certain well-structured aspects of bodily and interactional experience to abstract conceptual structures.
Rational thought is the application of very general cognitive processes
— focusing, scanning, superimposition, figure-ground reversal, etc. —
to such structures.

In the most general terms, the two theories contrast in the following ways:
— Where objectivist cognition views human thought as fundamentally disembodied, experientialist cognition sees human thought as essentially involving the kind of structured experience that comes from having human bodies, especially from innate human sensory-motor capacities.
— Where objectivist cognition sees meaning in terms of a "correspondence theory", as the association of symbols with external objects, experientialist cognition sees meaning as essentially involving an *imaginative projection*, using mechanisms of schematization, categorization, metaphor and metonymy to move from what we experience in a structured way with our bodies to abstract cognitive models.
— Where objectivist cognition sees thought processes as the manipulation of abstract symbols by a great many highly-structured algorithms, experientialist cognition posits a small number of general cognitive processes whose application to abstract highly-structured cognitive models constitutes reason.
Corresponding differences arise in the case of language. Since theories of cognition affect theories about the psychological status of a grammar,

these differences have equally great consequences for the conception of what a natural language is.

– Objectivist cognition, by definition, sees the syntax of a natural language as a set of algorithmic principles that manipulate symbols without regard to their meaning.

– Experientialist cognition sees the syntax of a language as
1. providing grammatical categories and constructions that are semantically-motivated,
2. giving the semantic and functional motivations for those categories and constructions, and
3. indicating the relationships among the constructions – relationships based both on form and on meaning.

Each grammatical construction is a form-meaning pairing with the structure of a cognitive model. Constructions are combined by superimposition and sentences are processed by general cognitive processes. The principles that provide semantic, pragmatic, and functional motivation for aspects of syntax are called *generative semantic principles*.

For a detailed example of grammatical constructions, the generative semantic principles that motivate them, and the relationships among constructions within a grammar, see Lakoff, 1987, case study 3.

Experientialist theories of cognition provide a view of the mind and of human nature that is very different from the view given by objectivist theories. It is therefore of the utmost importance that we consider the evidence that has led experientialist theorists to move to a very different view of mind. What is at stake is not merely an academic matter, but a view of what human beings are like in the most fundamental sense.

A Case of Philosophy Versus Science

Philosophy is most powerful when it is invisible. Over the course of centuries philosophical theories may become so engrained in our culture and our intellectual life that we don't even recognize them as theories; they take on the cast of self-evident truth, part of the intellectual landscape that serves as a background for theorizing. Such virtually invisible philosophical theories are often harmless. But when they are false and become widely accepted within important academic disciplines, invisible philosophical theories can stand in the way of scientific investigation. Because they are invisible, they are neither questioned nor taken into account.

This has occurred on a grand scale in the cognitive sciences. The philosophical theory in question is what Johnson and I (1980) have called "objectivism", which is essentially the same as what Putnam (1981) has referred to as "metaphysical realism". It is indicative of their pervasiveness and invisibility that the collection of philosophical views that we are referring to had no well-established name; we had to make up names for them. Yet those views have permeated establishment thinking in Anglo-American philosophy, linguistics, cognitive psychology, and artificial intelligence.

Before describing those views, it is important to see that there is important common ground between objectivism on the one hand and anti-objectivist views such as Johnson's and my experiential realism, Putnam's internal realism, and the views of cognitive linguists such as Langacker and Fauconnier. What we share with objectivism is *basic realism*:

− A commitment to the existence of a real world, both a world external to human beings as well as the reality of human experience. None of us are solipsists or pure idealists.

− A link of some sort between human conceptual systems and other aspects of reality.

− A conception of truth that is not based merely on internal coherence.

− A commitment to the existence of stable knowledge of the external world.

− A rejection of the view that "anything goes" − that any conceptual system is as good as any other.

− A commitment to standards of "objectivity" in science, that is, to standards within scientific communities that rule out the biases and prejudices of individual investigators.

None of this is being challenged. Realism and scientific objectivity are not the issues. The above philosophical assumptions are shared by all parties concerned, and it is worth stating them explicitly. Misunderstandings arise, however, when such a basic realism is confused with objectivism.

Objectivism (what Putnam calls "metaphysical realism") goes far beyond basic realism. Let us begin with *objectivist metaphysics*, which posits what Putnam (1981) has referred to as a "God's Eye View" of reality: In short, objectivism does not merely hold that there is a mind-free reality; it holds in addition that that reality is structured in a way that can be modeled by set-theoretical models, which consist of abstract entities (which model real-world entities), sets of abstract entities (defined by the common properties of their members), and sets of *n*-tuples (corresponding to relations among entities).

The basic tenets of objectivist metaphysics can be characterized by four intimately interrelated doctrines:

Doctrine 1: The world consists of entities with fixed properties and relations holding among them at any instant. This structure is mind-free, that is, independent of the understanding of any beings.

Doctrine 2: The entities in the world are divided up naturally into categories called *natural kinds*. All natural kinds are sets defined by the essential properties shared by their members.

Doctrine 3: All properties are either complex or primitive; complex properties are logical combinations of primitive properties.

Doctrine 4: There are rational relations that hold objectively among the entities and categories in the world. For example, if an entity x is in category A and if A is in category B, then x is in B.

These are interrelated doctrines. Natural kinds are correlates of essential properties of objects. Rational relations are defined in terms of categories (which correspond to properties). Logical combinations are understood in terms of rational relations. Doctrine 2, the doctrine of natural kinds, is central to objectivist metaphysics because it claims that categorization is built into objective reality — and it is categorization that links the properties and relations of doctrine 1 to the rational relations of doctrine 4 and the compositional structure of complex properties in doctrine 3. That is is why philosophers have paid so much attention to natural kinds in recent years. The doctrine of natural kinds is crucial to the entire enterprise, and it is that doctrine that we will be most concerned with.

Objectivist metaphysics is not a collection of self-evident truths: it is a *theory* about the nature of reality. It is not just a falsifiable theory; it is a false theory. It is demonstrably false for one of the most basic cases that it is supposed to work for: biological kinds. Ernst Mayr of Harvard, one of the principal figures in modern evolutionary biology, has taken pains to point out the fallacies in viewing biological species as natural kinds, that is, as sets defined by the essential properties of their members. The natural kind view was characteristic of pre-Darwinian biology, but has been known to be false since Darwin. Mayr (1984) cites seven properties of species that are at odds with the idea that they are sets defined by essential properties.

First, species do not have a homogeneous structure with all members sharing defining properties. Only statistical correlations among properties can be given.

Second, since a species is characterized partly in terms of reproductive isolation, it is defined not purely in terms of internal properties of individuals, but in large part with relation to other groups.

Third, a species is not defined only by properties of individual members. It is characterized in terms of its gene pool, though no individual has more than a small portion of the genes in the pool.

Fourth, if one considers populations distributed over broad areas, there is not always a distinct point at which one can distinguish one species from two.

Fifth, the concept "belongs to the same species as" is not transitive. There are documented cases of populations A, B, C, D and E in contiguous areas, such that A interbreeds with B, B with C, C with D, D with E, but A does not interbreed with E. Since "belongs to the same set as" is always a transitive relation, species cannot be sets.

Sixth, biological species do not always have necessary conditions for membership. Both interbreeding capacity and morphological similarity go into the characterization of a species. But they may not always go together. There are three kinds of cases: (a) One population may split into two, which may retain the same physical characteristics, but may no longer be able to interbreed. (b) Physical characteristics may change, while interbreeding capacity remains. (c) In cases of uniparental reproduction, interbreeding is not a factor.

Seventh, status as a separate species may depend on geographic location. There are two cases: (a) Two populations may interbreed in one habitat, but not in another. (b) Two populations in the same habitat may not interbreed at one point in history; neither population changes, but the habitat changes, and interbreeding becomes possible. Natural kinds, on the other hand, are not defined relative to habitat.

For all these reasons, evolutionary biology is inconsistent with the idea that natural kinds of living things are sets defined by the shared essential properties of their members. In its view of natural kinds as sets of this sort, objectivist metaphysics is in conflict with Darwinian biology, which is perhaps the best-substantiated scientific theory of the modern age. It is a case of philosophy versus science, and it required, in Mayr's words, "an emancipation of biology from an inappropriate philosophy".

Before we go on, let us stop to consider why this failure of objectivist *metaphysics* is important for cognitive science. Why, after all, should metaphysics matter in the study of cognition? It probably shouldn't. But in the objectivist theory of cognition, metaphysics matters plenty. In fact, it plays an extremely important role. The most essential feature of objectivist cognition is the separation of symbols from what they mean. It is this separation that permits one to view thought as the algorithmic manipulation of arbitrary symbols. The problem for such a view is how the symbols used in thought are to be made meaningful. The objectivist answer is that the symbols are meaningful by virtue of their association with things in the external world. This answer presupposes three philosophical doctrines in addition to those of objectivist metaphysics.

Doctrine 5. The doctrine of truth-conditional meaning: **Meaning** is based on reference and truth.

Doctrine 6. The "correspondence theory" of truth: Truth consists in the correspondence between symbols and states of affairs in the world.

Doctrine 7. The doctrine of objective reference: There is an "objectively correct" way to associate symbols with things in the world.

Here's where metaphysics comes in. Objectivist metaphysics is *required* at this point in order to guarantee that the world is structured in just the right way to accommodate these three doctrines.

It is worthwhile pausing for a moment to ponder this aspect of objectivist cognition. In claiming that meaning consists in the relation of symbols to the external world, the objectivist cognitive scientist is bringing *metaphysics* of a very special kind into to study of *cognition*. This is necessary for technical reasons. Algorithms are mathematical objects of a certain well-investigated kind.

They manipulate symbols and their manipulations are defined in such a way that they cannot take into account the meanings of the symbols. But they are mathematically precise, and precision is highly desirable. It is not the only kind of precision possible, but is one that proponents of objectivist cognition would like to make use of. But since thought is meaningful, it is necessary that the symbols be given meaning. Moreover, they must be given meaning in a way that does not compromise the mathematical precision of algorithms. The objectivist solution is to adopt doctrines 5 - 7, the objectivist doctrines of meaning, truth, and reference. This permits another well-investigated form of mathematics to be used: model-theory. If an objectivist metaphysics is assumed, then the set-theoretical models used in model-theory can be assumed to model the world accurately. Add doctrines 5 - 7 to give an account of reference, truth, and meaning, and the symbols used in the algorithms can be made meaningful. At present, this is the *only* idea that has been proposed for giving meaning to those symbols in a mathematically precise way.

We can now see why the doctrine that natural kinds are sets is so important. Most of our reasoning is not about individuals, but about categories. Even when we reason about individuals, we reason about them *as members of categories*. If I think about my desk, I rarely think about it as a unique object in itself distinct from all other objects. Rather I think about it as a desk, as a member of the category *desk*. If thought is viewed as symbol-manipulation, then many, if not most, of the symbols manipulated will represent categories, not individuals. Objectivist cognition claims such category-symbols can be made meaningful in only one way — by being associated with CATEGORIES IN THE WORLD. This brings in objectivist metaphysics. Categories of just the right kind must be assumed to exist objectively in the world if category-symbols are to made·meaningful. And if the mathematics of model-theory is to be used, the categories in the world must be sets — sets defined by necessary and sufficient conditions on their members. Otherwise, the mathematics of model-theory cannot be used to "give meaning" to category-symbols. The doctrine that natural kinds are sets of this sort is absolutely necessary if the mathematical apparatus of objectivist cognition — algorithms and models — is to be used.

It is at this point that evolutionary biology is in conflict with the mathematics used to make the philosophical theory of objectivist cognition work. Symbols for species would have to be given meaning via reference to sets defined by necessary and sufficient conditions on their members. But, as Mayr has taken great pains to point out, that is inconsistent with the concept of species needed for evolutionary biology.

It is particularly interesting that no empirical evidence is ever given *for* the view that natural kinds are sets defined by necessary and sufficient conditions on their members. It is simply assumed to be true. It is one of those many doctrines of objectivist philosophy that are assumed without question. The case of objectivist cognition versus evolutionary biology is particularly ironic. The whole point of objectivist cognition is to be scientific − to bring mathematical precision into the study of the mind, which is a highly laudable goal. But the peculiar way in which mathematical precision is achieved goes against the most thoroughly documented body of scientific knowledge of the modern age!

The Putnam Paradoxes

Objectivist cognition claims the advantages of mathematical rigor. Yet Hilary Putnam, one of our most distinguished philosophers of mathematics and of mind, has shown that, far from being rigorous, objectivist cognition suffers from fatal internal contradictions that undermines all claims to formal rigor. By looking closely at the mathematical properties of the apparatus of objectivist cognition, Putnam (1981) proved a theorem that can be used to show internal contradictions both within the objectivist doctrines of reference and meaning (doctrines 5 and 7 above). To see just where the contradictions occur, we need to look closely at both model theory and doctrines 5 through 7.

Within model theory, models consist of abstract entities and sets constructed out of those entities. Model theory provides a precise way of associating such entities and sets with meaningless symbols. The set-theoretical structures in the models are also meaningless in themselves. Model theory thus provides a way to associate elements of meaningless models with meaningless symbols. The question is whether such symbol-to-model associations can "give meaning" to meaningless symbols, as objectivist cognition requires.

Here is where objectivist metaphysics and the objectivist doctrines of meaning, truth and reference come in. Objectivist metaphysics says that the world has the structure of a set-theoretical model. Thus, it is the job of metaphysical doctrines 1 through 4 to give meaning to the otherwise meaningless models. Viewing a set-theoretical model as corresponding to the world is taken as making the model meaningful. A one-to-one model-to-world correspondence is presupposed. The doctrine of objective reference says that there is a "correct" way to assign elements of such a world-model to the meaningless symbols in terms of which we presumably think. Such a "fixing of reference" is supposed to make the meaningless symbols meaningful. The job is supposed to be accomplished through (1) the mathematics of model theory, (2) objectivist doctrines 1 through 7, and (3) one of the currently fashionable theories of reference.

Putnam has pointed out two major embarrassments for this pairing of perfectly good mathematics with objectivist philosophy. The embarrassments come from certain well-known mathematical properties of model-theory. The first embarrassment concerns the doctrine of objective reference. Within model theory a reference assignment function is a set of pairs (A,B), where A is a symbol and B is an element of a model. Let S be the set of pairs for such a reference assignment function. An initial embarrassment arises because reference itself is a human concept and a symbol like the word "refer" in English must be assigned a referent. Its referent must be the set of pairs S defining the reference assignment. For example, given that.

— "Candlestick Park" refers to Candlestick Park

the pair consisting of the name "Candlestick Park" and the stadium it names must be part of the set of pairs, S, referred to by "refer". That is, S is the set of pairs of the form

(linguistic expression, object or set)

for all expressions of the language that refer. Since "refer" itself refers to S, the pair ("refer", S) must be in S. But this yields the vicious circularity

S = {..., ("refer", S), ...}.

in which S is defined in terms of itself. The circularity is vicious, because the inner S must also be of the form:

S = {..., ("refer", S), ...}.

No matter how far we go, the reference of "refer" never gets pinned down. In short, it is nonsense to believe there is a reference relation of this kind.

One might try to avoid this embarrassment by providing a theory of reference that assigns some other relation R to "refer". But in the mathematical framework being used, such a theory can only be specified by some countable set of "sentences", that is, symbol sequences. The philosophical requirement (doctrine 7) says that reference must be objectively correct. That is, "refer" must be satisfied by one and only one set of pairs of the form

(symbol of the language, element of the model).

But now another mathematical property of model theory gets in the way of the philosophical doctrines: No countable sequence of symbols can be satisfied uniquely, that is, no sequence of sentences of a formal language is true in one and only one model. Other models always exist which can make any countable collection of sentences true. Therefore any theory of reference, which is such a sequence of sentences, cannot be satisfied uniquely. There is always more than one pairing of symbols and model-elements that will satisfy the sentences of any purported theory of reference. Kripke's causal theory of reference would be an example. In short, the unique, objectively correct account of reference that is required to give meaning to the symbols within objectivist cognition is not mathematically possible, given the proposed mathematical tools. The mathematics is just not appropriate.

Such an embarrassment would be bad enough. But Putnam has pointed out what seems to me to be an even worse embarrassment. It concerns a fundamental requirement that any adequate theory of meaning must meet:

— The meaning of the parts of a sentence cannot be changed significantly without changing the meaning of the whole.

Putnam takes a standard philosophical example, "Some cat is on some mat". He observes correctly that one should not be able to change the meaning of "cat" to cherry and "mat" to tree without changing the meaning of the whole sentence. He then shows how this can be done using model theory interpreted according to doctrines 1 - 7, that is, assuming that meaning is based on truth and reference, and reference is made to elements of models. Putnam then goes on to prove a theorem based on well-known properties of model theory showing that model theory cannot meet the fundamental requirement given above. The crucial fact made use of is the fact that elements of a model have no meaning in themselves; all they have is set-theoretical structure, and such structures can be distinguished only up to isomorphisms. For this reason, it is possible in model-theoretical semantics to change the "meaning" of the parts of a sentence — often radically — while keeping the "meaning" of the whole sentence constant. Thus, what model-theorists call "meaning" cannot be meaning. Whatever it is, it is not the concept that is needed to provide a theory of natural language semantics.

David Lewis (1984) has correctly perceived the powerful implications of Putnam's argument and has attempted to provide what he calls "saving constraints" to prevent Putnam's results. But I have been able to show (Lakoff, 1987, chap. 15) that Lewis' saving constraints cannot work, nor will any of the wide range of proposed saving constraints that I am familiar with. The mathematical tools of objectivist cognition — algorithms plus model theory — are inappropriate for the characterization of meaning.

Again we have an irony. Objectivist cognition became popular within cognitive science because it came with precise mathematical tools. Those mathematical tools are indeed, so precise that they can be shown to be inappropriate for what they were supposed to be used for. The irony is that the very precision of the mathematical tools used to justify objectivist cognition has been used to demonstrate its inconsistency.

Categorization

Since most of our reasoning concerns categories, the concept of what a category is is central to any account of cognition. Within objectivist cognition, conceptual categories are what have come to be called "classical categories":

Doctrine 8: Conceptual categories are designated by sets characterized by necessary and sufficient conditions on the properties of their members.

According to objectivist metaphysics, the only kinds of categories that exist in the world are sets. Given that the world is assumed to consist of entities with properties and relations, classical categories can be defined by necessary and sufficient conditions on the properties of entities. Conceptual categories are represented by symbols that designate real-world categories. Some of these symbols are complex — bundles of *features* that designate properties of category members. Such feature-bundles characterize the properties shared by all and only the entities in the category; they are the symbolic correlates of necessary and sufficient conditions defining classical categories in the world. Feature semantics is thus also a consequence of objectivist doctrine.

Within the past two decades an enormous amount of evidence has accumulated that shows that not all the conceptual categories used by human beings are classical categories, that is, that doctrine 8 is wrong. It should be understood at the outset that the failure of doctrine 8 does not imply that no conceptual categories have a classical structure. Some do. That is not the point. The point is that there are conceptual categories of many other kinds as well, and that the existence of such nonclassical categories is inconsistent with objectivist cognition.

I should also state at the outset that the nonclassical categories I will mainly be concerned with are *not* fuzzy sets (in the sense of Zadeh, 1965). Though fuzzy sets are not objectivist in the strict sense, the extension of objectivist cognition to admit fuzzy sets would not change things all that much. If one assumes the world is structured fuzzily (not too bold an assumption), one might well maintain that fuzzy conceptual categories could be represented by symbols that got their meaning by being associated with fuzzy real-world categories. This would still fit objectivist cognition. I assume that fuzziness is a real phenomenon in categories, but I will be concerned with other phenomena — phenomena that take the study of conceptual categories well beyond objectivist theories of cognition.

Each of the cases we will discuss is one in which a conceptual category has structure that cannot be accounted for by an association with something in objective reality. There are a number of kinds of cases:
— Cases where some imaginative aspect of the mind — schematic organization, metaphor, metonymy, or mental imagery — plays a role in the nature of the category.

— Cases where the nature of the human body (say, perception or motor capacities) determines some aspect of the category.

In both kinds of cases, the category is not a mere reflection, or representation, of nature. Rather, human bodily and imaginative capacities come into play. It should not be surprising that such conceptual categories exist. What is surprising is that a view of mind that excludes them could be taken seriously.

Color

Philosophers as far back as Locke have distinguished between "primary" and "secondary" properties. The primary properties are those that objects have as part of their very nature. The secondary properties are those that objects appear to have because of our perceptual apparatus. Color is the classic example of a secondary property. We now know an enormous amount about color. Color categories do not exist objectively in the world. Wavelengths of light exist in the world, but wavelengths do not determine color *categories*. Color categories seem to be determined by three factors:
— A neurophysiological apparatus.
— A universal cognitive apparatus.
— Culturally-determined choices that apply to the input of the universal cognitive apparatus.

The neurophysiological apparatus involves a system of color cones in the eye and neural connections between the eye and the brain. These determine response curves whose peaks are at certain pure hues: pure red, green, blue, yellow, white, and black. Other colors — for example, orange and purple and brown — are "computed" by a universal cognitive apparatus given neurophysiological input. A cultural-specific cognitive apparatus takes this input and determines a system of color categories by shifting color centers, determining major contrasts, etc. As a result, human color categories have certain general properties. They are not uniform — they have "central" best examples, which are either neurophysiologically determined pure hues or cognitively computed focal colors that are perceived as "pure" — pure orange, brown, purple, etc. Color categories are fuzzy at their boundaries, where response curves dip and overlap. Category boundaries vary greatly from culture to culture. Central colors do not vary much, but do show some variation due to culturally determined choices of contrast.

From all this it is clear that categories of color do not reside objectively in the world external to human beings. They are determined by the reflective properties of real-world objects plus our bodies and our minds. None of this would have surprised John Locke; color, after all, is a secondary property. But what does objectivist cognition have to say about color, or other "secondary" qualities? The answer is nothing. The objectivist tradition in philosophy has been concerned with primary qualities — what is assumed to be in the world independent of human perceptual and cognitive capacities. No theory of meaning at all is given for secondary properties that have no objective existence.

Color provides another embarassment to objectivist cognition. Color categories are, after all, real cognitive categories. Objectivist cognition must deal with them. But it has only one mechanism for doing so. It must represent color categories by arbitrary symbols and claim that they are made meaningful by reference to objectively-existing categories in the external world. But to do this is to treat color as if it were a primary property. For example, Barwise and Perry (1984) interpret their models as characterizing objective reality. They simply include a set of red things for the referent of "red", assuming that "red" has a referent in the objective world. Analyses of this sort are simply at variance with our present detailed and clear scientific understanding of color.

This is not a simple oversight or an easily correctable error. It is one of many fatal flaws of objectivist cognitive theories. To view meaning as residing only in the relationship between symbols and external reality is to make the implicit claim that neither color categories, nor any other secondary category, should exist as meaningful cognitive categories. Yet color categories are real categories of mind. They are meaningful, they are used in reason, and their meaning must be accounted for. But the mechanism of objectivist cognition cannot be changed to accommodate them without giving up on the symbolic theory of meaning. But to do that is to abandon the heart of the objectivist program.

Basic-Level Categories

The objectivist view of meaning for conceptual categories is often presented as being plausible on the basis of a certain range of examples of middle-sized physical objects: cats and mats and elephants and chairs and tables. Substances like gold and water are also used as examples. They usually seem like good examples of cases where there is some discontinuity in the external world that our conceptual categories fit well. In such situations, it doesn't seem implausible that our conceptual categories are symbols that acquire meaning by correspondence with real-world categories.

Brent Berlin, Eleanor Rosch, and their co-workers have studied examples of categories like this in great detail. They have shown that such examples, when understood, do not support an objectivist view of cognition; indeed, they provide strong counterevidence to objectivist cognition. What Berlin, Rosch, and others found was this: Examples like the above (cat, mat, elephant, gold, table) are instances of categorization *at a particular level.* It is a level that is cognitively basic; hence the term "basic-level".

The basic level is neither the highest nor the lowest level of categorization. It is somewhere in the middle. For example, *animal* is a superordinate category for *cat,* while *manx* is subordinate. The basic level is the level at which human beings interact with their environments most effectively and process and store and communicate information most efficiently. It is a level that is characterizable only in cognitive terms. Here are some of its properties:

— It is the level at which category members have similarly perceived overall shapes.

— It is the highest level at which a single mental image can reflect the entire category.

— It is the highest level at which a person uses similar motor programs for interacting with category members.

— It is the level at which subjects are fastest at identifying category members.

— It is the level with the most commonly used labels for category members.

— It is the level first named and understood by children.

— It is the first level to enter the lexicon of a language in the course of history.

— It is the level with the shortest primary lexemes.

— It is the level at which terms are used in neutral contexts.

— It is the level at which most of our knowledge is organized.

— It is the level at which most culturally-determined functions for objects are defined.

Basic-level categories are thus basic in four respects:
Perception: Overall perceived shape; single mental image; fast identification.
Function: General motor programs; general cultural functions.
Communication: Shortest, most commonly used and contextually neutral words, first learned by children and first to enter the lexicon.
Knowledge Organization: Most attributes of category members are stored at his level.

Let us consider some examples. Take mental images. We can form a general mental image for *cat* or *table.* But with superordinate categories like *animal* or *furniture,* there is no single mental image that covers the entire category. Thus, we have mental images for chairs, tables, beds, etc., but none for a piece of furniture that is not an image of a table, chair, bed, etc. Similarly, we have general motor programs for using chairs, tables, etc. But we have no motor programs for using furniture in general.

Or consider knowledge organization. We have a lot of knowledge about cars, which are basic-level. If you ask someone what they know about a car, it will turn out that they know a great deal. If you ask what they know about vehicles (the superordinate category), it will turn out not to be very much compared to what is known about cars. If you ask someone what they know about sportscars, it will not be very much more than what they know about cars. Thus, most of our knowledge is organized at the basic level.

The basic level is also the level at which people categorize real world objects most accurately. Berlin, Breedlove, and Raven (1974) and Hunn (1977), in massive studies of Tzeltal plant and animal names, found that at the basic level, folk terminology for plants and animals fit biological taxonomies almost perfectly. At higher and lower levels, accuracy dipped sharply. They hypothesized two reason for this, one having to do with the world and the other, with the nature of human perception and cognition. In the case of plants and animals, the basic level corresponds to the level of the biological genus. This is one level above the level of the species. In any given local ecosystem, one species of a given genus usually adapts better than other species. Thus, it is most common in a local environment to find only one species representing a genus. This results in relatively easy-to-perceive differences in overall shape among species in a locale. Since perception of overall shape is one of the determinants of the basic level, it makes sense that judgements of category membership are most accurate at this level.

Let us now return to the plausibility arguments often given for objectivist cognition, arguments based on the fact that conceptual categories like *cat, mat, elephant, table, gold,* etc. really do correspond to significant discontinuities in nature. There are two reasons why this is not evidence for objectivist cognition:

— First, superordinate and subordinate conceptual categories do not correspond to the discontinuities in nature all that well. Yet they are conceptual categories too. If the accuracy of categorization for basic-level categories makes objectivist cognition plausible, then the corresponding inaccuracy at other levels makes it implausible.

— Second, what defines the basic level is not present in the external world; the determinants of the basic level have to do with human bodies and minds. Basic-level categorization is defined not merely by what the world is like, but equally by how we interact with the world given our bodies, our cognitive organization, and our culturally-defined purposes. The level hierarchy is defined not just by what is in the world objectively, but by our nature as living beings and by our interactions within a real environment. Objectivist cognition, which posits a disembodied mind, is too impoverished to characterize the level hierarchy.

— Third, the level hierarchy is not fixed. It varies along certain limited parameters with age, culture, and individual knowledge and interests.

We appear to have a capacity for forming basic-level categories and categories at other levels. Objectivist cognition, in positing a disembodied mind, cannot characterize that capacity and therefore cannot account for variations in category level in different individuals and cultures.

Basic-level categorization points to an embodied, experientialist view of cognition rather than a disembodied, objectivist view.

Categories Defined by Schemas

What is the meaning of "Tuesday"? If, as objectivist cognition suggests, symbols get their meaning only by being associated with things in the world, then weeks must be things in the world. But weeks do not exist in nature. Different cultures have different lengths of weeks. In Bali, there are many kinds of weeks of various lengths, all of which exist simultaneously. Weeks are an imaginative creation of the human mind. In order to know what "Tuesday" means, we need to know what weeks are and how they are structured.

The kinds of imaginative structures required for the definition of concepts such as "Tuesday" have been called "frames" or "schemas". The central claim of contemporary cognitive anthropology is that most of our cultural reality resides not in the artifacts of society, but in the culture-specific schemas imposed by human beings (see Holland and Quinn, 1986). Complex collections of schemas that characterize the culturally-accepted structuring of domains of experience are called *folk theories*. Charles Fillmore has argued in a host of works on frame semantics (see annotated bibliography) that words are defined only relative to such schemas. "Tuesday" is meaningful only relative to a *weeks*-schema. The need for such schemas has become generally accepted throughout the cognitive sciences.

How do schemas of this sort square with objectivist cognition? Is a *week*-schema an "internal representation of external reality"? Does "Tuesday" refer to an aspect of "external reality" − reality external to human beings? Obviously not. That reality is constituted by the minds of human beings collectively − it is not an "external" reality. "Tuesday" cannot get its meaning by reference to a reality external to and independent of human minds. Neither can "bar mitzvah", "associate professor", "second base", "fiancee", nor any of the thousands upon thousands of realities defined by reference to cultural schemas. These realities reside in human minds, not in anything "external".

Such cultural schemas and the concepts defined only within them do not jibe with the objectivist theory of cognition, since they do not get their meaning by being associated with things external to the mind. One of the reasons that schemas have become popular within the cognitive sciences is that they can be represented as symbolic structures and manipulated algorithmically. The schemas are meaningful, but they do not derive their meaning via correspondence with an external reality. Culturally-defined schemas are a product of human imaginative capacities and, as such, do not have a place within objectivist cognition.

Again, this is not a trivial matter that can be adjusted merely by claiming that such schemas are made meaningful by reference to a mind-*internal* reality. This reason is this: In objectivist cognition, all thought is characterized as the manipulation of symbols that are *meaningless* without being associated with something external to the mind. The objectivist mind, in itself, contains nothing but meaningless symbols. There is nothing meaningful in the objectivist mind to give meaning to culturally-defined schemas.

For the working cognitive scientist, this is anything but a trivial matter. Take the question of definition. Much of cognitive science research involves natural language semantics, and every such study requires — explicitly or implicitly — an account of definition. Objectivist cognition comes with a doctrine on definition.

Doctrine 9: A complex concept is DEFINED by a collection of necessary and sufficient conditions on less complex (and, ultimately, primitive) concepts.

This constitutes the objectivist definition of "definition". It is a consequence of the doctrine of atomic primitives (doctrine 3 above) together with the central doctrine of objectivist cognition. Within the objectivist paradigm, this is the only way that a symbol can be given meaning in terms of other symbols; the other symbols must already have been made meaningful via an association with entities and categories in the world. It must be borne in mind that doctrine 9 is only a doctrine. It does not characterize what definition "really is".

Within Fillmore's frame semantics and other variations on it (e.g., theories of scripts, schemas, cognitive models, etc.) definition is defined very differently. Each word designates an element in a frame (or schema or script or cognitive model). Such frames are not defined as getting their meaning via correspondences with objectively characterized external reality. Frames are special cases of what I have called idealized cognitive models (Lakoff, 1987); they are idealizations and abstractions that may not correspond to external reality well or at all. Fillmore (1982b) looks in detail at the classic case of *bachelor,* which he argues is defined in terms of necessary and sufficient conditions — relative to an idealized cognitive model of social structure, not relative to reality. In the idealized model, everyone is heterosexual, marriage is monogamous, people get married at roughly a certain age and stay married to the same person, married men support their wives, etc. A bachelor is just an unmarried man of marriageable age, relative to this idealized model.

The model, of course, doesn't accord very well with reality. In the idealized model, the question of whether the following are bachelors does not arise: The pope, Tarzan, a moslem who is permitted to have four wives but only has three, a man who has been in a coma since childhood, etc. These are not good examples of bachelors, and whether one would want to call them bachelors at all depends on how one would want to stretch the definition. "Stretching the definition" means ignoring or modifying certain aspects of the idealized model — while leaving the necessary and sufficient conditions of the idealization intact.

In some cases, the cognitive models may be metaphorical in nature. A case in point is the English modal verbs (*must, may, can,* etc.) which Sweetser (in press) argues are defined via metaphor. Other such examples are given in Lakoff and Johnson (1980). Metaphorical definitions and various other kinds of definitions go beyond Fillmore's frame semantics and, correspondingly, beyond Putnam's stereotypes, and classical schema theory. For a detailed discussion, see Lakoff, 1987, chapters 5-7 and case studies 1 and 2.

Schemas Versus Objectivist Cognition

Let us consider a case where schema-based semantics comes into conflict with objectivist semantics. It is a case in which objectivist philosophers have proposed a semantic analysis based on objectivist cognition, proposing what they see as logical principles that are supposedly absolutely true in the real world. Counterexamples to the logical principles can be supplied, yet the principles do seem to have a certain validity, though not within objectivist cognition. Rather than being objectively true, the principles have the character of folk theories — schematically-represented commonplace ways of understanding experience, but which in many cases do not fit any external reality. The insights about the subject matter are basically correct, but the theory in which the insights are framed fails because it is based on objectivist cognition. Here is the example:

Barwise and Perry (1984) propose a logic of vision within their theory of situation semantics. Among the Barwise-Perry principles are:

Veridicality: If a sees P, then P.

Substitution: If a sees $F(t_1)$ and $t_1 = t_2$, then a sees $F(t_2)$.

These principles are justified by the following kinds of examples:

Veridicality:
If Harry saw Max eat a bagel, then Max ate a bagel.

Substitution:
 — Russell saw G.E.Moore get shaved in Cambridge.
 — G.E.Moore was (already) the author of *Principia Ethica*.

- Therefore, Russell saw the author of *Principia Ethica* get shaved in Cambridge.

It is easy to find counterexamples to such principles. Goodman (1978, chap. V) observes that well-known experiments in the psychology of vision (see Johansson, 1950, and Gilchrist and Rock, 1981) violate veridicality. For example, two lights, *A* and *B*, flashed in quick succession will appear to subjects as a single light moving from the location of *A* to the location of *B*. Suppose Harry is the subject in such an experiment. Then it will be true that

Harry saw a single light move across the screen

and false that

A single light moved across the screen.

This contradicts veridicality, which is supposed to be a *logical* principle − part of the *logic* of seeing − and which therefore is supposed to hold in *all* situations, not just normal ones.

Similarly, one can construct a situation that violates substitution. Imagine a story in which a prince has been turned into a frog. On the Barwise-Perry account, the following inference would be logically true.

The princess saw the frog jump into bed with her.

The frog was really the prince.

Therefore, the princess saw the prince jump into bed with her.

The conclusion does not clearly follow from the premises. The case is problematic to say the least. The inference should still follow, on the Barwise-Perry theory, even if the princess did not know the prince had been turned into a frog. One might claim that she did not know what she saw, but not that she did not see what she saw. Frogs don't look like princes. She saw a frog, but not a prince. The inference is not logically valid.

There is no question that the Barwise-Perry account of the semantics of seeing has certain validity − but not *logical* validity. It has folk-theoretical validity. We seem to have a folk theory of seeing. We take it for granted in normal cases, assuming certain *ceteris paribus* conditions: You are alive and awake, are functioning normally, have normal vision and relevant knowledge, are not being fooled, etc. The folk theory of vision goes like this:

- You see things as they are.
- You are aware of what you see.
- You see what's in front of your eyes.

If you see things as they are, then vision is veridical and the way things are described doesn't matter and substitution should hold.

The difference between the Barwise-Perry theory and the folk theory is all-important for the issue at hand, the question of whether objectivist cognition is correct. Is the word "see" to be given meaning via correspondence with a reality governed by the Barwise-Perry *logic* of seeing, a logic that must be valid in all situations? This is what is required if we assume that the mathematical constructions of their situation semantics is to be interpreted in terms of objectivist cognition, that is, if situations are taken as modelling reality directly. Under the objectivist interpretation (which Barwise and Perry give to their work) real contradictions arise, as we saw above. The contradictions can be avoided if the Barwise-Perry principles for seeing are interpreted as principles in a folk theory. The word "see" would then be defined relative to the cognitive schemas characterizing this folk theory. The folk theory would then provide a way of *understanding* a real-world situation, but only if the relevant *ceteris paribus* conditions held. In the counterexamples given, those conditions do not hold. To take the latter course is to give up on the idea that meaning is based on reference and truth and to give up on objectivist cognition. The reason is that the inferential properties of "see" would be characterized relative to a cognitive schema, which is not part of external reality.

To make the problem concrete, let us take a pair of sentences that cannot be made meaningful in a Barwise-Perry semantics for seeing:
− Harry saw *one light* move, but there were really many of *them* flashing in succession. He saw *it* move in a circle; but *they* were just arranged in a circle and were flashing rapidly in sequence.

Notice the use of pronouns. *It* is used for the single light that Harry saw, while *they* is used for the many lights that were actually flashing. Fauconnier's theory of mental spaces, which is a form of cognitive semantics, has no problem with such a case: The space that characterizes what Harry saw is distinct from the reality space. The former space has one light; the latter space has many. But the Barwise-Perry semantics of seeing can offer no such solution.

As we have seen, objectivist cognition fails in many ways in its account of semantics. Still more of its failures are documented in the works referred to in the annotated bibliography at the end of this paper. Objectivist cognition in general rests on its claim to be able to explain how arbitrary symbols get their meaning. The failure of objectivist semantics calls all the objectivist doctrines listed above into question, and warrants taking a very different general approach, not just to semantics but to cognition generally.

Let us now turn to a very basic semantic phenomenon that objectivist cognition can have little, if anything, to say about: systematic polysemy.

Systematic Polysemy as Evidence for a Cognitive Semantics

One of the most important and pervasive of semantic phenomena is polysemy − the fact that individual words and morphemes typically have many meanings that are systematically related to one another. Where such systematic relationships exist, it is part of the job of semantics to discover the general principles governing those relationships. Much of the cognitive semantics literature to date has been concerned with discovering such principles. I will limit myself here to the discussion of three kinds of principles that have been found: image-schema transformations, metaphor, and metonymy.

Kinaesthetic Image-Schemas

One of Mark Johnson's basic insights is that experience is structured in a significant way prior to, and independently of, any concepts. Existing concepts may impose further structuring on what we experience, but basic experiential structures are present regardless of any such imposition of concepts. This may sound mysterious, but it is actually very simple and obvious, so much so that it is not usually considered worthy of notice.

In *The Body in the Mind,* Johnson (1987) makes an overwhelming case for the embodiment of certain kinaesthetic image-schemas. Take, for example, a CONTAINER schema — a schema consisting of a *boundary* distinguishing an *interior* from an *exterior*. The CONTAINER schema defines the most basic distinction between IN and OUT. We understand our own bodies as containers — perhaps the most basic things we do are ingest and excrete, take air into our lungs and breathe it out. But our understanding of our own bodies as containers seems small compared with all the daily experiences we understand in CONTAINER terms:

Consider just a small fraction of the orientational feats you perform constantly in your daily activities — consider, for example, only a few of the many *in-out* orientations that might occur in the first few minutes of an ordinary day. You wake *out* of a deep sleep and peer *out* from beneath the covers *into* your room. You gradually emerge *out* of your stupor, pull yourself *out* from under the covers, climb *into* your robe, stretch *out* your limbs, and walk *in* a daze *out* of your bedroom and *into* the bathroom. You look *in* the mirror and see your face staring *out* at you. You reach *into* the medicine cabinet, take *out* the toothpaste, squeeze *out* some toothpaste, put the toothbrush *into* your mouth, brush your teeth, and rinse *out* your mouth. At breakfast you perform a host of further *in-out* moves — pouring *out* the coffee, setting *out* the dishes, putting the toast *in* the toaster, spreading *out* the jam on the toast, and on and on. (Johnson, 1987)

Johnson is not merely playing on the words *in* and *out.* There is a reason that those words are natural and appropriate, namely, the fact that we conceptualize an enormous number of activities in CONTAINER terms. Lindner (1981) describes in detail what is involved in this for 600 verbs containing the particle *out,* not just physical uses like *stretch out* and *spread out,* but in metaphorical uses like *figure out, work out,* etc. As Lindner observes, there are a great many metaphors based on the CONTAINER schema and they extend our bodily-based understanding of things in terms of CONTAINER schemas to a large range of abstract concepts. For example, emerging *out* of a stupor is a metaphorical, not a literal emergence from a container.

Let us consider some of the properties of this schema.

The CONTAINER Schema

Bodily experience: As Johnson points out, we experience our bodies both as containers, and as things in containers (e.g., rooms) constantly.

Structural elements: INTERIOR, BOUNDARY, EXTERIOR.

Basic Logic: Like most image-schemas, its internal structure is arranged so as to yield a basic "logic". Everything is either inside a container or out of it — P or not P. If container A is in container B and X is in A, then X is in B — which is the basis for modus ponens: If all A's are B's and X is an A, then X is a B. This is the basis of the Boolean logic of classes.

Sample Metaphors: The visual field is understood as a container: things *come into* and *go out of sight.* Personal relationships are also understood in terms of containers: one can be *trapped in a marriage* and *get out of it.*

The "basic logic" of image-schemas is due to their configurations as gestalts — as structured wholes which are more than mere collections of parts. Their basic logic is a consequence of their configurations. This way of understanding image-schemas is irreducibly cognitive. It is rather different from the way of understanding logical structure than those of us raised with formal logic have grown to know and love. In formal logic there are no such gestalt configurations. What I have called the "basic logic" of a schema would be represented by meaning postulates. This might be done as follows: Let CONTAINER and IN be uninterpreted predicate symbols, and let A, B and X be variables over argument places. The logic of the predicates CONTAINER and IN would be characterized by meaning postulates such as:

For all A, X, either IN(X,A) or not IN(X,A).

For all A,B,X, if CONTAINER(A) and CONTAINER(B) and IN(A,B) and IN(X,A), then IN(X,B).

Such meaning postulates would be strings of meaningless symbols, but would be "given meaning" by the set-theoretical models they could be satisfied in.

On our account, the CONTAINER schema is inherently meaningful to people by virtue of their bodily experience. The schema has a meaningful configuration, from which the basic logic follows, given basic cognitive operations such as superimposition and focusing. An example is given in Figures 1-4.

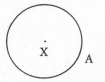

A is a CONTAINER-schema
with CONTENTS = X.

Figure 1

B is a CONTAINER-schema
with CONTENTS = A

Figure 2

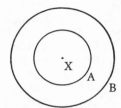

Superimposition of Figures 1 and 2

Figure 3

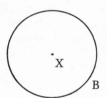

B is a CONTAINER-schema with CONTENTS = X.
This is the result of focusing on X and B in Figure 3.

Figure 4

On our account, the very concept of a set, as used in set theoretical models, is understood in terms of CONTAINER schemas (see Lakoff, 1987, case study 2 for details). Thus, schemas are not to be understood in terms of meaning postulates and their interpretation. Rather, meaning postulates themselves only make sense given schemas that are inherently meaningful because they structure our direct experience. The logician's meaning postulates are nonetheless useful as description in another vocabulary. From our point of view, they should be construed as precise statements of certain aspects of the logic inherent in schema-configurations.

Let us consider a few more examples of image-schemas.

The PART-WHOLE Schema

Bodily experience: We are whole beings with parts that we can manipulate. Our entire lives are spent with an awareness of both our wholeness and our parts. We experience our bodies as WHOLES with PARTS. In order to get around in the world, we have to be aware of the PART-WHOLE structure of other objects. In fact, we have evolved so that our basic-level perception can distinguish the fundamental PART-WHOLE structure that we need in order to function in our physical environment.

Structural elements: A WHOLE, PARTS, and a CONFIGURATION.

Basic logic: The schema is asymmetric: If A is a part of B, then B is not a part of A. It is irreflexive: A is not a part of A. Moreover, it cannot be the case that the WHOLE exists, while no PARTS of it exist. However, all the PARTS can exist, but still not constitute a WHOLE. If the PARTS exist in the CONFIGURATION, then and only then does the WHOLE exist. It follows that, if the PARTS are destroyed, then the WHOLE is destroyed. If the WHOLE is located at a place P, then the PARTS are located at P. A typical, but not necessary property: The PARTS are contiguous to one another.

Sample metaphors: Families (and other social organizations) are understood as wholes with parts. For example, marriage is understood as the creation of a family (a whole) with the spouses as parts. Divorce is thus viewed as *splitting up*. In India, society is conceived of as a body (the whole) with castes as parts, the highest caste being the head and the lowest caste being the feet. The caste structure is understood as being structured metaphorically according to the configuration of the body. Thus, it is believed (by those who believe the metaphor) that the maintenance of the caste structure (the configuration) is necessary to the preservation of society (the whole).

The LINK Schema

Bodily Experience: Our first link is the umbilical cord. Throughout infancy and early childhood, we hold onto our parents and other things, either to secure our location or theirs. To secure the location of two things relative to one another, we use such things as string, rope or other means of connection.

Structural Elements: Two entities, A and B, and LINK connecting them.

Basic Logic: If A is linked to B, then A is constrained by, and dependent upon, B. Symmetry: If A is linked to B, then B is linked to A.

Metaphors: Social and interpersonal relationships are often understood in terms of links. Thus, we *make connections* and *break social ties*. Slavery is understood as bondage, and freedom as the absence of anything tying us down.

The SOURCE-PATH-GOAL *Schema*

Bodily Experience: Every time we move anywhere there is a place we start from, a place we wind up at, a sequence of contiguous locations connecting the starting and ending points, and a direction. We will use the term "destination" as opposed to "goal" when we are referring to a specifically *spatial* ending point.

Structural Elements: A SOURCE (starting point), a DESTINATION (end point), a PATH (a sequence of contiguous locations connecting the source and the destination), and a DIRECTION (toward the destination).

Basic Logic: If you go from a source to a destination along a path, then you must pass through each intermediate point on the path; moreover, the further along the path you are, the more time has passed since starting.

Metaphors: Purposes are understood in terms of destinations, and achieving a purpose is understood as passing along a path from a starting point to an endpoint. Thus, one may *go a long way toward* achieving one's purposes, or one may get *sidetracked*, or find something getting *in one's way*. Complex events in general are also understood in terms of a source-path-goal schema; complex events have initial states (source), a sequence of intermediate stages (path), and a final state (destination).

Other image-schemas include an UP-DOWN schema, a FRONT-BACK schema, a LINEAR ORDER schema, etc. At present, the range of existing schemas and their properties is still being studied. Image-schemas provide particularly important evidence for the claim that abstract reason is a matter of two things: (a) reason based on bodily experience, and (b) metaphorical projections from concrete to abstract domains. Detailed evidence is provided by Johnson (1987). Johnson's argument has four parts:

— Image-schemas structure our experience preconceptually.
— Corresponding image-schematic concepts exist.
— There are metaphors mapping image-schemas into abstract domains, preserving their basic logic.
— The metaphors are not arbitrary, but are themselves motivated by structures inhering in everyday bodily experience.

For a detailed discussion, see Johnson, 1987, and Lakoff, 1987, chapter 17.

The Nature of Image-Schema Transformations

There are certain very natural relationships among image-schemas, and these motivate polysemy, not just in one or two cases, but in case after case throughout the lexicon. Natural image-schema transformations play a central role in forming radial categories of senses (Lakoff, 1987, chap. 6 and case study 2). Take, for example, the end-point-focus transformation. It is common for words that have an image-schema with a path to also have the corresponding image-schema with a focus on the end-point of the path, as Bennett, 1975, observed. Here are some typical pairs:

- Sam walked *over* the hill. (path)
- Sam lives *over* the hill. (end-of-path)

- Harry walked *through* that doorway. (path)
- The passport office is *through* that doorway. (end-of-path)

- Sam walked *around* the corner. (path)
- Sam lives *around* the corner. (end-of-path)

- Harriet walked *across* the street. (path)
- Harriet lives *across* the street. (end-of-path)

- Mary walked *down* the road. (path)
- Mary lives *down* the road. (end-of-path)

- Sam walked *past* the post office. (path)
- Sam lives *past* the post office. (end-of-path)

It should be noted that although such pairs are common, they are not fully productive.

- Sam walked *by* the post office. (path)
- Sam lives *by* the post office. (= *near;* ≠ end-of-path)

Here, *by* has a path schema, but no corresponding end-point schema.

- Sam ran *from* the house. (path)
- Sam stood three feet *from* the house. (end-of-path)

- Sam ran *to* the house. (path)
- *Sam stood (three feet) *to* the house. (≠ end-of-path)

From allows both path and end-of-path schemas, but *to* only allows a path schema.

   Path schemas are so naturally related to end-point schemas that people sometimes have to think twice to notice the difference. The same is true of the schema transformation that links multiplex (sometimes called "plurality") and mass schemas. It is natural for expressions like *all* and *a lot* that have a mass schema to also have a multiplex schema.

- *All* men are mortal. (MX)
- *All* gold is yellow. (MS)

- She bought *a lot of* earrings. (MX)
- She bought *a lot of* jewelry. (MS)

This schema transformation, of course, doesn't hold for all quantifiers:

- She bought *two* earrings. (MX)
- *She bought *two* jewelry. (MS)

There are also verbs which have both schemas:

- He *poured* the juice through the sieve. (MS)
- The fans *poured* through the gates. (MX)

The same systematic polysemy obtains for other verbs of liquid movement, such as *spill, flow,* etc.

- The wine *spilled* out over the table. (MS)
- The fans *spilled* out over the field. (MX)

There is a special case of the multiplex-mass transformation in which the multiplex entity is a sequence of points and the mass is a one-dimensional trajector (that is, a continuous line). A variety of prepositions permit both schemas.

- There are guards posted *along* the road. (MX)
- There is a fence *along* the road. (1DTR)

- He coughed *throughout* the concert. (MX)
- He slept *throughout* the concert. (1DTR)

- There were stains *down* his tie. (MX)
- There were stripes *down* his tie. (1DTR)

There is a natural relationship not only between a one-dimensional trajector and a sequence of points. There is also a natural relationship between a one-dimensional trajector and a zero-dimensional moving trajector (that is, a point) that traces a path.

- Sam *went* to the top of the mountain. (0DMTR)
- The road *went* to the top of the mountain. (1DTR)

- Sam ran *through* the forest. (0DMTR)
- There is a road *through* the forest. (1DTR)

- Sam walked *across* the street. (0DMTR)
- There was a rope stretched *across* the street. (1DTR)

Certain image-schemas have what Lindner (1981) refers to as "reflexive" variants, in which two distinct elements of a given schema are identified. As a result, the schematic relation holds not between two distinct entities, but between one entity and itself. "RF" indicates a reflexive schema and "NRF" indicates a nonreflexive schema. The natural relationship between reflexive and nonreflexive variants of a schema yields systematic polysemy for words like *apart, over, up, out,* etc.

Here are some examples:

- He stood *apart* from the crowd. (NRF)
- The book fell *apart.* (RF)

- He rolled *over* me. (NRF)
- He rolled *over*. (RF)

- The cat walked *up* to me. (NRF)
- The cat curled *up*. (RF)

- She poured the syrup *out* of the jar. (NRF)
- The syrup spread *out* over the pancakes. (RF)

Let us consider for a moment what is natural about these image-schema transformations.

Path-focus ↔ *end-point-focus*: It is a common experience to follow the path of a moving object until it comes to rest, and then to focus on where it is. Also, many paths are traveled *in order* to arrive at an endpoint that is kept in sight along the way. Such everyday experiences make the path-focus / end-point-focus transformation a natural principle of semantic relationships.

Multiplex ↔ *mass*: As one moves further away, there is a point at which a group of individuals, especially if they are behaving in concert, begins to be seen as a mass. Similarly, a sequence of points is seen as a continuous line when viewed from a distance.

0DMTR ↔ *1DTR*: When we perceive a continuously-moving object, we can mentally trace the path it is following, and some objects leave trails – perceptible paths. The capacity to trace a path and the experience of seeing a trail left behind make it natural for the transformation linking zero-dimensional moving trajectors and a one-dimensional trajector to play a part in semantic relations in the lexicon. (Incidentally, the word *path* itself is polysemous, with meanings that are related by this transformation).

NRF ↔ *RF*: Given a perceived relationship between a TR and a LM which are two separate entities, it is possible to perceive the same relationship between (1) different parts of the same entity or (2) earlier and later locations of the same entity, where one part or location is considered LM and the other TR.

In short, these schema transformations are anything but arbitrary. They are direct reflections of our experiences, which may be visual or kinaesthetic.

The fact that image-schemas are a reflection of our sensory and general spatial experience is hardly surprising, yet it plays a very important role in the theory of image-schemas. Perhaps we can see that significance most easily by contrasting the image-schema transformations we have described with the names we have given to them. Take the transformation name "MX ↔ MS". The name "MX" and "MS" are arbitrary relative to the character of what they name : a group of individual entities and a mass. The transformation is a natural relationship, but the name of the transformation is just a bunch of arbitrary symbols.

The distinction is important because of objectivist cognition. On one theory of image-representation — the "propositional theory" — visual scenes are represented by arbitrary symbols which are linked together in network structures. Arbitrary symbols such as X and Y are taken as standing for some aspect of a scene, such as a point or an edge or a surface or an entire object. Other symbols are used to express relations among these symbols, for example, "ABV(X,Y)" and "C(X,Y)" might represent relations which are supposed to correspond to "X is above Y" and "X is in contact with Y", but which, so far as the computer is concerned, are just symbols. Such a symbolization describes how various parts — points, edges, surfaces, etc. — are related to one another. Objects in a scene are described using such symbolizations.

According to objectivist cognition as applied to visual information and mental imagery (Pylyshyn, 1981), only such propositional representations are mentally real, while images are not real. This view stems from taking objectivist cognition *very* seriously. Since objectivist cognition requires that all cognitive processes work by the manipulation of such arbitrary symbols, objectivist cognition *requires* not only that visual perception and mental imagery be characterizable in such a "propositional" form, but also that such symbolic representations, and only those, are mentally real.

Our visual experience makes image-schema transformations natural and plausible on the assumption that they have an imagistic character. As relations among schematic *images*, they are natural; as relations among arbitrary symbols, they are unnatural and implausible. Moreover, the relationships defined by image-schema transformations do not exist objectively in the world external to human beings. They are relationships that are defined by the human perceptual and cognitive apparatus. Yet, relative to the English lexicon, they are *semantic* relationships, systematic relationships having to do with the meanings of words.

This is inconsistent with objectivist cognition, and the symbolic theory of meaning that it employs. On the objectivist view, all meaning concerns the relationship of symbols to external reality, and all semantic relations must be characterized in these terms. But the systematic semantic relations between senses of words that we have just discussed cannot be characterized by reference to external, mind-free reality. Those semantic relations have to do with image-schema transformations, which are characterized by the human perceptual and cognitive systems and not by any mind-free reality.

The very existence of systematic semantic relationships characterized by image-schema transformations thus conflicts with *both* parts of objectivist cognition.

— The fact that these *semantic* relationships (that is, relationships concerning the meanings of words) exist by virtue of the human perceptual and cognitive systems is in conflict with the idea that semantics can be characterized only by the relation between symbols and external mind-free reality.

— The fact that these cognitively real relationships between the meanings of words can be characterized naturally only in terms of schematic images and not in terms of arbitrary symbols is in conflict with the idea that meanings are represented cognitively only by arbitrary symbols, as the algorithmic view of thought demands.

Both the symbolic theory of meaning and the algorithmic theory of cognitive processes are inconsistent with the very existence of *any* such phenomena.

The existence of systematic semantic relationships of the sort we have just described places a constraint of major importance on the representation of meaning in the mind. Cognitively real representations of meaning must make use of image-schemas. Image-schemas are not finitary arbitrary meaningless symbols whose internal structure is irrelevant. Image-schemas are nonfinitary (that is, continuous), nonarbitrary, meaningful (via perceptual-motor experience), with a semantically-relevant internal structure.

The internal structure of image-schemas appears to be sufficiently rich and of the right character to permit one to characterize *general-purpose reasoning* in natural language in terms of image-schemas plus such general cognitive operations as superimposition, scanning, focusing, etc. operating on those schemas. This is significant for at least two reasons. It has been commonly assumed that reasoning in natural language makes use of finitary symbols and algorithmic operations using those symbols. This has resulted in a bifurcation between what has been called language-based or "propositional" reasoning on the one hand and the processing of mental images on the other. Kosslyn (1980) has argued that both kinds of processes exist. Pylyshyn has argued that only propositional operations exist and that the processing of mental images makes use of the algorithmic manipulation of finitary arbitrary symbols. The image-schema evidence points to the opposite conclusion — that natural language reasoning makes use of at least some unconscious and automatic image-based processes such as superimposing images, scanning them, focusing on parts of them, etc. It also raises the possibility that visual processing and reasoning using natural language may share some of the same cognitive operations.

Summary

Objectivist cognition is a false philosophical doctrine that stands in the way of research on the nature of meaningful thought. It brings with it a host of other false doctrines, doctrines about metaphysics, meaning, truth, reference, categorization and even definition. These doctrines have been rejected within the cognitive semantics tradition. The literature on cognitive semantics is now so voluminous that no introductory survey could do justice to it. The studies in this tradition have two aspects to them — a negative and a positive aspect. These works, in their negative aspect, argue against objectivist cognition, typically against the claim that semantics is characterized by the relationship between arbitrary symbols and mind-free reality. In their positive aspect, these works offer an alternative of a relatively clear character:

Meaning is based on the understanding of experience. Truth is based on understanding and meaning. Innate sensory-motor mechanisms provide a structuring of experience at two levels: the basic level and the image-schematic level. Image-schematic concepts and basic-level concepts for physical objects, actions, and states are understood directly in terms of the structuring of experience. Very general innate imaginative capacities (for schematization, categorization, metaphor, metonymy, etc.) characterize abstract concepts by linking them to image-schematic and basic-level physical concepts. Cognitive models are built up by these i-maginative processes. Mental spaces provide a medium for reasoning using cognitive models.

Even though most of these ideas are less than a decade old, they have been investigated and thought through in considerable detail. Here is a selective annotated bibliography so that the interested reader can begin to approach this literature. The most general overall accounts are Lakoff, 1987, and Langacker, 1987.

Selected Annotated Bibliography

BRUGMAN, CLAUDIA
1981   *Story of* Over, University of California, Berkeley, M.A., Thesis. Available from the Indiana University Linguistics Club, Bloomington, Indiana.
        This is one of the most detailed studies ever done of the relationships among the senses of a single lexical item. Brugman considers nearly 100 senses of over. She argues that the senses are characterizable by image-schemas and independently necessary metaphors applying to them. The senses form a radial structure, with a central sense and other senses linked to it by image-schema transformations and metaphors.
1983   "Extensions of Body-part Terms to Locating Expressions in Chalcatongo Mixtec", in University of California, Berkeley, Report No. 4 of the Survey in California and Other Indian Languages.
CASAD, EUGENE
1982   *Cora Locationals and Structured Imagery,* University of California, San Diego Ph.D. Dissertation.
        The studies by Brugman on Mixtec and Casad on Cora demonstrate that space is conceptualized in those languages in a way that is radically different from the conceptualization of space in Indo-European languages. In Mixtec, relative spatial location is conceptualized in terms of the metaphorical projection of body-part concepts onto objects. In Cora, there is an extensive system of locational morphemes. Each phoneme in such a morpheme designates an image-schema, and the meaning of the morpheme is given by the superimposition of all the schemas.

FAUCONNIER, GILLES
1985   *Mental Spaces*, Cambridge, Mass., MIT Press.
       *Within cognitive semantics, mental spaces play many of the roles that possible worlds
       and Barwise-Perry situations play in objectivist semantics. They are partial models. They
       contain (mental) entities. They permit the explicit statement of conditions of satisfac-
       tion. Entailment can be characterized relative to them. They bear relations to one another.
       But they are cognitive in nature; they are not interpretable as fitting objectivist metaphysics.
       Mental spaces provide the apparatus needed for a precise cognitive model theory, without
       the limitations of objectivist philosophy. Fauconnier's book presents a unified account
       of metonymy, presupposition and referential opacity making use of mental spaces, con-
       nectors, and cognitive strategies. The strategies are formalized versions of the following:*
       – *Avoid contradictions within a space.*
       – *Distinguish between foregrounded and backgrounded elements.*
       – *Maximize common background assumptions across adjacent spaces.*
       – *Currently foregrounded elements are subsequently backgrounded.*
       *Fauconnier demonstrates that these simple intuitive strategies provide a simultaneous
       solution for both referential opacity and the projection problem for presuppositions.*

FILLMORE, CHARLES
1975   "An Alternative to Checklist Theories of Meaning", in *Proceedings of the First An-
       nual Meeting of the Berkeley Linguistics Society.*
1976   "Topics in Lexical Semantics", in P. Cole (ed), *Current Issues in Linguistic Theory*,
       Bloomington, Indiana University Press.
1978   "The Organization of Semantic Information in the Lexicon", in *Chicago Linguistic
       Society Parasession on the Lexicon.*
1982a "Towards a Descriptive Framework for Spatial Deixis", in Jarvella and Klein (eds),
       Speech, Place, and Action, London, John Wiley.
1982b "Frame Semantics", in Linguistic Society of Korea (eds.), *Linguistics in the Morn-
       ing Calm*, Seoul, Hanshin.
1984   *Frames and the Semantics of Understanding*, unpublished ms., Department of
       Linguistics, University of California, Berkeley.
       *Within frame semantics, lexical items are defined relative to frames (which are akin
       to cognitive models, schemas, scripts, etc.). Frames characterize a unified and idealized
       understanding of an area of experience and Fillmore argues that meaning must be defi-
       ned in terms of such understandings, not in terms of truth conditions. The principle data
       that Fillmore draws on is the semantic relationships holding among words within semantic
       fields.*

GENTNER, DEDRE, and DONALD R. GENTNER
1983   "Flowing Waters or Teeming Crowds: Mental Models of Electricity", in D. Gent-
       ner and A.L. Stevens (eds), *Mental Models*, Hillsdale, N.J., Erlbaum.
       *The authors show that reasoning about electricity by students learning about it is done
       using metaphorical models. The students get different answers to problems based on the
       metaphorical models used. The study is significant for cognitive semantics since it
       demonstrates that metaphorical models are used in reasoning, which contradicts objec-
       tivist cognition and supports cognitive semantics.*

HOLLAND, DOROTHY, and NAOMI QUINN (eds.)
1987   *Cultural Models in Language and Thought*, Cambridge, Cambridge University Press.
       *This volume includes a number of papers that show the utility of cognitive semantics
       for characterizing culture-specific concepts. Quinn's paper is of special interest in its discus-
       sion of the use of image-schemas and metaphor in the characterization of the concept
       of marriage in America.*

JANDA, LAURA
1984   *A Semantic Analysis of the Russian Verbal Prefixes* ZA-, PERE- DO-, *and* OT-, Univer-
       sity of California, Los Angeles, Ph.D. Dissertation.
       *The semantics of the Russian verbal prefixes has been a perennial problem in Slavic
       linguistics. Using techniques of image-schematic analysis developed by Lindner, 1981,
       and Brugman, 1981, Janda is able to display for the first time the regularities among
       the many senses of four extremely complex verbal prefixes.*

JOHNSON, MARK
1987   *The Body In The Mind: The Bodily Basis of Reason and Imagination*, Chicago, University
        of Chicago Press.
        *Johnson argues that our everyday bodily experiences are preconceptually structured by
        image-schemas, and that such structuring in our bodily experience provides the basis for
        our understanding of image-schematic concepts. It is by this means that the body plays
        a central role in characterizing rational processes. Johnson's book plays a maior role
        in the characterization of experientialist cognition.*
KAY, PAUL
1979   *The Role of Cognitive Schemata in Word Meaning: Hedges Revisited,* unpublished ms.,
        Berkeley Cognitive Science Program.
1983   "Linguistic Competence and Folk Theories of Language: Two English Hedges",
        in *Proceedings of the Ninth Annual Meeting of the Berkeley Linguistics Society*, pp.
        128-137. Reprinted in Holland and Quinn.
        *The theory of objective reference is a key part of objectivist cognition. Within contem-
        porary philosophy there are two contending theories – Frege's view that sense deter-
        mines reference and the Putnam-Kripke theory of direct reference. Kay observes that
        English contains expressions such as* strictly speaking, loosely speaking, *and technical-
        ly whose meaning concerns the way reference is fixed. Strictly speaking and loosely
        speaking are defined relative to a folk version of the Fregean view, while technically
        is defined relative to a folk version of the Kripke-Putnam theory. Kay argues that this
        makes sense under Fillmore's theory that words are defined relative to cognitive schemata.
        In this case, the two cognitive schemata are about reference and are mutually inconsis-
        tent. But the meanings of these expressions cannot be given by association with anything
        in the external mind-free world. The reason is that the expressions are defined in terms
        of two mutually inconsistent accounts of reference, while at most one of these accounts
        of reference could be true objectively.*
LAKOFF, GEORGE, and MARK JOHNSON
1980   *Metaphors We Live By,* Chicago, University of Chicago Press.
        *The book presents evidence that the phenomenon of metaphor can best be explained
        in terms of conceptual mappings from one conceptual domain to another. Under such
        a characterization, the meanings of a large proportion of ordinary everyday language
        can be seen to involve such mappings. The book argues that such a view of meaning
        is inconsistent with objectivist cognition.*
LAKOFF, GEORGE
1987   *Women, Fire, and Dangerous Things: What Categories Reveal About the Mind,* Chicago,
        University of Chicago Press.
        *Since most reasoning concerns categories, empirical studies of categorization bear crucially
        on theories of the nature of meaningful thought. This book surveys research on categoriza-
        tion, especially research on basic-level categories and prototype theory. It argues that
        this research disconfirms objectivist cognition and confirms a version of cognitive semantics.
        The book also outlines a general theory of cognitive semantics and cognitive grammar
        and presents three detailed case studies that support the theory.*
LANGACKER, RONALD W.
1987   *Foundations of Cognitive Grammar,* Vol. 1, Stanford, Stanford University Press.
        *This is the first of two monumental volumes laying out foundations for a general theory
        of cognitive semantics and a theory of grammar based on it. Langacker gives a meticulously
        detailed and carefully thought out account of his theory of "images" (what I have called
        "image-schemas") and of the cognitive operations needed to operate on them. The volume
        contains a great many insightful analyses of semantic phenomena.*
LANGACKER, RONALD, and EUGENE CASAD
1985   "Inside and Outside in Cora Grammar", *International Journal of American Linguistics.*
        *An oversimplified version of one chapter of Casad's dissertation. It is an accessible and
        short discussion of one aspect of the conceptualization of space in Cora.*
LINDNER, SUSAN
1981   *A Lexico-Semantic Analysis of Verb-Particle Constructions with* Up *and* Out, Univer-

sity of California, San Diego, Ph.D. Dissertation. Available from the Indiana University Linguistics Club.

1982 "What Goes Up Doesn't Necessarily Come Down: The Ins and Outs of Opposites", in *Proceedings of the Eighteenth Regional Meeting of the Chicago Linguistic Society*. *Lindner's dissertation represented a major advance in the description of polysemy using image-schemas and metaphors. Lindner took up a question that was previously thought to be intractable: How are the senses of particles, such as the* out *of* figure out, space out, *and* fill out, *related to one another. Lindner took as data more than 600 examples of* out *and more than 1200 examples of* up *in verb-particle constructions. She showed that systematic semantic regularities appear once image-schemas and metaphors are taken into account in the semantics. In the process, she discovered the existence of reflexive variants of image-schemas.*

PUTNAM, HILARY

1981 *Reason, Truth, and History*, Cambridge, Cambridge University Press. *Prior to this book, Putnam was one of the principal figures in objectivist phylosophy. His functionalism thesis laid the contemporary philosophical foundation for objectivist cognition. In his classic paper "The meaning of* meaning*", he had both argued for the theory of direct reference and proposed a way of reconciling the objectivist account of meaning with a schema-based account of cognitive meaning (which he discussed under the rubric of "stereotypes"). In this book, Putnam rejects his former views about meaning and reference. He argues on the basis of a theorem proved in an appendix that all objectivist ("metaphysical realist") accounts of meaning and reference are internally incoherent, and that his own functionalist thesis, on which objectivist cognition depends, is equally mistaken.*

REDDY, MICHAEL

1979 "The Conduit Metaphor", in A. Ortony (ed.), *Metaphor and Thought*, Cambridge, Cambridge University Press. *This is a classic paper showing the role of metaphor in cognition. Reddy shows that most of our language about communication is based on a single metaphor — the conduit metaphor. Reddy discusses in detail how the metaphor is used in reasoning about communication and what aspects of communication the metaphor hides.*

SWEETSER, EVE E.

1984 *Semantic Structure and Semantic Change*, University of California, Berkeley Ph.D. Dissertation. Revised version to be published by Cambridge University Press. *Sweetser argues that the historical change of word meaning can only be accounted for by a cognitive semantics that makes use of image-schemas and metaphors. She also argues that the meanings of modal verbs in English (e.g., must, may, can, etc.) are metaphorical in nature and are based on Talmy's "force images".*

TALMY, LEONARD

1972 *Semantic Structures in English and Atsugewi*, University of California, Berkeley Ph. D. Dissertation.

1975 "Semantics and Syntax of Motion", in J. Kimball (ed.), *Syntax and Semantics*, Vol. 4, New York, Academic Press.

1978 "Relation of Grammar to Cognition", in D. Waltz (ed.), *Proceedings of* TINLAP-2 *(Theoretical Issues in Natural Language Processing)*, Champaign, Ill., Coordinated Science Laboratory, University of Illinois.

1985 "Force dynamics in language and thought", *Papers from the Parasession on Causatives and Agentivity*, Chicago, Chicago Linguistic Society. *Talmy's work, over many years, has contributed to the development of cognitive semantics in many areas, especially to the role of image-schemas in cognition. His was the earliest detailed research in this area.*

Other references

BARWISE, JON, and JOHN PERRY

1984 *Situations and Attitudes*, Cambridge, MIT Press.

BENNET, DAVID
1975   *Spatial and Temporal Uses of English Prepositions*, London, Longmans.
BERLIN, BRENT, DENNIS E. BREEDLOVE and PETER H. RAVEN
1974   *Principles of Tzeltal Plant Classification*, New York, Academic Press.
HUNN, EUGENE S.
1977   *Tzeltal Folk Zoology; The Classification of Discontinuities in Nature*, New York, Academic Press.
KOSSLYN, STEPHEN M.
1980   *Image and Mind*, Cambridge, Mass., Harvard University Press.
LEWIS, DAVID
1984   "Putnam's Paradox", *Australasian Journal of Philosophy* 62:3, 221-236.
MAYR, ERNST
1984   "Species Concepts and Their Applications", in E. Sober (ed.), 1984, pp. 531-540.
PYLYSHYN, ZENON
1981   "The Imagery Debate: Analogue Media versus Tacit Knowledge", *Psychological Review* 87, 16-45.
ZADEH, LOTFI
1965   "Fuzzy Sets", *Information and Control* 8, 338-353.

Wendy G. Lehnert

The Analysis of Nominal Compounds*

If one surveys the standard representational techniques for natural language that have evolved in linguistics and artificial intelligence, it is difficult to find much uniformity in the theories proposed. Distinctions are made between linguistic performance and linguistic competence, syntactic regularities and conceptual content, formal semantics and commonsense inference, structural models and process models. An innocent bystander could easily come to the conclusion that the study of language is both ill-defined and lacking in systematic research methodologies. The whole business is rather reminiscent of the three blind men who conclude that an elephant is like a tree, a snake, or a wall: what you find depends a lot on where you poke around.

It is not my intention here to sort out all the conflicting research premises and competing methodologies associated with the study of language. Instead, I will briefly identify my own position with respect to some of these larger issues, and then proceed to discuss a specific problem associated with my end of the elephant. My interest in language addresses language as a vehicle for communication. I am concerned with the conceptual content of sentences and the cognitive processes that extract conceptual content from a text or a discourse. These processes must be described in terms of human memory models and concerns for psychological validity or at least a healthy respect for psychological plausibility. But I am not a psychologist because I do not run experiments on subjects or analyze data. I conduct my research by writing computer programs that simulate language processing behavior. These complex computer programs allow me to develop theories and sometimes test competing explanations within a single theoretical framework. I am happy to borrow ideas from linguistics and psychology, but the theoretical foundations for my work come from artificial intelligence.

I have been involved with the design of many natural language systems, including question answering systems (Lehnert 1978), story understanding systems (Lehnert et al. 1983), and summarization systems (Lehnert 1982, 1984). More recently I have been concentrating on problems specific to conceptual sentence analysis (Lehnert and Rosenberg 1985), a crucial component for virtually all other language tasks. Over the last ten years we have seen tremendous progress in this area, and more than

* This research was supported by NSF Presidential Young Investigator Award NSFIST-8351863 and by DARPA grant N00014-85-K-0017.

a small amount of controversy over the relationship between syntactic and semantic analysis. Major contributions to the problem of conceptual sentence analysis have been made by a number of people in artificial intelligence (see for example, Charniak 1981, DeJong 1979, Dyer 1983, Gershman 1979, Lebowitz 1983, Lytinen 1984, Riesbeck & Martin 1985, Riesbeck & Schank 1976, Small 1980, Waltz & Pollack 1984, Wilensky 1981).

To state the problem simply, a conceptual analyzer must input a sentence (or sequence of sentences) and return a representational structure that captures the meaning of the sentence(s). This presumes a system for meaning representation that is suitable for higher level processes of inference and memory integration. One would also like the representational structures to be canonical in the sense that paraphrases of a sentence should produce identical (or very close to identical) meaning representations. Canonical meaning representations are motivated by psychological experiments which show that people are able to retain the general meaning of a sentence long after they have forgotten the precise wording of that sentence (Bransford & Franks 1971).

People who build conceptual sentence analyzers are necessarily concerned with the representations their analyzers produce, and all of the various arguments associated with competing representations. Syntactic parse trees are routinely dismissed since they were never intended to capture meaning in the first place. Lexical predicates and case frames do constitute an attempt at meaning representation but they tend to fall short of canonical form criteria because the predicates are typically determined by the main verb. For example, the two sentences:

"John gave Mary a book."
"John sent Mary a book."

result in two distinct predicate representations:

give (John, book, Mary)
send (John, book, Mary)

Extra rules have to be invoked if we are going to understand that these two representations are conceptually close. There is also a problem with lexical representations in that they do not address the problem of word sense ambiguity. The main event underlying "John gave Mary a book" cannot be distinguished from the event described by, "John gave Mary a kiss," or "John gave Mary a disease." Lexical representations do not attempt to make any such distinctions. To develop a representation that can capture appropriate word sense distinctions we have to resort to "deep" semantic representations which require decomposition into primitives.

A few people have developed conceptual representations based on primitive decomposition (Wilks 1972, Schank 1975, Lehnert 1979), and many systems employ primitives as a practical matter-of-course without a strong theoretical basis. Suffice to say, there is no "standard theory" for conceptual representation and it is likely to be a while before anyone presumes to offer a comprehensive solution. Many researchers believe we are pursuing a form of "applied epistemology" in which case it is not feasible to expect elegant solutions of great generality. The knowledge required to understand a newspaper story is different from the knowledge required to read a technical paper on hydrodynamics, so there is every reason to expect that the internal meaning representations associated with such disparate tasks will themselves be altogether different. Each knowledge domain may require its own set of event primitives and representational devices. Much exploratory work remains to be done before we can hope to look for general patterns and universal techniques.

Nominal Compounds

It is within this exploratory spirit that I would like to focus on a specific natural language construct that relates strongly to the question of internal meaning representations: nominal compounds. Simply defined, a nominal compound is a noun phrase consisting of nothing but nouns:

> dog leash
> computer terminal
> car mechanic
> leather book jacket
> steel doorknob plate screws

Within linguistics, nominal compounds have been studied and discussed for a number of languages. The major studies for English include (Koziol 1937, Jespersen 1942, Lees 1960, Marchand 1969, and Levi 1978). Nominal compounds have a shorter history within artificial intelligence but there has been some work addressing the phenomenon (Russell 1972, Finin 1982, Gershman 1979, Lebowitz 1984a). From the perspective of meaning representations, nominal compounds pose an interesting problem for information processing models. People manage to make sense of these noun phrases with little or no conscious effort. But the conceptual content of a nominal compound presumes a subtle understanding of semantic features and implicit relationships between concepts. There are structural regularities within nominal compounds that suggest a form of syntax, yet no one is ever taught these rules in school. For example, no one thinks twice about the meanings for:

> a dog collar   vs.   a flea collar

Yet the natural conceptual interpretations associated with these phrases are clearly distinct. A dog collar is a collar worn by a dog, but a flea

collar is a collar worn by a dog or cat for the purpose of killing fleas.
Conceptual distinctions can be found in any number of otherwise simple examples:

oil truck	(a truck that carries oil)
diesel truck	(a truck that runs on diesel fuel)
paper filter	(a filter made of paper)
coffee filter	(a filter for filtering coffee)
dress watch	(a watch to wear with formal dress)
gold watch	(a watch made of gold)
toy car	(a car that is a toy)
business car	(a car used for business travel)

In some cases, entirely different word senses must be selected for the
head noun:

play pen	(an enclosure)
fountain pen	(a writing instrument)
butcher block	(a piece of wood)
city block	(a region)
salary cap	(a maximal amount)
wool cap	(a hat)

Other features of nominal compounds surface when we examine longer
ones:

plastic cat food can cover
(a cover made of plastic that goes on a can filled with food for cats)

There are rules that regulate the proper word order for a noun group
of this complexity. We cannot refer to a "can food cat plastic cover"
or a "plastic food cover cat can", and expect to make any sense.

These examples suggest a number of interesting problems associated
with nominal compounds which we will discuss from a representational
perspective. The problems we will consider are not well understood, but
they may provide us with some intriguing glimpses of conceptual information processing at work.

Lexicalization

One representational strategy for nominal compounds is commonly
referred to as lexicalization. A noun phrase is considered to be "lexicalized" if it assumes the status of a lexical dictionary entry. In this case the
noun phrase effectively becomes a single vocabulary item that happens
to contain some blank spaces thrown in among the alphabetical characters.

In artificial intelligence, this same idea has been suggested by the notion of a "phrasal lexicon" (Becker 1975).

In a computational model, a lexicalized noun phrase can be handled very simply. All we have to do is make sure we can find the lexicalized phrase in our dictionary, and then we can retrieve any ready-made definition we wish to associate with the given phrase. There is no need for "run-time" analysis or complicated procedures that attempt to construct a meaning representation dynamically. It is all just a straightforward problem of dictionary access.

The idea of limited lexicalization is quite reasonable. Certain phrases do seem to be rather specialized in their meaning, and it is unlikely that anyone would ever manage to construct their meaning from general principles. Some likely candidates for lexicalization include:

night stand	stop watch
hay ride	water closet
ball park	bank shot

It seems quite plausible that these phrases are simply memorized as units and effectively treated as lexical items. It is not possible to paraphrase these expressions as we might with other nominal compounds. A "dried grass trip" just doesn't work as an alternative to a hay ride and "sphere park" is not likely to conjure images of hotdogs and crowds. Further evidence for lexicalization can be found in the etymology of agglutinated words. Many words start out as noun groups and then attain full lexical status through popular usage:

sundial	gunrunner
hellfire	shoelace
motorboat	mothball

But the extreme position on lexicalization claims that *all* nominal compounds should be handled as pre-defined dictionary entries. This position is not feasible for computational models of language processing since it requires that we anticipate all possible noun groups. In principle, one could argue that this presupposes an infinite dictionary, since it is possible to construct noun groups of arbitrary length. An argument based on infinite dictionaries is admittedly stretching things a bit since there is a limit to how much people can handle in practice. It is possible in some sense to use the phrase:

"plastic cat food can cover retail package manufacturer rebate deadline"

in referring to the deadline on a rebate offered by a company who packages for sale the plastic covers that go on cat food cans! But one would not expect to find such a construct in reasonable discourse. So we will dismiss the infinite dictionary argument as an argument about linguistic competence.

From a performance perspective, we can still combat the extreme lexicalization position by noting that strong regularities govern compound
noun groups. We must assume that regularities have evolved in language
because they make it easier for people to process language quickly and
effectively. If all noun groups are handled by a simple process of dictionary access, what purpose is served by their structural regularities?
How is it possible for people to make sense of a new noun group the
first time it is encountered? In time, a specific noun phrase that is frequently used may become lexicalized for a given speaker. But that does
not preclude the possibility of dynamic noun phrase analysis for other
speakers, nor does it follow that all lexicalized noun phrases start out
as such. As one becomes more familiar with the concept underlying a
frequent noun phrase, it may be that lexicalization occurs as a side-effect
of concept acquisition. The relationship between lexicalization, conceptual analysis, and concept acquisition appears to be a worthy problem
for the cognitive scientists among us.

In any case, we will assume that people have some cognitive facility
for processing novel noun groups and extracting conceptual content from
such constructs without the benefit of a phrasal lexicon. In order to better understand what this facility must accomplish, we must examine the
regularities present in nominal compounds and consider the underlying
memory mechanisms that exploit these regularities.

Specialized Meanings

If we hope to find general mechanisms for meaning extraction, we must
understand that such mechanisms will be limited and may not be capable
of producing certain associations commonly attributed to complex
nominals. Many of these idiosyncratic associations can be attributed to
specialized domain knowledge and are often described as extralinguistic
because they depend on a speaker's education, ethnic background, oc-
cupation, and so forth.

For example, about ten or twelve years ago the term "fern bar" sur-
faced in American discourse. The term was popular among urban singles
who frequented the bar scene. It referred to bars that catered to a particular type of upwardly-mobile clientele (forerunners of the YUPPIE
phenomenon). Many of these bars shared a common decor: exposed brick
walls, the menu on a blackboard, oversized plate-glass windows, blond
woodwork, and lots of hanging ferns. People began to refer to these
establishments as fern bars. The reference was mildly derogatory, as it
conveyed a hint of condescension toward those misguided souls who
would tolerate overpriced drinks for the sake of running with the in-
crowd. So on one level, the term meant a bar containing ferns, but it
also carried a specialized meaning that went far beyond that simple con-

cept. By now, the term is so specialized that it is possible to have a fern bar without any ferns.

Whenever a term carries a specialized meaning which cannot be derived by general mechanisms, that term must be lexicalized (for those speakers who understand its extralinguistic associations). If it weren't, how would those associations be accessed? Many complex nominals, especially noun-pairs, carry specialized meanings which cannot be derived by general mechanisms. The question of how specialized meanings are acquired is an interesting one. I can recall the first time I heard the term "fern bar" in casual conversation: I understood immediately what was meant by the reference. The concept had been present in my mind beforehand, but I had no concise linguistic description for easy reference. The name fit the concept and the specialized meaning required no explanation for me. It is probably more often the case that specialized meanings have to be described and explained.

Whatever the process of concept acquisition is for specialized meanings, we will not attempt to account for that aspect of conceptual understanding with general mechanisms of meaning extraction. Specialized meanings require lexicalized dictionary entries, so there is no point in trying to account for their presence on the basis of conceptual analysis. We will be satisfied to acknowledge their existence, and then concentrate on those constructs that can be processed by general processes of conceptual analysis.

Evidence for Conceptual Analysis

The processing of a noun phrase can be complicated by the fact that there is sometimes uncertainty as to exactly when a noun phrase is being terminated. Under certain circumstances, these situations result in "garden path" sentence processing. A garden path sentence is one that leads the understander "down the garden path" into an incorrect interpretation as the sentence is being processed. Once the error is caught, it is then necessary to revise the original interpretation by going back and trying to understand the sentence one more time. Garden path sentences can result from syntactic ambiguities as well as lexical ambiguities, but we will restrict this discussion to those that occur because it is unclear whether a particular word should be interpreted as a noun or a verb. Such ambiguities are easy to construct:

sentry stands	paper wraps	log rolls
building blocks	dog runs	wood tops
silk dresses	baby toys	steel slides

Various mechanisms have been proposed to account for the ways that people process potentially ambiguous word pairs of this type. For example, one could assume that there is natural preference for noun-noun interpretations wherever possible, so noun-noun interpretations are always tried first. But if this were true, garden path sentences could only result from constructs that should be taken as noun-verb combinations. In such cases a noun-noun interpretation would cause a garden path before the correct noun-verb interpretation could be considered. But there seem to be many examples of garden path sentences that start out as noun-verb interpretations and end up as noun-noun interpretations:

The sentry stands were rusty.   (vs. The sentry stands alone.)
The toy rocks are green.   (vs. The toy rocks back and forth.)
The knife cuts hurt.   (vs. The knife cuts poorly.)

If you were not conscious of any garden path processing when you read the above sentences, you might like the idea of a limited look-ahead capability (Marcus 1980). When a sentence is processed with limited look-ahead, one is effectively allowed to take a peek at some fixed number of subsequent sentence constituents (or words) before committing the system to any particular interpretation. By using limited look-ahead, it is possible to argue for deterministic sentence analysis, which means that it is never necessary to revise an interpretation (unless the critical information needed is further away than the look-ahead facility can go). But limited look-ahead theories have difficulty making predictions about which sentences will cause people to follow a garden path.

Given any fixed length for look-ahead, it is possible to construct a sentence with a local ambiguity that is not resolved until after the look-ahead capability is exhausted. But sentences can be found that confound even the most minimal look-ahead requirements. For example, people do not have any difficulty understanding a sentence such as:

"The prime number 2 is the only even prime."

Yet many people have difficulty understanding the following as a complete and grammatical sentence:

"The prime number few."

Both sentences are potentially ambiguous up to, "The prime number..." So why does only one sentence cause difficulty? In these cases, the limited look ahead model is not feasible, since the look ahead needed for "The prime number few", is as minimal as possible (one word). If limited-look-ahead is what people use, both of these sentences should be understood without garden paths.

Of course, one cannot pose serious arguments about psychological validity on the basis of subjective judgements. In this case, it is useful to collect reaction time data in order to test one's process model. If a sentence is processed as a garden path sentence, it will take longer for subjects to understand the sentence than would otherwise be the case.

Since any potential garden path can (in principle) be understood without going down the garden path, it is possible for some subjects to understand such a sentence only after considering the garden path while others understand the sentence the first time through without any difficulties. If the resolution of a local ambiguity is made randomly, we would expect to see both types of processing: roughly half of a subject pool should go down the garden path while the remaining subjects do not.

A purely syntactic parser like the one proposed by Marcus (op. cit.) must be arbitrary when it cannot resolve an ambiguity by looking ahead. But reaction time data indicates that people are not arbitrary when they confront potential garden path sentences (Coker & Crain 1979, Crain & Coker 1979). Rather, there appear to be semantic processes that influence the resolution of local ambiguities.

In one set of experiments, local ambiguities of the noun-noun vs. noun-verb type were studied (Milne 1982). After controlling for variables in syntactic complexity, it was found that the reaction times collected for potential garden path sentences could be explained by the "Semantic Checking Hypothesis." This model argues for a semantic process which is triggered whenever a word pair is encountered that could be interpreted as noun-noun. This process examines the word pair and returns some judgement as to whether or not the word pair should be interpreted as a noun phrase. If the judgement favors a noun phrase interpretation, that is how the ambiguity is resolved. If the judgement for a noun phrase is weak, alternative interpretations are then considered before resuming sentence analysis. So the "Semantic Checking Hypothesis" considers noun-noun interpretations first, but may reject the noun-noun interpretation on purely semantic grounds before continuing with the sentence.

As Milne admits, his experiments have not attempted to take into consideration possible predictive factors from a larger sentence processing context. A sentence that requires garden path processing in isolation may not be a garden path sentence when it is encountered in some larger context. But his experiments do argue convincingly for a semantic mechanism that must play at least a part in the overall process model.

We cannot say precisely how Milne's semantic checking mechanism operates. Does it compute a confidence rating on each potential noun phrase and then accept the noun-noun interpretation only if that confidence passes threshold? Or is the judgement purely binary (a yes or a no)? More importantly, how is the conceptual content of a noun-noun construct represented in memory? If we find a likely noun phrase interpretation, how do we encode that interpretation in memory? One can argue for surface representations in the case of certain lexicalized noun pairs, but other noun pairs must be encoded at a deeper level. If you ask someone to paraphrase a newspaper story about an "alleged killer", it is quite likely that the paraphrase might refer to a "murder suspect" or even "murderer". Similarly, a "highrise office complex" might become

a "skyscraper", and a "cellar door" could become the "basement entry."
The representational issues associated with nominal compounds are
sometimes subtle but nevertheless intriguing. Complex noun groups may
provide us with a useful "window on the mind" if we approach them
with care.

Recoverably Deletable Predicates

Within linguistics, nominal compounds can be studied in terms of grammatical derivations. Some linguists have claimed that the semantic relationships within complex nominals are impossible to categorize, leaving
the problem of systematic derivation far beyond the machinery of
generative grammar (Jespersen 1942). But recent efforts suggest that this
need not be the case. In particular, Judith Levi has suggested that there
is one type of derivation that accounts for most complex nominal surface structures (Levi 1978).

According to Levi, the majority of semantic relationships can be
characterized as recoverably deletable predicates (RDP's). More importantly, it is possible to break this class of predicates into nine subgroups.
We will list these nine groups here along with some examples:

CAUSE	tear gas	drug death	cigarette smoke
HAVE	picture book	lemon peel	church bells
MAKE	daisy chain	glass jar	coffee machine
USE	steam iron	water pipe	charge card
BE	target site	passport book	soldier ant
IN	house dog	kitchen table	spring breeze
FOR	dog collar	baby food	student government
FROM	sea breeze	olive oil	country crafts
ABOUT	tax law	price war	product brochure

According to Levi, these predicates have been deleted by a transformation that changes relative clauses into complex nominals. For example,
"student government" is derived from "government which is for students"
and "water pipe" comes from "pipe which uses water."

At first glance, these nine categories seem reasonable enough, but if
one tries to categorize random noun pairs using this taxonomy, it is
sometimes difficult to know which category to use. Should "cigarette
smoke" be "smoke which is caused by a cigarette" or "smoke which is
made by a cigarette"? Is a "dog collar" a "collar which is for a dog" or
"a collar which a dog has"? While some noun pairs seem to qualify for
more than one deletable predicate, many semantic relationships fail to
be differentiated in this taxonomy. A "kitchen table" describes a locative
relation, while a "spring breeze" describes a temporal relation. But both
kitchen tables and spring breezes fall into the single predicate "in". For
that matter, one could distinguish a number of semantic relationships

that are only generally represented by the "in" predicate:

INHABIT	house dog	(a dog which inhabits a house)
GROW-IN	water lilies	(lilies which grow in water)
DURING	spring breeze	(a breeze which occurs during spring)
LOCATION	kitchen table	(a table which is located in the kitchen)
PART-OF	car lighter	(a lighter which is part of a car)
ABSTRACT-LOC	system bugs	(bugs which are associated with a system)

If one wishes to work with a set of RDP's, what criteria should be used in selecting the proper set? How much generality or specificity is needed? According to Levi, an RDP analysis must capture "... all the *productive* aspects of complex nominal formation and thus, all the information that a grammar can in any case be expected to predict." That is, Levi is interested in grammatical derivations which can be characterized by semantically equivalent paraphrases. It is enough to know that each noun pair associated with a given RDP can be paraphrased by the same relative clause construction:

house dog	(a dog which is in a house)
water lilies	(lilies which are in water)
spring breeze	(a breeze which occurs in the spring)
kitchen table	(a table which is in a kitchen)
car lighter	(a lighter which is in a car)
system bugs	(bugs which are in a system)

It is not necessary to break apart the "in" RDP any further since each of these different semantic relations can be expressed by the same relative clause using the preposition "in". If the relative clauses are semantically ambiguous, the associated RDP should remain ambiguous as well.

As a model in generative linguistics, the notion of a recoverable deletable predicate may provide an adequate description of compound nominals. Unfortunately, RDP's are not adequate for computational models of language processing. In order to construct the semantic checking mechanism proposed by Milne, we must build a memory model that allows us to assess the credibility of concepts underlying noun groups. Any such credibility measure must be based on fine-grained semantics: if our language allows us to make periphrastic distinctions between two instances of an RDP, these distinctions must be grounded in the underlying semantic component. Even a conservative view of semantic representation would claim that our semantic foundation must be *at least* as refined as our linguistic expressions.

Of course, one does want to limit the link-types allowed in a semantic network, and the selection of appropriate links is no small task. What would happen if we tried to build a memory model that was too "coarse"? Let's see what would happen if we had a semantic memory that used only links based on Levi's RDP's.

Consider the concept node for a "truck." A truck has parts: an engine, tires, doors, etc. So we would have HAVE links going from the truck node to all the various truck parts. Trucks also run on oil and either gasoline or diesel fuel so we would have USE links pointing to oil, gasoline, and diesel fuel. Trucks are also used for carrying things, so we could have FOR links going to all the things that trucks carry: cement, lumber, freight, etc. Now consider the problem of understanding two noun pairs:

oil truck
diesel truck

In principle, these are both ambiguous. An oil (diesel) truck could either be a truck that carries oil (diesel) or a truck that runs on oil (diesel). But most people would be inclined to agree that an oil truck is a truck which carries oil while a diesel truck is a truck which uses diesel fuel. One could explain this by claiming that these terms are lexicalized, but that would be pushing lexicalization further than is necessary. It is much easier to account for these interpretations in terms of a memory model that is somewhat stronger than the one we've described.

Everyone knows that *all* trucks burn oil, so it would be uselessly redundant to describe a truck as an oil truck if that description only referred to the USE link between trucks and oil. On the other hand, it is not the case that all trucks run on diesel fuel, so a diesel truck should be interpreted in terms of the USE link much more readily. This distinction cannot be made on the basis of a simple USE link. It must rely on more refined memory associations, such as NECESSARY-USE and OPTIONAL-USE. One could further argue that the optional links pointing to gasoline and diesel fuel should themselves be conjoined by an OR link, but we cannot make that argument on the basis of compound nominals alone.

If we are willing to look beyond complex nominals just a little bit, we can see how semantic interpretations based on Levi's RDP's would not be adequate for many simple analysis tasks. Consider the sentence:

Boomer's dog collar was too tight.

Anyone who understands this sentence will conclude that Boomer is a dog. Now consider:

Boomer's flea collar was too tight.

Here we may feel uncertain about whether Boomer is a dog or a cat, but we are not likely to consider the possibility that Boomer might be a flea. Unfortunately, this is the only possibility that a simple FOR predicate could produce. If a "dog collar" is a collar which is for dogs, and a "flea collar" is a collar which is for fleas, then there is nothing we can use to distinguish the conceptual meanings underlying these two senses of "for". The missing concepts are crucial:

dog collar = a collar which is worn by dogs
flea collar = a collar which is worn by dogs or cats in order to kill fleas.

It is possible to produce lots of examples like these. If our goal is to produce conceptual representations for sentences, we are going to have to go beyond the simple notion of RPD's in designing our underlying memory representation.

Semantic Categories

If we want to move beyond the notion of general surface predicates, it will be necessary to organize memory acording to some set of semantic categories. Originally, semantic markers were used to resolve word sense ambiguities (Katz and Fodor 1964). In order to analyze the conceptual content of noun groups, we will use semantic markers to resolve conceptual ambiguities that explain how words relate to one another. In creating a system of semantic memory, we are confronted with the usual problem of choosing appropriate semantic categories. The arguments that can be made for a given set of categories are ultimately empirical, and therefore critically dependent on actual computer programs that can be run to conduct experiments. For this reason, it is instructive to look at an early computer program for noun-pair processing that created multiple representations for ambiguous noun-pairs, and ranked these competing interpretations according to their credibility (Russell 1972).

In Russell's program, the analysis of noun-pairs was based on a set of 21 possible dependency functions between two nouns. Each dependency function specified semantic criteria for its application, and a resulting conceptual representation consistent with the theory of conceptual dependency (Schank 1975). If more than one dependency function could be applied, multiple interpretations were ranked according to a fixed priority assigned to each dependency function. It was therefore possible to compute only the "most likely" interpretation by applying each dependency function in the order of descending priorities until one function was found to apply.

A few dependency functions are described below:

FUNCTION NAME	PRIORITY	EXAMPLE	CRITERIA
COMPOSITION	20	rubber knife	N1 = + matter and − fluid N2 = + phys and − animate
R__GOAL	17	kitchen table	N1 = + env and + man-made N2 = − matter and + man-made
POSSESS	10	horse shoe	N1 = + animate or + inst N2 = + man-made (use: read, wear)

PART__INAL__RECIP   2   arm chair   N1 = + part
                                               N2 = obj or category of
                                                    objs of which N1 is
                                                    an inalienable part

In examining the semantic criteria required by each dependency function, we see that this model of noun-pair processing does require some semantic structures that go beyond strict semantic features. For example, in order for PART__INAL__RECIP to apply, we must be able to confirm that N1 is in fact a part of N2. Such semantic checks cannot be handled by semantic features alone. Similarly, POSSESS requires that N2 refer to an object that can be read or worn, and more importantly, read or worn by the referent of N1. A "horse tie" should not be interpreted the same way as a "horse shoe".

Russell designed this system to fit into the framework of conceptual information processing being developed at the time by Roger Schank (op. cit.), so there was no reason for her to restrict her dependency criteria to semantic features alone. However, some of the tests required by her system could not have been implemented with full generality, at least not on the basis of the semantic memory model described by Russell. For example, Russell never tells us exactly how one is supposed to know that a horse can wear shoes but not a tie. Furthermore, a memory model that does not distinguish between horse shoes and human shoes requires some more work.

However, Russell's work is provocative and well worth exploring. What kind of memory access is required beyond the semantic features? Do the features suggested by Russell really provide reliable coverage for a large class of examples? Do the 21 dependency functions provide broad coverage? Are static function priorities adequate or should credibility judgements be sensitive to the relative strength with which the function criteria are satisfied? What would it mean to satisfy a dependency criterion with relative degrees of strength?

Whatever the answers are, at least Russell attempted to produce a conceptual representation for the noun-pairs being analyzed. It seems that Russell was working under something of a disadvantage in that regard, since the formalisms of conceptual dependency are strongly event-oriented. If it were possible to map her concepts into a system of primitive decomposition that were more object-oriented, that resulting interpretation might be even more impressive. One such system has been proposed (Lehnert 1979), but its application to nominal compounds has never been investigated.

Semantic Memory vs. Episodic Memory

In describing her work on noun-pair analysis, Russell was careful to characterize her enterprise in terms of certain limitations. She states,

'... all our features represent conceptual rather than cultural knowledge. The features generally satisfy the criterion of being "inherent" properties rather than unstable situations or conditions.' The distinction she makes can be properly described as the difference between semantic memory and episodic memory.

This distinction was first popularized by Endel Tulving (Tulving 1972) as the difference between universal knowledge and knowledge about specific individuals or events. For example, semantic memory would be responsible for telling us that cats are animals, but episodic memory would tell us that Morris is a cat who sells cat food on television commercials. For many years, it was assumed that only semantic memory was required for sentence comprehension. This assumption seemed reasonable at the time, but only because no one was looking beyond single isolated sentences. As researchers began to consider the inference processes required for connected text (paragraphs or stories), a case for the importance of episodic memory in language processing began to emerge (Schank and Abelson 1977).

In order to make appropriate inferences that connect sentences together, it is necessary to access complex knowledge structures. These knowledge structures can provide information that is only implicitly present in the original sentences, thereby allowing the reader to complete important causal connections and fill in many details that were never explicitly mentioned. If a knowledge structure is well-designed, it organizes information efficiently so that irrelevant information does not need to be accessed or examined. One famous example of a scriptal knowledge structure was popularized by Roger Schank (op. cit.) in order to explain how people make inferences about stereotypic behavior in restaurants.

While episodic memory structures are enjoying a healthy following within natural language processing circles, it is very difficult to say where semantic memory stops and episodic memory begins. Semantic markers are presumably a feature of semantic memory, but everything else has become somewhat controversial. Consider a typical proposition about penguins: "Penguins have skin".

This certainly looks like a universal truth, which should qualify it as semantic knowledge according to Tulving. It is easy to construct an "is-a hierarchy" to handle the appropriate generalizations we would like to manage. For example, we would probably not want to store the feature skin under penguins directly. It is better to create a structure which can tell us that a penguin is a bird and birds have skin. It is then up to some deductive retrieval mechanism to figure out whether or not penguins have skin. The same general mechanism would be used for propositions about canaries, chickens, and so forth and so on.

But is this how people store such information? An episodic alternative is also possible. Suppose you are asked the question "Do chickens have skin?" and you are someone who loves fried chicken. If you eat a lot of fried chicken, and take particular pleasure in eating the crisp skin of fried chicken, you might access episodic structures about eating chicken in order to answer that question. Figure 1 shows a fanciful picture of semantic penguin memory vs. episodic chicken memory to illustrate the difference more concretely. The general point is simple: given any "semantic" proposition, it is possible to imagine an episodic structure that could encode the information under consideration.

Does a penguin have skin?

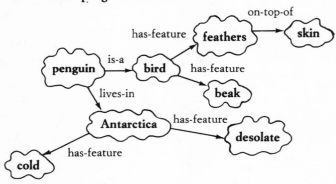

Does a chicken have skin?

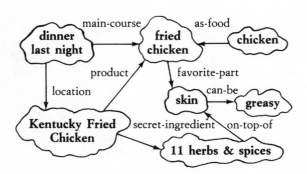

Figure 1. Semantic memory vs. episodic memory

While linguists typically dismiss the idea of episodic memory as a "pragmatics" issue, artificial intelligence workers must grapple with the problems of pragmatics every day. The controversy in artificial intelligence between semantic and episodic memory goes far beyond natural language processing applications. Proponents of production-based expert systems are banking on semantic knowledge, while people who argue for case-based reasoning are committing themselves to episodic memory structures. Semantic knowledge provides a natural foundation for deductive reasoning (the programming language PROLOG is nothing more than a simple deductive mechanism operating over semantic knowledge bases). At the same time, some very interesting work is also being done on inductive reasoning within episodic memory (Lebowitz 1983b).

The question of underlying memory structures is important for any systematic study of nominal compounds. We have to account for the memory processes that tell us "chicken skin" makes sense. It is one thing to say that a semantic checking mechanism executes a test to see if chickens have skin. It is something else to specify the precise memory model that allows us to find correct answers. A complete process model for nominal compounds must therefore address complex issues of memory organization − it is not possible to finesse these problems (at least not knowingly) when the time comes to define an actual test function.

Memory Access and Knowledge Acquisition

A text in a specialized knowledge domain can be either easy to understand or difficult to understand depending on whether or not the reader has knowledge of the underlying domain. Terms like "base plate insulator welds" or "ship-shore tty sat communications" can render a text incomprehensible if the reader has no conceptual foundation for the objects being described (Marsh 1983). In many cases (especially technical text), it is necessary to build new conceptual structures into memory at the same time a text is being processed. At first it may seem that the problem of memory access is then compounded by the problem of knowledge acquisition. But recent work in this area suggests that the knowledge acquisition problem goes hand-in-hand with memory access, and may even serve to simplify matters when it comes to complex noun phrases (Lebowitz 1983a, 1984a).

Lebowitz has implemented a system called RESEARCHER that maintains a knowledge base for patent abstracts describing computer hardware. This program has processed about 100 abstracts using a vocabulary of about 1200 words. Patent abstracts are characterized by a large number of long and complicated noun phrases, so RESEARCHER must maintain a rich knowledge base of relevant concepts and the relationships between them. What makes RESEARCHER unique is its ability to add knowledge to its memory as it reads new patent descriptions. This facility for knowledge acquisition makes RESEARCHER more robust in its text processing than would otherwise be possible. The very processes of memory access can be changed over time to reflect newly-acquired concepts and generalizations created by RESEARCHER. The implications of this for the analysis of nominal compounds are dramatic. Lebowitz sums it up rather casually: "... *As with noun group processing* (my italics) it is possible to develop heuristics that handle most cases, but they are complex and do not seem to be the right way to go for robust understanding." Using techniques that Lebowitz first developed for newspaper stories (Lebowitz 1983a), RESEARCHER builds a "generalization-based memory" which is a form of inheritance hierarchy. The important point about this memory is that it automatically creates a hierarchy of object descriptions from examples. This type of memory provides a powerful foundation for semantic checking mechanisms during noun phrase analysis.

For example, suppose we are trying to understand the phrase:

magnetic read/write head enclosure

and we must decide whether "magnetic" is supposed to modify "read/write head" or "enclosure". Rather than test for semantic features or possible semantic features under each concept, we can examine the general concepts for a read/write head and an enclosure first, and then search through a tree of successively more specific concept instances until we find an example where one or the other is magnetic. This approach can only work if memory is sufficiently "fleshed-out", but the advantages seem worth the cost of some initial start-up overhead. In the event that no helpful instances can be located in memory, one could always fall back on heuristics of the sort described by Russell.

To understand better exactly how RESEARCHER uses memory to extract conceptual representations for nominal compounds, consider a simple noun-pair:

"a motor spindle"

Figure 2 shows a trace of RESEARCHER as it would process this phrase when there is no relevant information available in memory.

Running RESEARCHER at 3:19:26 PM
(A MOTOR SPINDLE)

Processing:

A   :New instance word — skip
MOTOR   :Memette within NP; save and skip
SPINDLE   :MP word — memette DRIVE-SHAFT #
New DRIVE-SHAFT # instance (&MEMO)
> > >Looking for relation between MOTOR # & MEMO (DRIVE-SHAFT #)
New MOTOR # instance (&MEM1)
Assuming &MEM1 (MOTOR #) and &MEMO (DRIVE-SHAFT #) are functionally
   related
Establishing UNKNOWN-PURP-REL relation; SUBJECT: &MEM1 (MOTOR #);
   OBJECT: &MEMO (DRIVE-SHAFT #) [&REL1]

Text Representation:

——————————————————A-0 M0 DRIVE-SHAFT #
——————————————————A-1 M1 MOTOR #

A list of relations:

Subject:	Relation:	Object
[&REL1/A] &MEM1 (MOTOR #)	{UNKNOWN-PURP-REL}	&MEMO(DRIVE-SHAFT #)

Figure 2. 'Motor spindle' with memory empty

Conceptual analysis begins after the head noun "spindle" is encountered.
RESEARCHER then works backwards from the concept definition for a
spindle (DRIVE-SHAFT #) to the concept definition for motor (MOTOR #)
and tries to determine the relation (UNKNOWN-PURP-REL) between these
two concepts. It searches memory for instances of drive shafts and motors,
but finds no relevant examples. At this point RESEARCHER is forced to
conclude that there is an indeterminate functional relation between these
two objects.

Now suppose we have relevant information available in memory.
Specifically, suppose RESEARCHER had previously processed the noun
phrase:

EX1:   "a drive with a motor on top of a spindle"

Figure 3 shows the internal memory representation that RESEARCHER
produces for this concept.

Text Representation:

```
    |  ——————————— A-1 M0 DRIVE #
——————————— 0 | ——————————— A-2 M1 MOTOR #
——————————————————————————— M2 DRIVE-SHAFT #
```

A list of relations:

Subject:	Relation:	Object:
[&REL1/A] & MEM1 (MOTOR #)	{R-ON-TOP-OF}	&MEM2 (DRIVE-SHAFT #)

Figure 3. Setting up memory

Here we have an instance of a disk drive (DRIVE #) (in memory with "on top of" relation between the motor (MOTOR #)) and the spindle (DRIVE-SHAFT #) used in the disk drive. If we now try to process "a motor spindle" with this information in memory, the conceptual analysis proceeds very differently. Figure 4 shows a trace of RESEARCHER's processing in this case.

Running RESEARCHER at 3:18:11 PM
(A MOTOR SPINDLE)

A   :New instance word – skip
MOTOR   :Memette within NP; save and skip
SPINDLE   :MP word – memette DRIVE-SHAFT #
New DRIVE-SHAFT # instance (&MEM3)
> > >Looking for relation between MOTOR # and &MEM3 (DRIVE-SHAFT #)
New MOTOR # instance (&MEM4)
Establishing R-ON-TOP-OF relation; SUBJECT: &MEM4 (MOTOR #)
    OBJECT: &MEM3 (DRIVE-SHAFT #) [&REL2]

Text Representation:

```
——————————————————————————— B-3 M3 DRIVE-SHAFT #
——————————————————————— B-4 M4 MOTOR #
```

A list of relations:

Subject:	Relation:	Object:
[&REL2/B] &MEM4 (MOTOR #)	{R-ON-TOP-OF}	&MEM3 (DRIVE-SHAFT #)

Figure 4. "Motor spindle" with EX1 in memory

When RESEARCHER looks for a relation between DRIVE-SHAFT# and MOTOR#, it finds the relevant example (figure 3) and assumes that the proper relation between a DRIVE-SHAFT# and a MOTOR# must be an "on top of" relation.

If RESEARCHER had previously processed a different example before encountering the phrase "a motor spindle", its conceptual analysis might have been different. For example, suppose that instead of hearing about "a drive with a motor on top of a spindle," RESEARCHER had previously encountered:

EX2: "a drive with a motor that includes a spindle"

In this case RESEARCHER would construct a part/assembly relation between the motor (MOTOR#) and the spindle (DRIVE-SHAFT#) as shown in figure 5.

Running RESEARCHER at 6:40:31 PM
(A MOTOR SPINDLE)

Processing:

A   :New instance word − skip
MOTOR   :Memette within NP; save and skip
SPINDLE   :MP word − memette DRIVE-SHAFT#
New DRIVE-SHAFT# instance (&MEM3)
> > >Looking for relation between MOTOR# and &MEM3 (DRIVE-SHAFT#)
New MOTOR# instance (&MEM4)
Assuming &MEM3 (DRIVE-SHAFT#) IS PART OF &MEM4 (MOTOR#)

Text Representation:

───────────── 4│ ───────────── 3 M3 DRIVE-SHAFT#
                                  M4 MOTOR#

A list of relations:

Subject:	Relation:	Object:
[none]	[none]	[none]

Figure 5. 'Motor spindle' with EX2 in memory

As a result, RESEARCHER's interpretation of "a motor spindle" would now be based on this example, and the system would assume that a "motor spindle" must be a drive shaft contained in a motor.

As these last two examples illustrate, multiple interpretations for nominal compounds are possible in RESEARCHER. This raises the question of how the system should resolve conceptual ambiguities in the event that memory contains more than one relevant example, leading to more than one possible interpretation. Lebowitz believes that in such cases, the instances located closest to the "top of the tree" provide the best interpretations. Examples high in the tree structure correspond to the most general object descriptions, so this seems like a reasonable heuristic. For example, if a system has encountered 10 examples of oil trucks, one would expect that most of these instances would be describing trucks that carried oil. If one of the references described a truck that used oil for fuel, that example should be located further down in the tree structure since it is more specific (by virtue of the fact that there was only one). For more details on exactly how these trees are constructed, see (Lebowitz 1983b).

By accessing a dynamic memory structure that changes and grows the more it reads, we are much closer to simulating a system that learns domain expertise much as a person does. Some generalizations may be incorrect, and competing interpretations might be resolved differently depending on what the system has seen, but these imperfections can correct themselves as the system's exposure to its domain increases. Generalization-based memory may not be perfect, but does have the potential for being self-correcting (Lebowitz 1984b). RESEARCHER is an exciting example of how episodic memory structures might be used to handle low-level problems in language analysis.

Conclusions

By examing a number of approaches to the problem of nominal compounds, we have seen a variety of memory models and representational devices proposed. Three distinct memory models have been described drawing from work in generative linguistics, modified formal semantics, and heuristic memory modelling. By comparing and contrasting these three approaches, we have tried to emphasize the different research goals and theoretical premises that characterize each. The ostensible topic of interest has been nominal compounds throughout. But individual treatments of this topic vary considerably across theoretical frameworks.

From an interdisciplinary vantage point, there seems to be a clearly defined sense of evolution and direction. We are moving from a purely linguistic paradigm that manages to avoid the problem of internal meaning representation altogether, toward a process model paradigm that embraces not only the problems of conceptual representation but global memory organization as well. This trend may not be welcomed or even acknowledged by all concerned, but it is an inevitable fact for those of us who wish to design detailed process models for natural language processing. If we are willing to confront language in terms of its cognitive facilities, language processes become inseparable from processes of memory. This perspective on language can entice us with great promise but it probably boasts the greatest difficulties as well. Let us hope that it inspires our most diligent research efforts in return.

Bibliography

BECKER, J.D.
1975   "The phrasal lexicon", in *Theoretical Issues in Natural Language Processing*, M.I.T., Cambridge, Ma. pp. 60-63.
BRANSFORD, J.D. & J.J. FRANKS
1971   "The abstraction of linguistic ideas", *Cognitive Psychology*, 2, 1971, pp. 331-350.
CHARNIAK, E.
1981   "A Parser with Something for Everyone", Technical Report No. CS-70, Department of Computer Science, Brown University, Providence, RI.
COKER, P. & S. CRAIN
1979   "Lexical access during sentence processing", a paper presented at the Linguistic Society of America Annual Meeting, University of California at Irvine.
CRAIN, S. & P. COKER
1979   "A semantic constraint on parsing", a paper presented at the Linguistic Society of America Annual Meeting, University of California at Irvine.
DEJONG, G.
1979   "Prediction and substantiation: a new approach to natural language processing", *Cognitive Science* 3, 1979, pp. 251-273.
DYER, M.
1983   *In-Depth Understanding: A Computer Model of Integrated Processing for Narrative Comprehension*, Cambridge, Ma., M.I.T. Press.
FININ, T.W.
1982   "The interpretation of nominal compounds in discourse" Technical Report MS-CIS-82-3, Moore School of Engineering, University of Pennsylvania.
GERSHMAN, A.V.
1979   "Knowledge-Based Parsing" (PhD thesis) Research Report # 156, Department of Computer Science, Yale University, New Haven, CT.
JESPERSEN O.
1942   *A Modern English Grammar on Historical Principles*, Copenhagen, Ejnar Munksgaard.
KATZ J.J. & J.A. FODOR
1964   "The structure of a semantic theory", in Fodor J., Katz J. (eds.), *The Structure of Language*. Englewood Cliffs, N.J., Prentice-Hall, Inc.
KOZIOL, H.
1937   *Handbuch der Englischen Wortbildungslehre*, Heidelberg, Carl Winter's Universitätsbuchhandlung.
LEBOWITZ, M.
1983a   "Memory-Based Parsing", *Artificial Intelligence* 21, 4, pp. 363-404.
1983b   "Generalization from natural language text", *Cognitive Science*, 7, 1 pp. 1-40.
1984a   "Using Memory in Text Understanding", in *Proceedings of the 1984 European Conference on Artificial Intelligence*, Pisa, Italy.
1984b   "Conceptual processing when things go wrong", *Cognition and Brain Theory* vol. 7, no 3-4, pp. 375-398.

LEES R.B.
1960 "The grammar of English nominalizations", *International Journal of American Linguistics* 26, Publication 12.
LEHNERT, W.
1978 *The Process of Question Answering*, Hillsdale, N.J., Lawrence Erlbaum Associates.
1979 "Representing Physical Objects in Memory" in Ringle, M. (ed.), *Philosophical Perspectives on Artificial Intelligence*, Atlantic Highlands, N.J., Humanities Press.
1982 "Plot units: a narrative summarization strategy" in Lehnert W., Ringle M. (eds.), *Strategies for Natural Language Processing*, Hillsdale, N.J., Lawrence Erlbaum Associates, pp. 375-414.
1984 "Narrative Complexity based on summarization algorithms", in Bara B., Guida (eds.), *Computational Models of Natural Language Processing*, Amsterdam, North-Holland, pp. 247-259.
LEHNERT, W., DYER, M., JOHNSON, P., YANG, C.J., HARLEY, S.
1983 "BORIS — An experiment in in-depth understanding of narratives", *Artificial Intelligence* vol. 20, 1983, pp. 15-62.
LEHNERT, W. and S. ROSENBERG.
1985 "The PLUM Users Manual" CPTR # 1, Department of Computer and Information Science, Amherst, Ma., University of Massachusetts.
LEVI, J.
1978 *The Syntax and Semantics of Complex Nominals*. New York, Academic Press.
LYTINEN, S.
1984 "The organizaion of knowledge in a multi-lingual, integrated parse", (PhD thesis) Research Report # 340, Department of Computer Science, Yale University, New Haven, Ct.
MARCHAND, H.
1969 *The Categories and Types of Present-Day English Word Formation* (2nd edition) Munich, C.H. Beck'sche Verlagsbuchhandlung.
MARCUS, M.P.
1980 *A Theory of Syntactic Recognition for Natural Language*, Cambridge, Ma., M.I.T. Press.
MARSH, E.
1983 "Utilizing domain-specific information for processing compact text", in the *Proceedings of the Conference on Applied Natural Language Processing*, Irvine, Ca., pp. 99-103.
MILNE, R.W.
1982 "Predicting garden path sentences", *Cognitive Science* vol. 6, no. 4, pp. 349-373.
RIESBECK, C.K. & C.E. MARTIN
1985 "Direct memory access parsing", Research Report # 354, Department of Computer Science, Yale University, New Haven, Ct.
RIESBECK, C. and R. SCHANK
1976 "Expectation-Based analysis of sentences in context", Research Report # 78, Department of Computer Science, Yale University, New Haven, Ct.
RUSSELL, S.W.
1972 "Semantic categories of nominals for conceptual dependency analysis of natural language", Standard Artificial Intelligence Project MEMO AIM-172, STAN-CS-72-299, Computer Science Department, Stanford University.
SCHANK, R.
1975 *Conceptual Information Processing*, New York, American Elsevier.
SCHANK, R. and R. ABELSON
1977 *Scripts, Plans, Goals and Understanding*, Hillsdale, N.J., Lawrence Erlbaum Associates.
SMALL S.
1980 "Word expert parsing: A theory of distributed word-based natural language understanding" (PhD thesis) TR-954, Department of Computer Science, University of Maryland.
TULVING E.
1972 "Episodic and semantic memory", in Tulving E., Donaldson (eds.) *Organization of Memory*, New York, Academic Press.

WALTZ D.L. and J.B. POLLACK
1984 "Phenomenologically plausible parsing", in *Proceedings of the 1984 American Association for Artificial Intelligence Conference*, pp. 335-339.
WILENSKY, R.
1981 "A knowledge-based approach to language processing", in *Proceedings of the Seventh International Joint Conference on Artificial Intelligence*, pp. 25-30.
WILKS, Y.
1972 *Grammar, Meaning, and the Machine Analysis of Language*, London, Routledge & Kegan Paul.

Roger Schank and Alex Kass

Knowledge Representation in People and Machines

Introduction

The central questions of cognitive science are very easy to state: What is the nature of knowledge and how is this knowledge used? These questions are old ones and they have held fascination for a broad range of thinkers. Although they have not always stated it exactly the way we do, answering these questions has been the goal of many within psychology, linguistics, philosophy of mind, and our own field, artificial intelligence (henceforth AI).

The methodology of AI provides a unique vantage point from which to view these questions. The AI researcher tries to program a computer so that it can understand and interact with the outside world. At first this may seem to be a rather different goal from say, the psychologist's, and for some AI researchers it is different. But if you believe, as we at the Yale AI Project do, that the best way to approach the problem of building an intelligent machine is to emulate human cognition, then the goal of AI converges with those of the other cognitive sciences, to understand what knowledge looks like and how it is used. Rephrased in AI terms, the questions are, what data structures are useful for representing knowledge and what algorithms operate on those knowledge structures to produce intelligent behavior? All the AI work done in our lab is aimed at answering these questions by designing structures for representing knowledge and writing computer programs that manipulate those knowledge structures to understand the world, to plan, and to learn. This paper is about some of that work. Our aim is to present some knowledge structures that we have found to be important, and to describe the mental/computational tasks that we use these for.

Understanding Language

When we first started our work in AI we began by working on mental representation in a rather narrow sense; we began as computational linguists designing a theory of representing the meaning of natural language utterances. We wanted to develop a language-free representation that would form a theory of how humans represent information communicated by natural language and could also be used as the basis of intelligent language understanding programs. The result of this work was

Conceptual Dependency theory (henceforth CD) [Schank 72], which we discuss in some detail later on. CD proved to be rather successful at the role for which it was designed (representing the propositions communicated by a natural language sentence in a form that was convenient for manipulation by AI programs). However, as our work on intelligent programs progressed, the need for larger, more complex organizational structures became evident. It became clear to us that in order to truly understand natural language with anything like human levels of ability, it would be necessary to simulate human cognitive abilities such as problem solving and learning that on the surface had little to do with language understanding but in fact had everything to do with it.

The philosophy that has developed in our natural language work, and has guided us towards the investigation of seemingly non-linguistic issues, can be summed up in the following straightforward propositions:

1) The function of language is to communicate concepts between people.

2) Therefore, in order to understand language one must be prepared to understand the underlying concepts represented by that language.

To the "naive" reader the above propositions may seem extremely obvious, and in fact they are. But it is important to realize that much work on language within the linguistics community and even within parts of the AI community, has ignored or denied these straightforward notions. It is frightening to many scientists to realize that understanding language is as difficult as understanding thinking. As a result, most researchers have tended to back away from the admittedly difficult task of representing the knowledge that language communicates, in favor of maintaining a narrow focus on the formal structural properties of language. We have chosen to take the road less traveled, to attack the tough problems of knowledge representation and organization rather than ignoring them. As we have progressed in this direction our work has become less and less specific to language processing, but has remained quite relevant to it. The highlights of this progression are traced in the sections that follow.

Conceptual Dependency

CD is a theory about the representation of the meaning of sentences. But how does one judge such a representation scheme? How does one decide whether something is a good way to represent a particular meaning? The answer is that one can judge a representational system only in relation to how well it facilitates performing a given set of tasks.

One of the tasks in mind when CD was designed was machine translation (MT). MT programs translate text from one language to another. The early MT programs operated essentially via word-by-word dictionary lookup. For each word in the input language, the program would simply consult its dictionary for the corresponding word in the target language. The assumption was that if the dictionaries were large enough and the lexicography good enough, then the programs would be able to do quality translation. It took some time to learn that language is more complicated, and more interesting than that. Even when MT programs were augmented with syntactic knowledge of the input and output languages they remained rather glaring failures. It eventually became clear that as long as no attempt was made to deal with the meaning of translated sentences that quality MT would remain an unreachable goal.

The problem is that language is ambiguous and elliptical. Much of the meaning conveyed by a sentence is conveyed only implicitly (and can't be extracted by examining the words in isolation). Thus it is necessary to represent the meaning in a non-linguistic form — a form that would not suffer from the same ambiguity problems — in order to reliably generate output that is synonymous with the input. The task of MT would then be a two-part one: map the sentences from the input language into this language-free interlingua and then map from the interlingua into the output language. CD was designed to be this interlingua. Of course, an interlingua like CD is useful for more than just mechanical translation. Almost any reasoning is facilitated by a language-free representation like CD, since it frees the reasoning system from the quirks of a particular language; languages evolved to communicate ideas between people, not for representing ideas internally. It is not surprising that the requirements of the two tasks are quite different.

The design of CD was guided by a few related principles. CD structures should represent meaning:

A) Canonically. For any two sentences that are identical in meaning (even if expressed in different tongues) there should be only one representation. In addition, it is helpful if nearly synonymous sentences have representations that are nearly identical; conceptualizations that represent similar concepts should be alike structurally. The most important argument for this constraint is that it greatly facilitates writing inference rules. If one uses a system that has multiple ways of expressing the same concept, then one must write families of inference rules to cover the entire set. A canonical representation ensures that this will not happen.

B) Unambiguously. A CD structure, unlike a natural language sentence, should have only one meaning. This is the main point of having a language-free representation. There are good reasons that languages are ambiguous; being unambiguous can be tiresome. Since understanders have many means of disambiguation at their disposal, and because efficiency of communication is at a premium in languages, it is worth paying the price of ambiguity. However, the priorities are different for an internal representation that will not be used as the basis of communication, but rather as the basis of reasoning. Combined with principle A this ensures that there will be a one-to-one mapping between concepts and CD structures.

Principles A and B have an important corollary. CD structures must represent meaning:

C) Explicitly. Information that is expressed implicitly in the utterance should be made explicit in the internal representation.

The approach used to meeting the requirements of principles A, B, and C in CD theory is to build meaning representations by combining a small set of primitive meaning elements. Breaking down meaning into a set of primitive meaning elements allows individual features of a concept to be represented explicitly. The small size of the primitive vocabulary helps ensure canonicalness.

The CD primitives are the atoms of meaning representation within the system. The basic propositional molecules of CD are called conceptualizations. A conceptualization can represent either an action or a state. Conceptualizations consist of a main predicate and some number of case-slots. For action conceptualizations the main predicate is one of the primitive actions (called ACTs). For state conceptualizations it is one of the primitive states. Each slot can be filled by either a symbol or another conceptualization. Action conceptualizations have an actor, object, direction and sometimes an instrument case. The instrument is another action, which was performed in order to accomplish the main action. State conceptualizations specify an object and the value (along some arbitrary scale) of some state that the object is in. In general, CD theory has paid more attention to the actions than the states because they seem to be more crucial to representing much natural language.

The eleven ACTs of CD theory are as follows:

ATRANS   The transfer of an abstract relationship such as possession, ownership, or control. Thus, one sense of "give" is ATRANS something to someone else. "Buy" is made up to two conceptualizations that cause each other, one an ATRANS of money, the other an ATRANS of the object being bought.

PTRANS   The transfer of the physical location of an object. Thus, "go" is PTRANS oneself to a place; "put" is PTRANS of an object to a place.

PROPEL   The application of a physical force to an object. PROPEL is used whenever any force is applied regardless of whether a movement (PTRANS) took place. In English, "push", "pull", "throw", "kick", have propel as part of them. "John pushed the table to the wall" is a PROPEL that causes a PTRANS. "John threw the ball" is a PROPEL that involves the ending of a GRASP act at the same time.

MOVE   The movement of a body part of an animal by that animal. MOVE is nearly always the ACT in an instrumental conceptualization for other ACTs. That is, in order to throw, it is necessary to MOVE one's arm. MOVE foot is the instrument of "kick". Examples of MOVE as the main ACT include "kiss", "raise your hand", and "scratch".

GRASP   The grasping of an object by an actor. "grab", "let go", and "throw" inolve a GRASP or the end of a GRASP.

INGEST   The taking in of an object by an animal to the inside of the animal. Examples of INGEST are "eat", "drink", "smoke", and "breathe".

EXPEL   The expulsion of an object from the body of an animal. This is the opposite of INGEST. Words for excretion and secretion are described by EXPEL, among them, "sweat", "spit", and "cry".

MTRANS   The transfer of information between animals or within an animal. We partition memory into two pieces: The CP (conscious processor where something is thought about), and the LTM (long term memory where things are stored). The various sense organs can also be the originators of an MTRANS. Thus, "tell" is MTRANS between people, "see" involves an MTRANS from eyes to CP, "remember" is MTRANS from LTM to CP, and "learn" is the MTRANSing of new information into the LTM.

MBUILD   The construction of new information from old information. Thus, "decide", "conclude", "imagine", "consider" are common examples of MBUILD.

SPEAK   The action of producing sounds. Many objects can SPEAK, but human ones are usually SPEAKing as an instrument of MTRANSing. The words "say", "play music", "purr", and "scream" involve SPEAK.

ATTEND   The action of attending or focusing a sense organ towards a stimulus. ATTEND ear is "listen", ATTEND eye is part of "see". ATTEND is very often the instrument of an MTRANS.

In addition to the primitive actions, CD theory employs a number of primitive states. The states are things like JOY, ANGER, HEALTH, and PHYSICAL-STATE. By convention they were all measured on a scale of -10 to +10, with lower meaning worse condition (for example, HEALTH(-10) means dead, HEALTH(0) means doing fine, HEALTH(10) means ready to win the decathlon. JOY(-10) means severely depressed, JOY(10) means ecstatic). The set of states were never as well fixed in the theory as were the ACTs, and different instantiations of the theory have used different sets. In practice the numerical values have been used only for rough comparison — no sort of state calculus has ever been attempted. Conceptualizations often represent state changes as the result of an action. For example, pleasing someone is represented as doing something that causes that person's JOY to increase.

Let's look at some example sentences and their CD representations. We have expressed the CD representations in a lisp-like notation (modelled after that used in *Inside Computer Understanding*, which is a notational variant on the original):

English: Mary gave John her car.
CD: (ATRANS (ACTOR (PERSON (NAME (MARY)))
             (OBJECT (PHYS-OBJ (TYPE (CAR))))
             (DIRECTION (FROM (PERSON (NAME (MARY))))
             (TO (PERSON (NAME (JOHN)))))))

Note that the above contains representations like: (PERSON (NAME (MARY)). This might be the output of an analyzer, although internally most CD-based programs have a more detailed description of the objects mentioned. Usually, a pointer to this internal representation is substituted into the conceptualization at some point in the processing. To enhance readability, the rest of the examples will be even more concise, and use only the person's name in the representations. Keep in mind that this is for notational convenience only.

English: Mary read *Fine Dining In New Haven*.
CD: (MTRANS
        (ACTOR (MARY))
        (OBJECT (INFORMATION))
        (DIRECTION (FROM (BOOK (NAME "Fine Dining...")))
                   (TO (CP (PART-OF (MARY)))))
        (INSTRUMENT
          (ATTEND
            (ACTOR (MARY))
            (OBJECT (EYES (PART-OF (MARY))))
            (DIRECTION
              (TO (BOOK (NAME "Fine Dining...")))))))

English: Mary was pleased to eat ice cream.
CD: (CASUAL (RESULT (STATE-CHANGE
             (OBJECT (MARY))
             (STATE JOY)
             (DIRECTION (FROM ?X) (TO > ?X)))
          (CAUSE (INGEST (ACTOR (MARY))
                   (OBJECT (ICE-CREAM))))))

It should be clear to the thoughtful reader that there are really two levels of claims to CD theory. First of all there are the general claims about what an interlingua should look like — the desirability of a language-independent meaning representation, the need for primitives, etc. Secondly, there is the specific content theory — the set of primitive ACTs and states, and the way they are combined to form the conceptualizations that represent various language sentences.

Both portions are important. In some sense, the lesson to take home from CD theory is the general portion. This conception of what properties a meaning representation should have has been transfered to other domains in academia and industry by developing alternate sets of conceptual primitives (see, for example, [Carbonell 79] and [Gershman 84]). However, the guiding principles alone are too vague to be a theory. So CD takes its particular content theory, its specific set of primitives, very seriously. Without this commitment there is not enough of a theory to defend or attack. The fact that we have been able to develop a specific vocabulary in which we can represent a healthy variety of natural language utterances in a form useful for intelligent programs is important evidence that our theory is a good one. In the next section we briefly describe one of the programs that has been based on CD theory.

Margie – A CD-Based Program

The Margie system was a program based on conceptual dependency theory. It was capable of reading natural language sentences, drawing inferences from them, and paraphrasing them. It was made up of three independent modules: The Conceptual Analyzer [Riesbeck 75] took English sentences as input and produced CD conceptualizations as output, the Conceptual Inferencer [Rieger 75] took the output of the analyzer and produced inferences from them (in the form of other conceptualizations), and the generator [Goldman 75] (also known as BABEL) took the conceptualizations and produced natural language (English) output. Margie was primarily implemented for English, although there was nothing in principle that tied the program to that particular language. In fact, since the analyzer and generator were independent modules, they could use different natural languages, making Margie a mechanical translation system. Translation wasn't the main goal of the system – we were more interested in the theoretical issues of language understanding – but a small amount of German was generated by the BABEL portion of the program simply to make the point that translation is merely paraphrasing in another language.

Margie could run in two modes: In paraphrase mode the inferencer was turned off and the output of the parser was sent directly to the generator. In inference mode the output of the parser went to the inference module, and the inferences were sent to the generator. Below is a small amount of sample I/O from the program:

PARAPHRASE MODE
INPUT: John killed Mary by choking her.
OUTPUT: John strangled Mary.
INPUT: John advised Mary to drink the wine.
OUTPUT: John told Mary that drinking the wine would benefit her.

INFERENCE MODE
  INPUT: John gave Mary an Aspirin.
  OUTPUT1: John believes that Mary is sick.
  OUTPUT2: Mary is sick.
  OUTPUT3: Mary wants to feel better.
  OUTPUT4: Mary will ingest the Aspirin.

  INPUT: John told Mary that Bill wants a book.
  OUTPUT1: Mary knows that Bill wants a book.
  OUTPUT2: Bill wants to come to have a book.
  OUTPUT3: Bill wants someone to cease to have a book.
  OUTPUT4: Bill wants to read a book.

Margie was an exciting program for us because it convinced us that
CD really could be used as the basis of a program that processed natural
language. We won't talk much about the analyzer or generator in this
paper, although we considered them important successes at the time. The
analyzer showed that it was possible to translate from English to CD,
and that it was possible to guide the translation process by associating
predictions with the conceptual case-slots. The generator showed that
it was relatively straightforward to translate back again, and to preserve
the essential meaning of the original input. Aside from being evidence
for the validity of CD, the interesting aspect of Margie for the purposes
of this paper are the issues related to Margie's middle man, the conceptual inferencer.

The Need for Inference

At first glance, it might not be clear that natural language processing
should require inferencing at all. Some readers may be wondering to
themselves, "Surely inferential capabilities are necessary for some
cognitive tasks but are they really part of language processing?" The
answer is yes and the simple reason is very nicely expressed by Rieger
in [Rieger 75]: Natural language users presuppose that speaker and hearer
share a common frame of reference, expressed in the large storehouse
of knowledge they share about the way the world works. "Because of
this, no natural language utterance is ever more than a very lean allusion
to the very rich set of circumstances it describes."

When people understand natural language they understand not just
the lean allusions but also that which is being alluded to. They fill in
the blank spaces easily and unconsciously. To use a simple example, if
one is told that Mary took an aspirin, one simply cannot be said to have
understood the sentence unless one expects that Mary feels ill and wishes
to feel better. Or with a multiple-sentence fragment, suppose one is told:
Bill gave Mary an aspirin. Later, Mary felt better. To be worthy of be-

ing called an understander, a system had better realize (i.e. somewhere have represented) that Mary ingested the aspirin, that this is the reason Bill gave her the aspirin, and that it was the medicinal effects of the aspirin that led to Mary's improved condition. Understanding texts involves more than building representations of the component sentences; it is also important to recognize how those sentences are connected. People do this so easily that they are rarely even aware that it is going on. But computers would be unable to make such connections without modelling human inferential abilities. Rieger's program was an attempt to provide the Margie system with such abilities.

Rieger attacked the inference problem by defining classes of inferences and attaching programs he called inference molecules for each class of inference to each of the primitive ACTs. Each new conceptualization that was added to memory (for example, the output of the analyzer) was then fed to the inference molecules, which inferred new conceptualizations. These inferred facts were then fed back to the inference molecules, resulting in long chains of inference radiating from each input. Connections between inputs were recognized when these chains intersected. These connections represented the coherence of the text.

Although it was a good start, it now seems clear that the process theory implemented in Margie failed to account for a key aspect of human understanding: People process familiar situations much more easily than unfamiliar ones. They are very slow at processing novel situations, in which they lack specific expectations about what will come next. Margie treated every situation as if it were unfamiliar. The next section describes a knowledge structure that was developed to fix this problem.

Scripts — A Theory of Top-Down Guidance

The biggest problem with Margie was that although its parser used top-down predictions to process individual sentences, above the sentence level the system was quite bottom up. The inferencer dealt with each sentence in isolation; it made little use of context to understand a story. There was a good reason for this: Margie was based on CD theory and CD, as we have said, was a theory about representing the meaning of sentences, not of texts. To some extent, Rieger's inference molecules were capable of bridging the gap between sentences, but the unconstrained nature of the inferencing process in Margie led quickly to a combinatorial explosion of inferences, with useless (i.e. irrelevant) inferences flooding the useful ones. It became clear after finishing Margie that a more top-down theory of understanding was needed. In order to develop such a theory it would be necessary to come up with some knowledge structure to provide the top-down guidance.

Schank and Abelson [Schank and Abelson 77] conceived of Scripts as a solution to this problem. A Script is essentially a pre-packaged inference chain relating to a specific routine situation. To simplify things, one can imagine a script as a sequence of conceptualizations, with some variables in them (called script variables). In fact, scripts were somewhat more complex structures than this, but that isn't important for our purposes here. Once a script is activated, understanding the text covered by the script is much easier since the script already has encoded within it many of the inferences that will be needed. Let's look at a simple restaurant script. The lines in a script are represented using conceptual dependency but for readability we'll paraphrase in English. Underlined words refer to script variables.

THE RESTAURANT SCRIPT
1) <u>Actor</u> goes to a <u>restaurant</u>.
2) <u>Actor</u> is seated.
3) <u>Actor</u> orders a <u>meal</u> from <u>waiter</u>.
4) <u>Waiter</u> brings the <u>meal</u> to <u>actor</u>.
5) <u>Actor</u> eats the <u>meal</u>.
6) <u>Actor</u> gives money to the <u>restaurant</u>.
7) <u>Actor</u> leaves the <u>restaurant</u>.

Obviously, this script is intended to capture a person's knowledge of the sequence of events that occurs when dining out at a restaurant. The script variables for this script would include the actor, the restaurant and the meal. The task of understanding a story about restaurants in terms of this script is largely reduced to binding the script variables to their appropriate values and instantiating conceptualizations in the script using these variable bindings.

People understand a story much more easily when they have experienced something like it many times in the past. Schank and Abelson proposed that this was the case because the knowledge picked up from these past experiences is encoded in a script and this process does not have to be recapitulated once the script is built.

An understander armed with an appropriate script has a number of advantages over a system armed only with the general inference molecules like those in Margie's inferencer. For example, specification inferences are much easier with script-based processing. Suppose that a story contained the following sequence, "John ordered a hamburger. After eating, John went home." It is reasonable to expect an understander to know that what John ate was a hamburger, even though this isn't specifically stated. When the first sentence in the story matches line 3 in the restaurant script, the meal variable is bound. Since this is the same variable that appears in line 5, the instantiated script will represent the fact that John ate a hamburger.

Scripts also help the program to infer what unstated actions took place.

It would be useful for an understander to recognize the fact that John probably paid for his meal even though this line in the script is skipped in the story. Script-based understanders make this type of inference very easily since they can assume that when a script finishes normally that intermediate actions in the script occurred even if they are not explicitly mentioned in the story. Of course it is not the case that a bottom up inferencer would be completely incapable of making these inferences (given enough time and memory), it is just that scripts allow the relevant inferences to be made more naturally and efficiently.

Scripts also turn out to be useful for language generation since they provide structure to a series of events, distinguishing the constant features from those that vary. For example, when paraphrasing a story about a restaurant, it would not be necessary to indicate that the diner was seated, if one assumes that the reader of the paraphrase will have a restaurant script and will therefore assume as much. One need only indicate what the script-variable bindings were (and in the case of more complex scripts with choice points in them, which choices were taken). Along the same lines, scripts suggest a very efficient way to store episodes in long term memory. Rather than store the entire episode, one need only record it as an instance of a particular script with a certain set of variable bindings. The episode can then be reconstituted whenever needed.

In short, scripts provide a way to package one's domain-specific knowledge and make it readily available for processing stereotyped events. The guidance provided by the overall context of a story, as encoded in a script, allows the understander to circumvent the combinatorial explosion that occurs when one tries to make the required inferences without such guidance.

SAM − A Program Based on Script Theory

SAM (Script Applier Mechanism [Cullingford 78]), was a computer program that used Scripts to help it understand stories. SAM possessed scripts covering a number of domains, including car accidents and state visits, and could process real newspaper articles in such domains. SAM could summarize and answer questions about the stories it read by refering to the instantiated scripts that it produced. Like Margie, SAM contained an analyzer and generator, but unlike Margie, it used a Script-based approach to generating the inferences necessary to understand the story.

MOPs − A Theory of Memory Organization

Scripts are simple knowledge structures that provide considerable predictive power to an understanding program. However, our experience with scripts led us to recognize shortcomings in them as well. Many of these shortcomings have to do not with the kind of knowledge that scripts encode, but with the way that they are organized. The problems in the theory became especially clear to us when we began to think seriously about the ways in which scripts might be retrieved from a realistically large memory, and the ways in which scripts could be modified dynamically. Originally we thought of each script as a separate structure that was unrelated to other scripts regardless of how similar they were. Scripts did not share components with each other, nor was there any well-developed theory of how scripts themselves might be arranged in memory.

MOPs (Memory Organization Packets) [Schank 82] were proposed as a replacement for scripts that would address these issues. MOPs represent temporal sequences the way scripts do, but they do so in a more modular, interconnected fashion. The idea behind MOPs is to break down the script into small units, called scenes, and to have the same scene shared by many MOPs, each of which can indicate the variations (called colorations) that it imposes on the scene. For example, in the original script theory one might have a script that describes a visit to the doctor and one that describes a visit to the lawyer, both of which mention waiting in a waiting room. However, the similarity between these two would not be explicitly represented. In MOP theory, the two MOPs would both point to the same waiting room scene. There are two important advantages to this scheme. First of all there is an efficiency argument; it seems silly to have the same information represented in different places. But more importantly, this organization greatly facilitates learning since something you learn about waiting rooms in one MOP will be available when processing with another one. MOP theory represents the first time in our research when our concerns moved beyond designing representations that would be easy to apply during language understanding. At this point we became very interested in organizing the memory as a whole so that MOPs could be created and modified dynamically.

In *Dynamic Memory* [Schank 82], Schank also proposed that MOPs be linked together just as MOPs linked scenes together. First they would be linked together by a set of abstraction hierarchies. The doctor visit MOP and the lawyer visit MOP are both instances of the professional office visit MOP. Second, they would be connected by a set of packaging links. Packaging links connect together other MOPs that often occur together in some larger context. For example, the business-trip MOP would package together, among other things, the plane-trip MOP, the hotel MOP and the business-lunch MOP, since each of these occurs as subparts of the larger business trip MOPs. In addition, Schank also proposed organizational structures whose purpose was to connect episodes that shared more abstract similarities. These structures he called TOPs (Thematic Organization Points). TOPs were designed to capture things like the connection between *Romeo and Juliet* and *West Side Story*, in which the actual events are quite different although the two stories are quite similar thematically.

IPP and CYRUS — MOP-Based Programs

Several programs have been written based on MOP theory. Among these are IPP [Lebowitz 80] and CYRUS [Kolodner 80]. IPP was a story understander, like the programs we have mentioned above. But IPP had a MOP-based memory in which it actually stored representations of the newspaper stories it had read so that it could recognize repeated occurrences and make generalizations based on them. For example, after reading several stories about killings in Northern Ireland, IPP could learn that they were often performed by the IRA and that the victims were often British authority figures. CYRUS was able to index episodes in a MOP-based memory. It then could use a set of heuristics to search its memory for an episode that would allow it to answer questions posed by the user.

Dynamic Memory theory is a more developed notion of how to organize high-level knowledge to make expectations available when understanding events or stories that conformed to those expectations. The question that naturally arose from this work was what to do when those expectations failed. When people are faced with failed expectations they find themselves attempting to explain those expectation failures in order to understand the current situation and to improve their models of the world. An investigation of the explanation process is the research project in which we are currently engaged. This work in progress we describe in the pages that follow.

Explanation Patterns — Dealing with Anomalies

The basic notion in our earlier work on natural language processing involved activating an appropriate knowledge structure and then using the expectations provided by that structure to guide the processing of the input. However, the most interesting stories often contain anomalies — events that are not handled by active expectations. When we encounter anomalies we feel the need to explain them.

Explaining an anomaly means bringing knowledge to bear that will tie the anomalous action to something we understand, and thus render it non-anomalous. But the problem is that there is a tremendous amount of knowledge that could conceivably be brought to bear and combined in arbitrarily complex ways. This combinatorial explosion of inference problem is similar to the one that confronted Margie. Our solution has also been similar: We designed a knowledge structure (which we call an

Explanation Pattern or XP) to store useful explanations so that explanations don't have to be built up from scratch every time they are used. Thus, an XP is a frozen explanation in much the same way that a script is a frozen plan. The function of both is to exempt the understander from having to build the inference chain over and over.

XPs differ from scripts and MOPs in that the latter are meant to provide an overall view of some group of events (such as a doctor's visit or a meal at a restaurant), while the former are designed to be a detailed trace of the reasoning that was used to answer a particular problem that could arise in such a group of events (such as the waiter not bringing your food). The beliefs in an XP are linked together in a causal network containing pointers to the inference rules that were used to build the XP.

Consider the following story: "Swale, a successful 3-year old race horse, was found dead in his stall a week after winning the Belmont Stakes race." Most people who read this story find the death to be an anomalous event, which they feel the need to explain. We will now describe the components of an XP in the context of an example XP that might be retrieved when considering an early death such as Swale's. This XP is taken from [Schank, forthcoming].

POVERTY-BRINGS-EARLY-DEATH-XP
1) *An anomaly that the pattern explains*: Early death.
2) *A set of relevant indices under which the it can be retrieved*: Early death; poverty; lack of food.
3) *A set of states of the world under which the pattern is likely to be a valid explanation*: Prior lack of health; poor childhood.
4) *A set of states under which the pattern is likely to be relevant, even if it can't be directly applied*: shortage of necessities; harsh conditions.
5) *A pattern of actions, with the relationships between them, that show how the event being explained could arise*:
   Lack of money prevents buying enough food.
   Lakc of money prevents adequate health care.
   Lack of food causes bad health as does lack of health care.
   Bad health causes early death.
6) *A set of prior explanations that have been made possible by use of this pattern*: Lives of immigrants; people in Africa.

The idea is that when an anomaly is encountered while reading a story or having an experience in the real world, that the understander uses features of the anomaly to retrieve XPs that might explain the anomaly. Once an appropriate XP is found, it helps in the understanding of the anomaly.

For any anomaly an understander encounters, there are four possibilities:
1) An XP can be retrieved from memory that applies perfectly to anomaly. In this case it is easy to explain the anomaly.

2) None of the XPs retrieved from memory apply directly, but some relevant XPs can be modified (we call this tweaking) to create new XPs that are applicable. This case is more difficult, but it is also more important, since at the end of the process the system has created and learned a new XP.

3) No XP is retrieved that can even be tweaked to apply. An XP must be built from scratch out of the primitive inference rules. This case is hard. Generally an understander will only bother to do this if the anomaly is really important. Most models of explanation deal only with this case.

4) The system does not even have the inference rules to allow it to build an appropriate XP. In this case the system simply is not equipped to understand the anomalous experience.

Most of our experiences fall into categories 1 and 2; we explain them by retrieving an existing XP and either applying it directly or modifying it to fit the new situation. Thus XPs must be well indexed so that they will be easy to retrieve; it must be possible to evaluate how well they fit any given situation, and it must be possible to modify them intelligently, so that old XPs can provide the basis for learning new ones. A theory of how these processes are performed is currently being developed in our laboratory and implemented in the SWALE program, which we describe briefly below.

SWALE — An Explanation-Based Understander

SWALE is a program that produces novel explanations by retrieving old XPs and modifying them to fit new situations. Thus SWALE is both an understanding program and a learning program. Its actions are driven by the goal of discovering an explanation that will help it understand an anomalous event, and in doing so it learns new explanations, and stores them for future use. The algorithm is:

1: ANOMALY DETECTION
Attempt to fit story into memory.
If successful DONE; otherwise an anomaly has been detected.

2: XP SEARCH
Search for an XP that can be applied to explain the anomaly.

3: XP ACCEPTING
Attempt to apply XPs.
If successful then skip to step 5.

4: XP TWEAKING
If unable to apply XPs directly then attempt to tweak them into XPs that might apply better.
If successful send these tweaked XPs back to step 3.

5:   XP INTEGRATION AND GENERALIZATION
If any results accepted, integrate results back into memory making appropriate generalizations.

We have begun our work on the SWALE program by attempting to process the example story we mentioned earlier about Swale's untimely death. Our goal is to have the SWALE program use the above algorithm to come up with as many interesting explanations as possible by applying the XPs we have indexed in its XP library and by applying tweaking strategies to create new variations of these XPs. There is a library of modification strategies available; the strategy chosen depends on the failure encountered when the explanation is applied. These strategies do things like splice two XPs together or substitute causally equivalent actions. Many of these strategies make use of the causal links in the XP to decide what changes can reasonably be made to the XP.

Unfortunately, there is no room in this paper to give a detailed description of the SWALE program. We will limit ourselves to a brief description of XPs we have equipped the program with, the explanations the program develops, and a very brief summary of one run of the program. For a more detailed discussion refer to the appendix of (Schank, forthcoming).

SWALE begins with the following library of prior XPs:

The Jim Fixx XP < *episode-based* > :
Joggers jog a lot.
Jogging results in physical exhaustion because jogging is a kind of exertion and exertion results in exhaustion.
Physical exhaustion coupled with a heart defect can cause a heart attack.
A heart attack can cause death.

The Janis Joplin XP < *episode-based* > :
Being a star performer can result in stress because it is lonely at the top.
Being stressed-out can result in a need to escape and relax.
Needing to escape and relax can result in taking recreational drugs.
Taking recreational drugs can result in an overdose.
A drug overdose can result in death.

The Too-Much-Sex XP < *folklore-based* > :
Having too much sex can kill you.

The Preoccupation XP *<basic causal pattern>:*
Being preoccupied about something can cause you to be inattentive.
Being inattentive can result in walking into traffic.
Walking into traffic can result in you being hit by a vehicle.
Being hit by a vehicle can cause death.

The Despondent Suicide XP *<basic causal pattern>:*
Thinking about something you want but that you don't have can make you despondent.
Being despondent can result in suicide.

The following is a brief trace of a SWALE run in which it develops some variations on explanations contained in its library. This is intended to give the reader some feel for the way that SWALE's processing proceeds:

- Use routine search to find XPs concerning premature death in animals.
- Find *death from illness.*
- These XPs can't apply, since Swale wasn't sick. The failures are severe enough to abandon these XPs without trying to tweak.
- Look for XPs indexed by unusual features of Swale. Racehorses are in excellent physical condition; death + excellent condition pulls up the Jim Fixx XP.
- Swale wasn't a jogger, so the Fixx XP can't apply. Try to tweak.
- Since the problem was invalid-theme, try the repair strategy *substitute alternative theme.* (A theme is an action that a actor performs often or a role that an actor normally fills). Swale's known themes are horse-race and eat-oats.
- The horse-race theme is selected because it involves running, and the tweaked XP is *Since Swale had a heart defect, the exertion from running overtaxed his heart.*
- Check whether the XP is believable. It's reasonable, but since the heart defect can't be confirmed, continue looking for other XPs.
- No more regular XPs are found, so try folkloric explanations of death. Pull up the old wive's tale *too much sex will kill you.*
- Racehorses aren't allowed to have sex while racing. But they do have a lot of sex when they retire to the stud farm. Try to tweak.
- Since the problem was that the death happened too early, try the tweaking strategy *substitute anticipation.* Could Swale have died just from thinking about life on the stud farm?
- The new XP is unconvincing. Try tweaking to strengthen support.
- To strengthen, use the strategy *find connecting XP.* Effects of thinking about sex are distraction, excitement, and depression (if you're thinking about not having it). Distraction can be linked to death

by the XP *death from stepping in front of a bus*. Excitement can cause *death by heart-attack*. Depression can cause *death from suicide*.
- The three XPs are possible, but still not convincing. Search continues.
- No more XPs are found.
- Each of the new explanations depends on conditions which can't be confirmed. Since the Fixx XP was the possibility located most directly by the searcher, the tweaked version of Fixx is accepted as the most likely explanation.
- The causally-significant feature Fixx and Swale shared was that they did physical exertion. The XP is generalized to apply to people who have an exertion theme.
- The generalized XP is installed in memory for future use.

Here is a list of the explanations that SWALE has come up with so far:

The Jim Fixx Reminding Explanation:
Swale had a congenital heart defect. The exertion of running in horse races strained his heart and brought out the latent defect. He had a heart attack and died.

The Drug Overdose Explanation:
Swale's owner was giving him drugs to improve his performance. He accidentally gave him an overdose, which killed him.

THE STUD FARM TRILOGY
SWALE's processing brings it to consider the idea that thinking about sex too much caused Swale's demise. It then attempts to imagine ways in which this might have occurred and develops the three explanations that follow:

The Sexual Excitement Explanation:
Swale was thinking about his future life on a stud farm. Since he was an excitable creature, thinking about the prospects proved to be too much strain for his heart. He had a heart attack and died.

The Hit-By-A-Bus Explanation:
Swale was thinking about his future life on a stud farm. Being preoccupied with visions of the delightful prospects, he absent-mindedly wandered out into the street and was struck by a bus.

The Despondent Suicide Explanation:
Swale was thinking about his forced chastity during his racing career. He became despondent and killed himself.

Although SWALE is still in its formative stages, we are very excited by the preliminary results. The program possesses an important trait that previous understanders did not: For SWALE, understanding is literally a creative act. The program does not merely attempt to fit input into pre-existing knowledge structures, and give up when no structure is available. When expectations fail, the program attempts to form new hypotheses for understanding the events. This is an important component of flexible, human-style understanding.

We feel that we have the basic control structure for the SWALE program in place now. Our goal now is to provide the program with a much larger library of XPs (and to index them cleverly so that the program will have ready access to useful XPs even when its library contains many irrelevant ones), and to equip it with a much larger array of XP modification strategies, so that it will be able to come up with new and unexpected explanations for a range of anomalies. When the system develops interesting explanations that its authors have never thought of, then we will consider it a real success.

Conclusion

The problem of knowledge representation is at the center of cognitive science. At the Yale AI project we have developed a number of structures for representing knowledge, which were intended both as theories of representation within the human mind and as data structures that would be useful to AI computer programs. Each has proven itself by allowing us to build a new generation of programs that was more flexible and more powerful than the last — in other words, a step further along the long road leading toward human-level abilities. The AI methodology works by writing programs to stretch one representation to its limits and then designing a new one to do what the last could not.

We began with Conceptual Dependency, a theory of representing the meaning of sentences, and this allowed us to write programs that could understand simple stories. Next we worked on higher level structures (such as scripts and MOPs), which represented the relationship between actions, and these allowed us to build more powerful programs that could understand real newspaper stories on a range of topics and could make generalizations about them. Explanation Patterns represent inference chains about MOPs. This has allowed our current work on explanation-based understanding to push the frontiers back yet a bit further, with a program that understands creatively, building novel explanations for things it hasn't seen before. The SWALE program has the potential to be genuinely creative because it has explanatory knowledge of the way things work, and can therefore think about them in new ways.

Bibliography

CARBONELL, J.
1979   *Subjective Understanding: Computer Models of Belief Systems*, Technical Report 150, Yale U. Department of Computer Science, Ph.D. Thesis.
CULLINGFORD, R.
1978   *Script Application: Computer Understanding of Newspaper Stories*, Ph.D. Thesis, Yale University.
GERSHMAN, A., JOHNSON, P., and SCHWARTZ, S., and WOLF, T.
1984   "CD Meets the Real World", *First Annual Workshop on Theoretical Issues in Conceptual Information Processing*.
GOLDMAN, N.
1975   "Conceptual Generation", in *Conceptual Information Processing*, Amsterdam, North-Holland.
KOLODNER, J.L.
1980   *Retrieval and Organizational Strategies in Conceptual Memory: A Computer Model*, Technical Report 187, Yale U. Department of Computer Science, Ph.D. Thesis.
LEBOWITZ, M.
1980   *Generalization and Memory in an Integrated Understanding System*, Technical Report 186, Yale U. Department of Computer Science, Ph.D. Thesis.
RIEGER, C.
1975   "Conceptual Memory and Inference", in *Conceptual Information Processing*, Amsterdam, North-Holland.
RIESBECK, CHRISTOPHER C.
1975   "Conceptual Analysis", in *Conceptual Information Processing*, Amsterdam, North-Holland.
SCHANK, R.C.
1972   "Conceptual Dependency: A Theory of Natural Language Understanding", *Cognitive Psychology* 3 (4).
1975   *Conceptual Information Processing*, Amsterdam, North-Holland.
1982   *Dynamic Memory: A Theory of Learning in Computers and People*, Cambridge, Cambridge University Press.
forthcoming   *Explanation Patterns: Understanding Mechanically and Creatively*, in Preparation.
SCHANK, R.C., and ABELSON, R.
1977   *Scripts, Plans, Goals and Understanding*, Hillsdale, N.J., Lawrence Erlbaum Associates.

Acknowledgements

David Leake and Christopher Riesbeck provided several helpful rounds of comments on earlier drafts of this paper. The SWALE program is being developed by David Leake, Christopher Owens, Christopher Riesbeck and the authors. This work is being supported in part by the Advanced Research Projects Agency of the Department of Defense and monitored under the Office of Naval Research under contract N00014-82-K-0149.

Bas van Fraassen

Identity in Intensional Logic: Subjective Semantics*

After the wonderful success of possible world (truth and reference) semantics in the sixties and seventies, we now gallop off in many directions, to escape its confines. In this paper I shall describe, more or less informally, one of these directions, and the initial findings therein. As focus for our attention I chose *identity*.

Like many others I have been convinced by Kripke and Putnam that there is a distinction between necessity and the *a priori*. In addition I think that logic is not the study of what is necessary, but exactly of what is *a priori*. By "logic" I mean here pure logic, the ground in which can flourish many applied logics — some of which do describe necessity in its various forms and guises. From pure logic I want something different, something more fundamental. Such propositions of identity as "Cicero = Tully", which are arguably necessary if true but generally not *a priori*, provide therefore a touchstone for the purity of our logic. To arrive at this touchstone, however, we need to travel some ways along my chosen direction — reflecting first of all on the criteria of equivalence in various logics, then on how we can represent reasoning (including *reasoning under suppositions*), and on quantification and abstraction. I commend to you the story of the Zen minds (section 6), offered as the image to replace possible worlds.

I. Distinctions of fact and of reason

1. Modal logic began early in this century with C.I. Lewis' discontent with a certain feature of then current theories of language. If two sentences have the same truth-value they could be substituted, one for the other, everywhere — similarly for two names with the same referent. We now say that he was discontent because the logic of his day was *extensional*. That means, the criterion of total equivalence was sameness of extension. The term "extension" which means "class of instances"

* Research support by the National Science Foundation is gratefully aknowledged. I also wish to thank Richmond Thomason and Nuel Belnap for helpful discussions. Subjective semantics (the attempt to elucidate logical connections in language through models of reasoning that use the language, rather than models of entities and worlds referred to and described in the language) has taken various forms. I have learned most from the "probabilistic semantics" initiated by William Harper and Hartry Field, and the "epistemic semantics" of Brian Ellis.

when it is applied to a predicate, is here used in a wider sense: the extension of a term is its referent, the extension of a sentence is its truth-value. Thus we have in extensional logic the following three valid inference patterns:

Sentences	Predicates	Terms
$A \equiv B$	$(x)\ (Fx \equiv Gx)$	$a = b$
- -A- -	- - -F- - -	- - -a- - -
- -B- -	- - -G- - -	- - -b- - -

I am thinking of logic here as applicable to our natural language, and the interpretation of the logical signs in the above table is supposed to be the usual one in terms of truth value and extension.

Total equivalence amounts to intersubstitutivity everywhere, and I'll call a logic *extensional* if it has the above three criteria for total equivalence. For example, in an extensional logic, the criterion for total equivalence of two predicates F and G is that $(x)\ (Fx \equiv Gx)$ be true. With respect to the reasoning depicted ("governed") by such a logic this means: if $(x)\ (Fx \equiv Gx)$ be assumed (to be true), then F and G may be systematically substituted for each other everywhere.

2. A logic is generally called *intensional* if it is not extensional, but let us distinghish at once between *intensional in its narrow sense*, or as I shall also say *modal*, and other sorts of non-extensional logic. In a modal logic there will be a necessity sign, used to formulate its criteria of total equivalence:

$\Box(A \equiv B)$	$\Box(x)\ (Fx \equiv Gx)$	$\Box(a = b)$
- - -A- - -	- - -F- - -	- - -a- - -
- - -B- - -	- - -G- - -	- - -b- - -

In the usual semantic account we now say that between necessary equivalents, there is no difference in any possible world. The Medievals said: even God could not create a case of the one which is not a case of the other.

I do not intend to deride possible world semantics, which I think is fine as far as it goes. Its way of looking at things does anyway not date from the fifties, but has for example characterized Anglo-Saxon philosophy for a century. Examples may be found in William James' essay "The Dilemma of Determinism" (1884: especially his treatment of the example of a choice of walking home by either Divinity Ave or Oxford Street) and Bertrand Russell's *The Problems of Philosophy* (1912: see especially in Ch. VII, his discussion of 2 + 2 = 4 and all men being mortal).

But I do think that, just as extensional criteria of total equivalence wipe out important distinctions, so do the modal criteria.

3. Turning now to non-modal non-extensional logic, there is no uniform nomenclature. We hear "hyper-intensional logic" and "fine-grained distinctions", but mostly there are names for specific such logics, all of which are regarded with suspicion by almost everyone besides the adepts.

The Medievals discussed distinctions of fact (*in re*) but also distinctions of reason. Among the latter the simplest was the one where there is a possibility of a distinction of fact — the case in which God could have, though actually did not, create a case of the one which was not a case of the other. Such is the distinction between rational animal and featherless biped. But there are further distinctions, distinctions of reason where even God could not tear asunder.

Duns Scotus is especially known for the *formal distinction* between transcendentals, i.e. between properties which everything must have. In terms equally reminiscent of Plato's *Sophist*, we can mention the transcendentals of being and unity: everything that is, is one — and everything that is one, is — and no exceptions could exist; yet there is a distinction. We should also mention especially Francis Suarez, "On the Various Kinds of Distinction", *Disputationes Metaphysicae*, Disp. VII.[1] But in our century, too, and indeed recently, such distinctions have been drawn.

4. I shall refer, for now, to only one case. The discussion of proper names by, for example, Russell, Ruth Marcus, and Kripke, led to the latter's theory of rigid designators and the well-known view that "Cicero = Tully" is necessary if it is true at all. Hilary Putnam added a corresponding view for common nouns: "water = H_2O" is necessary if true at all. But for neither example would it be plausible to say that it could be known *a priori*. In a strict sense, their truth is independent of the way the world is; yet no amount of reasoning could have led to them as conclusions.

It is sometimes argued that this distinction is already observed in modal logic. Only the sentence "Cicero = Cicero", but not "Cicero = Tully" is a *theorem* of modal logic (sound and complete under the standard interpretation) although the proposition expressed is necessary in both cases. But that is not sufficient to show that the relevant distinctions are genuinely observed. For the most general necessity operator $\Box$ — the one that literally corresponds to truth in all possible worlds — we can define

"$A \mapsto B$" for "$\Box (A \supset B)$"
"$A \equiv B$" for "$(A \mapsto B) \& (B \mapsto A)$"

and then $A \equiv B$ entails the substitutivity of A for B everywhere — their total equivalence. But in these terms we have the theorems

(Cicero = Cicero) $\mapsto$ (Cicero = Tully) . or .
(Cicero = Tully) $\mapsto$ (Cicero $\neq$ Cicero)

[1] Tr. C. Vollert, Marquette University Press, 1947.

and

$$(\text{Cicero} = \text{Tully}) \equiv (\text{Cicero} = \text{Cicero}) \; . \; \text{or} \; .$$
$$(\text{Cicero} = \text{Tully}) \equiv (\text{Cicero} \neq \text{Cicero})$$

These theorems express the fact, built into logic, that an identity statement must have the same status as *either* a tautology *or* a self-contradiction. Unlike other statements, its status (although we may not know it) cannot be anywhere between these two extremes. The case is exactly analogous to the retort a disciple of Quine could have given to the call for modal logic: "Cicero = Cicero" may be materially equivalent to "Socrates is Greek", but that is not a theorem. Indeed; but it is a theorem of extensional logic that

$$(\text{Cicero} = \text{Cicero}) \supset (\text{Socrates is Greek}) \; . \; \text{or} \; .$$
$$(\text{Socrates is Greek}) \supset (\text{Cicero} \neq \text{Cicero})$$

$$(\text{Socrates is Greek}) \equiv (\text{Cicero} = \text{Cicero}) \; . \; \text{or} \; .$$
$$(\text{Socrates is Greek}) \equiv (\text{Cicero} \neq \text{Cicero})$$

and with such theorems, involving the strictest expressible equivalence proper to that logic, the language cannot accomodate the sought-for distinctions.

I urge therefore the need for a "purer" logic — one in which "Cicero = Tully" can have, in any given model, a status different from the *a priori* truth and also from the *a priori* falsehood. This must be urged for the same reasons, *mutatis mutandis*, as we urge against extensional logic that "Socrates is Greek" should not be constrained to have *either* the status of "Cicero = Cicero" *or* that of "Cicero = Cicero".

II. Subjective Semantics: Minds and Propositions

5. So I am going to talk about pure logic, the theory of the *a priori* and I mean to do so still from a semantic point of view. Now I don't want to say anything against the usual semantics of truth and reference, but for the present purpose it is obviously not far-reaching enough. It may perhaps be supplemented by something more that is sometimes called *subjective* or even solipsistic semantics, because it does not proceed in terms of what does or even could exist. I profess no imperialism on its behalf. On the other hand, I realize that even if (or rather, especially if) it can be successfully developed, there will be special problems of coexistence for the two sorts of semantics. But reduction of one to the other, or replacement by one for the other, like any sort of imperialistic solution, is probably just the wrong thing to try.

6. I really think that the proposition (by which I mean, the semantic value to be associated with a sentence) is the basic topic of concern in semantics. But I don't want to start with propositions, because that would make them seem like some Platonist realm of strange entities.

In possible-worlds-truth-and-reference semantics (let's say, standard semantics), propositions are constructs: they are sets of possible worlds. *First* you say: a proposition is true or false in each world. *Then* you add, we may as well *identify* a proposition with the class of worlds in which it is true. You might as well, because you are anyway unable to draw distinctions between propositions which are true in exactly the same worlds.

So let me try this: there are minds, conceivable minds, and they *suppose* some propositions. By this I mean they treat them as "given" or regard them so, or suppose them to be true, as basic premises for all reasoning. And now I'll add: we might as well identify a proposition with the set of minds in which it is supposed, or as I shall also say, all minds in which it is *held* (to be true).

Of course, you may think that this is only to replace one metaphysical metaphor by another, and will result only in a verbal difference. But there is one major difference in that a mind may easily suppose neither a given proposition, nor any incompatible with it. In addition, I hasten to point out that there are obvious relations among minds which have no counterparts on worlds. First of all, some minds are more dogmatic, or *stricter* than others:

$$x \leq y, \text{ x is } \textit{at least as strict as } \text{y, exactly if}$$
$$\text{x supposes all that y supposes.}$$

As gloss and symbol suggest, this is a partial ordering. At the very bottom lies the strictest mind of all, which holds all propositions as suppositions. Ever increasing assumptions or dogmatism on more and more subjects has driven it to insanity − it is called $\emptyset$, the abnormality, the *memento mori* of dogmatic thought. As you go up in the structure, you find freer and freer minds; at the top are *Zen minds* which are subordinate to none but the other Zen minds, holding or supposing only what all minds suppose.

7. We must widen this relationship among minds. Let us say that one mind x is *subordinate* to a set W of minds (briefly, x *Sub* W) exactly if x holds (supposes) whatever all members of W hold.[2] This must be a primitive relation in our construction; the *preceding* $\leq$ is a special case (x is at least as strict as y exactly if x is subordinate to the set $\{y\}$). But it must be a relation such that we will be able to say: x is subordinate to W exactly if x is a member of every proposition which includes W as a subset. It follows then that subordination needs to have the following properties:

(a) If x is a member of W then x is subordinate to W

---

[2] This notion of subordination is analogous to the construal of superposition in quantum logic, which suggested some of the constructions that follow. For reasons to think of quantum logic, like intuitionistic logic, as belonging to the family of modal logics, see Dalla Chiara.

(b) if all members of U are subordinate to W, and x is
    subordinate to U, then x is also subordinate to W.
(c) the abnormal mind is subordinate to every set W.

If W is a set of minds let us call the *span* of W exactly the set of minds
that are subordinate to W – and denote this span as [W]. It follows
now from the above properties that [...] is a so-called closure operation.
Also since a proposition is to be identified with the set of minds which
hold (suppose) it, a proposition must contain all the minds subordinate
to it. Hence we have now a precise way to capture this proposal concerning the propositions.

a *proposition* is a closed set of minds; that is, a set W such that W = [W].

We also have a precise way to characterize the Zen minds, at the top
of our hierarchy:

x is a Zen mind exactly if it is subordinate to a set W only if [W]
contains all minds.

i.e. only if [W] = K, the set of all minds. We may also call [{x}] the span
of the mind x; then this becomes

x is a Zen mind exactly if its span is K, the set of all minds.

These minds hold or suppose only what all minds hold, and are free from
peculiar beliefs of their own; they are completely undogmatic. (The span
of a mind is, as it were, the conjuction of all the propositions it holds.)
    In classical logic, also classical modal logic, the propositions always
form a Boolean algebra. This need not be so here, and indeed, pure logic
should not be so parochial. We have the result:

Theorem The propositions form a complete lattice of sets, with
$\Phi = \{\emptyset\}$ as minimum, K as maximum, partially ordered by
the relation of set inclusion, set intersection as *meet* ("conjunction") and the operation $\uplus X = [UX]$ as *join* ("disjunction").

This follows at once from elementary results about closure operations.
Almost every logic known to mankind allows of a full set of models in
which the propositions form this sort of structure. This includes most
certainly classical, intuitionistic, quantum, and relevance logics.

8. I have been saying "hold" and "suppose" as if they were inter-
changeable. Really they are not. To hold a belief is the most definite,
positive epistemic attitude one can have. To suppose something, on the
other hand, is not even to hold it momentarily, but to hold it momentarily with a mental reservation, "for the sake of argument". Yet this

is a very important act, for reasoning would be completely impotent if it could not include reasoning under suppositions. This is what we must now explain.

Let the span of the mind x be briefly denoted as [x]. The mind x holds a proposition P exactly if [x] is part of P. We can imagine this mind x adding one more proposition, say A, to what it holds. Then it becomes a different mind, whose span is equal to [x] ∩ A. Let us therefore call this different mind x^A — x *conditioned on* A. But instead of changing in this way, the mind x could merely imagine itself doing so, and ask itself what it would hold if it added A to all it does hold. This is reasoning under the supposition that A. If it finds that this other mind x^A holds B, then it can say of itself that it holds B *on the supposition that* A, or holds the proposition (B *if* A).

It appears therefore that we can introduce a *conditional* or *implication operation* as follows:

x is a member of (A → B) exactly if $x^A ∈ B$.

But now we face several questions. First, if x is a mind, and A a proposition, is there also such a mind as x^A — that is, another mind whose span equals [x] ∩ A? And secondly is this set (A → B) really a proposition — that is, is it a closed set? The answer to both questions will in general be *no*. If it is *no*, we are dealing with a model of minds which are not capable of reasoning under suppositions. Of course, it is of great interest to look at the sorts of mind which are capable of this.

9. By a *frame of minds* I shall mean a set K (call the members *minds*) with a special member $\emptyset$ and a special relation *Sub* (subordination) such that (a) - (c) in section 7 are satisfied. Now I want to look at the sort of frames in which the minds are capable of conditional reasoning. Let us first define a kind of conditional subordination. This is a defined and not a primitive relationship:

x is A-*subordinate* to W exactly if
for all propositions C: if $y^A ∈ C$ for each y in W, then $x^A ∈ C$.

Thus subordination *simpliciter* is the same as K-subordination, because $y^K = y$ always. Let us now call I-*frame* any frame for which the following postulate is satisfied:

Postulate If x is a mind and A a proposition, then x^A is a mind too, and moreover, subordination always implies A-subordination.

This last clause means: if x is subordinate to W, then also x is A-subordinate to W.

Now we have a very nice theorem: the logic by which these minds reason, is *intuitionistic logic*. That is, the I-frames are really models of that logic, and intuitionistic logic is complete with respect to these models. (See the appendix for a proof-sketch.)

I called this a very nice theorem, but perhaps you were dismayed — must pure logic lead so quickly to intuitionistic logic? What if that is not your favorite? Well, there are other sorts of frames of minds, which you may prefer.

Let us consider a relation different from subordination, namely *radical disagreement* or *orthogonality*. Such a disagreement must be experienced when one mind holds a proposition which another rejects. We have as yet no notion of rejection, but we can see intuitively that this relation of disagreement, to be written as $\perp$, must have the following properties:

$x \perp x$ if and only if x is the abnormal mind,

$x \perp y$ only if $y \perp x$,

$x \perp \emptyset$ for every mind x.

Such a relation I shall call an *orthogonality* relation on the frame. For the one that represents disagreement, there must be a connection with subordination. Suppose that x is subordinate to W, and z is orthogonal to every member of W. Since x holds whatever the members of W hold in common, z must also be in disagreement with x. Thus:

(a)   x is subordinate to W only if $z \perp W$ implies $z \perp x$, where $z \perp W$ means that $z \perp y$ for each member y of W. (To say that z *rejects* proposition P evidently means that $z \perp P$.)

Conversely, let us suppose that any z which is orthogonal to W is also orthogonal to x. If that orthogonality is radical disagreement, should we conclude that x is subordinate to W? Well suppose x is not subordinate to W. Then there is some proposition A held by all members of W but not by x. It is possible to imagine then a mind z which holds all that x holds, and holds nothing else, but rejects A. (This could be x itself!) In that case z would be orthogonal to all members of W but not to x. Thus we conclude also:

(b)   x is subordinate to W if $z \perp W$ implies $z \perp x$.

This is enough to go on; let us call an *O-frame* one for which there exists an orthogonality relation $\perp$ such that (a) and (b) hold. In O-frames, closure has a second meaning:

(c)   [W] = the set of minds such that for all minds y, if $y \perp W$ then $y \perp x$.

We have again a very nice theorem: the minds in an O-frame of minds reason in accordance with orthologic ("baby quantum logic" as it is sometimes called). That is, the O-frames are in effect models of orthologic, and orthologic is complete with respect to this set of models. (Again, see the Appendix for a proof sketch.)

But you may still be dismayed, if you are of a more classical turn of mind. You may then prefer C-frames, n. l. the sort of frame which is at once an I-frame and a O-frame. *Classical logic* is sound and complete with respect to the C-frames of mind. So there is room for all the usual logical persuasion. It would be nice to have a further story of this sort to accommodate relevance logics. The new result of Alasdair Urquhardt makes one conjecture wistfully that this area, always closely associated with lattices, can also be brought into the present fold; but I don't know.

III. Quantification and Identity: Transformation Semantics[3]

10. In semantics, you describe models for language. In models of subjective semantics we could have some familiar denizens of truth and reference semantics, such as propositions (though differently conceived). But it would make no sense to try and introduce counterparts to most of the familiar entities to be found there. For example, I think it would be a mistake to introduce some counterpart of a domain of discourse, such as a mental picture gallery or set of individual concepts, or whatever, to function as surrogate referents. Some such things may eventually appear, but they can't play a basic role. I have two reasons for saying this.

The first comes from thinking about pictures. A picture of Socrates has propositional content; it shows Socrates in repose or excited, sitting or running or flying. So a representation can't be like a bare referent; and indeed there must be many pictures of any one thing, and they never just represent it. So they cannot be good surrogate referents, since we really refer to only one thing by means of many of them, and may only *refer* to it, without describing it.

The second reason comes from thinking about reference without representation. I could even speak about there being things which never have been and never will be pictured, described, or conceived individually. So the surrogates would never be enough anyway.

No, if we are going to do subjective semantics, we must eschew not only reference but also all surrogate reference. Representation there may be, but surrogate reference it is not.

What this means is that I shall make up everything from propositions and operations on propositions. But beforehand I'll motivate it in two ways. The first way is to explain how we can use syntactic analogues, while keeping their referential interpretation "bracketed". The second is to sketch a continuation of our new metaphysical metaphor of conceivable minds engaged in supposition.

---

[3] This section contains an informal exposition of my "Quantification as an act of mind" (briefly, QUAAM); the ideas are not entirely unchanged. Specifically, I think I now understand better what it means to suppose a general proposition.

There is a certain Correspondence Principle that has always guided semantics: the semantic value of a complex expression $F(E_1,..,E_n)$ is a function $\Psi(|E_1|,..,|E_n|)$ of the semantic values $|E_1|,..,|E_n|$ of its parts. This *suggests* but *does not imply* that a proposition is a complex entity of the sort Russell envisaged, built up from parts which are referred to by parts of the sentence that express the proposition. A set of possible worlds has no such parts, neither does a closed set of minds. But once you observe this, you may be able to let the Correspondence Principle guide you to other correspondences. The significant correspondences, I shall submit, are between operations or transformations acting on sentences and acting on propositions. For example, Fb comes from Fa by the substitution of b for a. Well, the proposition |Fb| comes from |Fa| by a corresponding operation, which I shall posit.

Of course it is no use just positing operations any more than propositions themselves — we need a metaphysical metaphor to light our way. So let us see what a mind can suppose.

Imagine I ask you to suppose that Tom Schneider is rich, happy, handsome, a bit small for his age but rather paunchy, ... You have no idea who Tom Schneider is. You do have the idea that the world has a limited number of inhabitants, and if you did identify Tom, it would be as one of them, but you have made no particular identification. All this is plausible, is it not? But now, *what exactly are you supposing?*

Before answering that, consider the ordinary language of real number algebra, with such sentences in it as

(1) $2 + 3 = 6$
(2) $a + b = c$
(3) $(x)(x + x + a = 2x + a)$

I could ask you to suppose (1), as initial premise of a *reductio*; if you do, you become $\emptyset$. Can I ask you to suppose that $a + b = c$? Certainly; we can use that as a premise and begin a deduction. If you suppose that $a + b = c$ you are *not* treating this as implicitly quantified — you are supposing *neither* that $(x)(y)(z)(x + y = z)$ *nor* merely that $\exists x \exists y \exists z(x + y = z)$. But neither is there a specific numerical identity, like (1), that you are supposing. Only if you *had* identified a as 2, b as 3, c as 6, would you be supposing (1). Well, what exactly are you supposing?

I'll offer an answer to such questions. You are supposing a proposition, but it is a proposition which depends on certain parameters a,b,c, which you may or may not identify as specific entities — you may or may not "fix their values". This proposition is a sort of generic proposition, "general" in the sense, derided by Berkeley, of Locke's general triangle.

Syntactically, the sentence $a + b = c$ can be transformed by substitution in two ways: into $a + a = c$ or into $a + 2 = c$. The first substitutes a parametric term a for b; the second substitutes a numerical constant for

b. I will introduce two corresponding operations on propositions: *variation* and *instantiation* (or *fixing*).

At some point we should ask the question (answered for the dyadic operation → in terms of the operation that transforms mind x into x^A) what operations or relations between minds can engender these operations on propositions. At the moment I do not have a satisfactory theory about that, so let us look into the abstract theory.

11. Let us talk about propositions again. Before looking at them from close up, let me list the features of a collection of propositions that could make up a model.

I. The proposition form a complete lattice, with top element K (the *a priori*), bottom element Φ (the *absurd*), partial ordering ≤ (implication relation), conjunction (meet) ∧, disjunction (join) ∨, ("complete" in that every set of propositions has a conjunction and disjunction).

Any such lattice will do, for the time being; and this assumption is so minimal that no logic I know is disqualified by it. But I will add one feature that does limit the subject a bit.

II. There is an "implication" operator → ("ply"), such that A → B = K if and only if A ≤ B

Quantum logic and relevance logic are the usual exceptions to assumptions about conditionals, but they are not ruled out by the assumption that all models may have *this* feature. So the field is still very wide. We can define our strongest equivalence here by

"A ↔ B" for "(A → B) ∧ (B → A)"

We notice that (A ↔ B) = K if and only if A = B, so that condition certainly guarantees substitutivity everywhere (when the syntax is interpreted in such a model).

12. Now I want to talk about quantification, and I shall use syntax as a *pons asinorum*. From the sentence Fa we can make up the therm âFa, and from Fb, the term b̂Fb — these two terms stand for the properties that a and b must have, respectively, for Fa and Fb to be true. But of course, these must be the same property. The sentence (x)Fx says that this property is universal, everything has it, so it can be written as UâFa.

We can look upon this situation in two ways. The first is to think of a proposition which is "generic" like Locke's general triangle, something like

$$A = (\text{a certain entity is } F)$$

and then imagine this generic proposition being made definite into one in which the subject is "fixed":

$$A_1 = this \text{ entity is } F$$
$$A_2 = \alpha \text{ is } F$$
$$A_3 = \beta \text{ is } F$$

and so forth. The second way we can look at it is by imagining that some "specific" proposition is changed by altering its subject:

$$B = \text{this entity is F}$$
$$B' = \text{that entity is F}$$
$$B'' = \alpha \text{ is F}$$
$$B''' = \beta \text{ is F}$$

and so forth. The two processes are different: A is "made more specific" while B is altered in a way that leaves it "equally specific". But each of the processes we have imagined is a very general one. They are:

Take this parameter and fix its value at_ - - - - -

Take this fixed value and alter it to - - - - -

Each of these processes is a *transformation* of all propositions at once (though it does not affect all equally). The transformation preserves structure; if it be called f we have

$$f(A \wedge B) = f(A) \wedge f(B) \qquad f(\bigwedge_i A_i) = \bigwedge_i f(A_i)$$
$$f(A \vee B) = f(A) \vee f(B) \qquad f(\bigvee_i A_i) = \bigvee_i f(A_i)$$
$$f(K) = K$$

When these equations hold, and only then, will I call the function a transformation. If it additionally has the nice feature

$$f(A \rightarrow B) = f(A) \rightarrow f(B)$$

I'll call it *normal*.

13. We have found two sorts of transformations that are somehow associated with abstraction and quantification. Should we now choose one to start with? Actually, we can discover quite a bit about these two topics without making any choice, but just thinking about transformations generally. Let us define:

An *abstractor* is a set of transformations.

If b is an abstractor, the *b-abstract* of proposition A is the set
$$bA = \{gA : g \epsilon b\}.$$

If $bA = \{A\}$ we call b *irrelevant* to A, or say that A does not depend on b.

I write "gA" as short for "g(A)", the proposition that A is turned into by g. In terms of the syntactic *pons asinorum*, âFa is being associated with the set of all propositions that Fa can be turned into, so as to keep everything unaffected by abstraction from a: Fa,Fb,Fc, − etc. (But the syntax may give out here; perhaps not all the relevant propositions are expressed in the language.)

The *universal quantifier* $\forall_b$ associated with abstractor b is defined by
$$\forall_b A = \bigwedge (bA)$$

The abstract bA is a set; $\forall_b A$ is the meet of that set. (Note that quantifiers are here not pieces of language but operations in the models for language.)

Theorem   Let b be any abstractor and let $\forall$ be its associated quantifier.

Then:

     (a) $\forall K = K$
     (b) if $A \leq B$ then $\forall A \leq \forall B$
     (c) if $\wedge X \leq B$ then $\wedge\{\forall A : A\epsilon X\} \leq \forall B$
     (d) $\forall A \leq gA$ if $g \epsilon b$
     (e) $\forall A \leq \forall\forall A$ if, for any $g,g' \epsilon b$, the proposition
         $gg'A$ is also in bA.

Let us just look at what all this means.

(a) This corresponds to the rule of simple universal generalization: if A is *a priori*, so is $\forall A$.

(b) This corresponds to conditional reasoning with the quantifier (generalized universal generalization): if A implies B, then $\forall A$ implies $\forall B$.

(c) This generalizes the rule still farther, to infinite sets of premises.

(d) This corresponds closely to universal instantiation. Suppose $(x)Fx$ is written UâFa, and F1 is a relevant variant of Fa; then UâFa implies F1.

(e) Here we see the principle of vacuous quantification; the proviso holds specifically in two interesting cases:

     (e1) b is *destructive*: if $B \epsilon bA$ and $g \epsilon b$ then $gB = B$.
     (e2) b is a *semigroup*: if $g,g' \epsilon b$ then so is gg'.

Clearly if you fix the value of a parameter at a certain point, and then you try to fix it again, nothing happens because it has changed from fixable to fixed already. (The syntactic analogue is the transformation of "a man is happy" or "x is happy" into "Peter is happy".) Hence at least the first sort of transformation we looked at is destructive.

The importance of the theorem is this: if you think of universal quantification as the simultaneous assertion of all results of a set of transformations, you immediately get the right basic properties — plus in addition a framework for introducing new assumptions (in terms of what the abstractors are like) which may lead to interesting sorts of models.

14. I said that terms âFa and b̂Fb must stand for the same property, sentences UâFa and Ub̂Fb for the same propositions. So there must be some relation between the two sorts of expressions that allows this to happen.

You will have noticed that I think of abstractors in a curious, "active" way, as sets of transformations. One intuition is that of fixing a value; the generic proposition A, which depends on some parameter, is transformed into another, by fixing a value for that parameter. All the transformations being thought about there, do the same sort of job — fixing the value of *that* parameter. This close association allows us to identify the parameter with the abstractor whose members fix the value of that parameter. Think of it this way:

    $b = h(b,1), h(b,2),...$ $h(x,i)$ fixes the value of
    $a = h(a,1), h(a,2),...$ parameter x at i

This looks a little circular; but really it has the unobjectionable form of "the Jones family = { The father of the Jones family, the mother of the Jones family,...}". Now we can alter a proposition which depends on parameter b, by changing its dependence to parameter a; we can also think of fixing the values of parameter a and b in the same way. At this point drop the picture, toss away the ladder; but you must keep the idea that between the members of abstractors a and b there can be a systematic correlation.

The easiest way to do this is to think of a set G^* of Ur — functions whose members take abstractors into members of those abstractors:

if a is an abstractor and $g \in G^*$ then $g^a \in a$;

moreover, $a = \{g^a : g \in G^*\}$.

In addition, the transformation that changes a proposition dependent on b into one with exactly similar dependence on a, may be called (a-b) — read it as "a for b" — and then we must have:

The functions:

$g^a g^b$

$g^a(a\text{-}b)$

$g^b(b\text{-}a)$

are all the same function.

This is again easiest to understand in analogy with the syntax. Let s(x,i) replace the term x by the numeral i, and let (x/y) replace all occurrences of y by occurrences of x:

s(a,1)s(b,1)Rab = R11

s(a,1)(a/b)Rab = s(a,1)Raa = R11

s(b,1)(b/a)Rab = s(b,1)Rbb = R11

If our abstractors are correlated in this fashion we can deduce:

Theorem If A = (a-b)B and B = (b-a)A,
      then aA = bB and $\forall_a A = \forall_b B$.

The antecedent says that A and B depend on a and b respectively in exactly the same way.

From now on I shall assume we have a correlated set of abstractors; their members g^a I shall call *instantiations* (of a), and the transformations (a-b) I shall call *variations*. These are my precise mathematical correlates of the two processes I described intuitively above.

Obviously the properties of these abstractors and variations between them need to be spelled out further than I have here. I will just assert, without proof, that a few minimal assumptions suffice to yield all required properties. Their theory has a certain completeness, in that if the abstractors are *normal* (i.e. contain only normal transformations) then all functions defined by composing instantiations and variations are strictly calculable.

15. I turn now to identity. To begin, I propose to regard a name as the label of an abstractor. Suppose "Cicero" is a name, and "Cicero is hap-

py" is a sentence that stands for the proposition A. The abstractor a which "Cicero" stands for produces the abstract denoted by "Ĉicero (Cicero is happy)" which is also denoted by "Ĉato (Cato is happy)". Thus aA contains all the propositions that could be expressed by sentences of form " − is happy". (Note: "could be", not merely "are".)

Now what proposition does "Cicero = Tully" stand for?

Well, what happens if I replace "Cicero" by "Tully" in this sentence? It becomes a tautology. Similarly for the sentence "If Cicero is rich then Tully is rich", and for many others, like "Either Cicero is rich or Tully is not". That is really important in this case, because the sentence "Cicero = Tully" when introduced as a premise, sanctions exactly that substitution transformation.

On the side of propositions, we have the case of a transformation into the *a priori* proposition, K. Define, therefore, for a transformation f:

$$C(f) = \{A : fA = K\} \quad - \text{ the } core \text{ of f}$$
$$I(f) = \wedge C(f) = \wedge \{A : fA = K\} \quad - \text{ the } identity\ proposition \text{ of f.}$$

How much can we deduce here if we know very little about the transformation? Let us assume that f is idem-potent   (ffA = fA) and that it is normal. Both assumptions hold already for our variations as well as instantiations.

Theorem (a) $I(f) \leq A$ iff $f(A) = K$
          (b) $I(f) \leq (A \rightarrow fA)$
             $I(f) \leq (fA \rightarrow A)$
          (c) provided $K \rightarrow A = A$ for all A;
             $I(f) = \wedge \{A \leftrightarrow fA: A$ a proposition$\}$
          (d) provided $A \wedge (A \rightarrow B) \leq B$ for all A,B:
             $I(f) \wedge A \leq fA$
             $I(f) \wedge fA \leq A.$

The provisos in (c) and (d) hold even in quantum logic.

These are all generalized versions of parts of Leibniz' principles of the identity of indiscernibles and its converse. Consider these syntactic analogues;

(a) a = b implies Rab if and only if Raa is logically true
(b) a = b implies that Fa and Fb imply each other
(c) a = b is equivalent to the conjunction of all sentences of form Fa ≡ Fb
(d) a = b and Fa together imply Fb
    a = b and Fb together imply Fa.

The only thing we need for such desirable theorems (which contain as good as the whole theory of identity) is to find a transformation f for which we can say: "(Cicero = Tully)" expresses the identity proposition of f.

But there is an obvious candidate: the *variation* (a-b) in which a, b are the abstractors which are labelled by the names "Cicero" and "Tully". Let us write simply "Iab" for "I((a-b))". Then the above theorem tells us certainly that most of what we want to say about Iab definitely holds. There is more that is needed or desired, and here is my wish-list:

(a) Iab is in effect a transitive, reflexive, symmetric relation:
Iaa = K
Iab = Iba
Iab ∧ Ibc ≤ Iac
(b) if a,b are not the same, Iac = (c-b)Iab and Icb = (c-a)Iab
(c) Iab = K only if a,b are the *same* abstractor
(d) Even if Iab ≠ K, it still need not imply everything.

All this *except* (d) follows from our definition and the properties of variations (subject to the *modus ponens* proviso A ∧ (A → B) ≤ B for the last part of (a)). However we can also show that (d) holds in non-trivial models, and that there are such models.[4]

16. Let's step back now, and see what this means about identity. The proposition expressed by "Cicero = Tully" was identifiable — the meet of all propositions that become true *a priori* if their dependence on Cicero is changed to dependence on Tully. But Cicero, the semantic value of "Cicero", was not an entity, not the person Cicero, but an abstractor, something active and mobile, a small army of transformations acting on propositions.

This had to be so, since we set out to do *subjective* semantics, in which there can be no use of the person Cicero at all. The abstractor is, if you like, a concept — such a concept as traditionally, but not recently, have been associated with names — but it is not at all the individual concept of a person who is Cicero, nor is it the concept of satisfying descriptions of Cicero. It is instead the action of abstracting *from* Cicero, the action of turning a proposition "about Cicero" into a large family of propositions (of which the original may be one of course) that are not about Cicero (at least in the same way).

17. The project of a Pure Logic has been approached here in the semantic way, that is, by discussing what the most general models for language should be. The building blocks were minds, whose only activity is to suppose, and to conceive of other minds which differ from themselves in what they suppose. From these blocks we can build lattices of proposi-

---

[4] QUAAM, (11-10) says, if a,b are distinct then g^aIab = Ig^b. In this case Iab ≠ K; it is the minimal proposition Φ only if Ig^b is (since g^b (Φ) = Φ if b is irrelevant to Φ, which it must be if anything is). So the conditions of interest is that g^b should not turn incompatible propositions into K — without which the model would be useless. See also the Appendix of QUAAM for concrete models.

tions. If we then ask what it is like, in detail, for a mind to suppose something, we have to look as the strange case of supposing a general proposition — something we do even in elementary forms of abstract reasoning. This led to the introduction of a new set of important items: the transformations of those lattices of propositions. Using sets of such transformations we can reconstruct quantification, identity, and abstraction. The pleasing result, for whose sake in part the project is undertaken, is that identity propositions are not constrained to have the same status as either tautologies or self contradictions.

APPENDIX (to section 9)

It is quite easy to explain intuitionistic logic in algebraic terms. In each model, the propositions form a lattice, with minimum and maximum K, and a binary operation $\rightarrow$ much that the Great Law of Implication holds:

(Imp) A implies B $\rightarrow$ C exactly if A $\wedge$ B implies C

where "implies" denotes the partial ordering of the lattice. The pseudo-complement is defined by: $\neg$ A = (A $\rightarrow$ Φ). It follows automatically that these lattices are distributive; they are called Heyting lattices.

To check that the propositions in an I-frame form a Heyting lattice, we must show that Imp holds. Suppose first that A $\subseteq$ B $\rightarrow$ C, i.e. that if x ϵ A then x^B ϵ C. A fortiori, if x ϵ A $\cap$ B it follows also that x^B ϵ C; but in that case x = x^B, so x ϵ C. That establishes Imp in one direction. Conversely, suppose that A $\cap$ B $\subseteq$ C and that x is in A. Then clearly x^B ϵ A $\cap$ B and hence in C, so x ϵ B $\rightarrow$ C.

More interesting is the precondition that A $\rightarrow$ B must be closed if A and B are. This means: any mind subordinate to A $\rightarrow$ B is also a member of it. Suppose therefore that x is subordinate to A $\rightarrow$ B. By the special condition on I-frames, this entails that x is also A-subordinate to A $\rightarrow$ B. Therefore, for any proposition C, if all y^A ϵ C for all y in A $\rightarrow$ B, then also x^A ϵ C. A fortiori, if all y^A ϵ B for all y in A $\rightarrow$ B, it follows that x^A ϵ B. But the antecedent is true by definition; and the consequent is the conclusion that indeed, x is in A $\rightarrow$ B.

Turning now to the completeness question, we note that the lattice of propositions in an I-frame is always a complete Heyting lattice. However, every Heyting lattice can be embedded in a complete one, so this feature does not obstruct completeness.

Suppose then that L is a complete Heyting lattice, and define F(L) to be the frame whose elements are the elements of L and whose subordination relation is defined by: x is subordinate to U exactly if x $\leq$ V U, the complete join of elements of U. In that case [U] = [VU], i.e. the principal ideal generated by the element VU. By another standard theorem (see e.g. R. Balbes and P. Dwinger, *Distributive Lattices*, Ch. IX, section

4, thm. 2) L is isomorphic to the lattice of its own principal ideals. Thus we have L isomorphic to the lattice of propositions of frame F(L), for a proposition is a closed set. Note then that if P is a proposition, then $x \in P$ iff $x \leq \vee P$.

In the frame F(L) define $x^A = x \wedge (\vee A)$. Then $[x^A] = [x] \cap A$ as required, if A is a proposition. Next suppose that x is subordinate to U, i.e. $x \leq \vee U$, and let us try to prove that it is then also A-subordinate to U. So let C be a proposition such that for all y in U, y^A is in C. Because A is a principal ideal, let A = [a], and let C = [c]. Thus we have for all y in U, $y \wedge a \leq c$. It follows that $(\vee U) \wedge a \leq c$ and hence that $x \wedge a \leq c$, i.e. that x^A is in C. Thus we conclude that F(L) is indeed an I-frame.

Turning to orthologic, our work is made easy by an article of Rob Goldblatt. This is a logic which has a negation; besides the principles reflecting lattice laws it has only

$P \wedge \sim P$ implies Q
P implies $\sim \sim P$ and conversely
if P implies Q then $\sim Q$ implies $\sim P$

as fundamental principles. Goldblatt provides a semantic analysis in terms of what he calls orthoframes (studied earlier by Foulis and Randall under the name *orthogonality spaces*). The proof of soundness and completeness for orthologic with respect to O-frames follows of course the same pattern as the above proof for intuitionistic logic, except that subordination is defined in terms of the orthogonality relation: x is subordinate to W, by definition, exactly if for all y, $y \perp W$ only if $y \perp x$. Thereafter we can follow Goldblatt's paper so closely that we need not give details here.

As to the classical case, a C-frame is an I-frame in which $x \perp A$ can be defined as: x is subordinate to $A \rightarrow \emptyset$. The latter proposition is the intuitionistic negation of A. If we now require this frame to be also an O-frame, then the law of double negation is imported which reduces intuitionistic logic to classical logic. Completeness is not sacrificed in this way of providing a semantic analysis for classical logic. The reason lies in the fact that every Boolean algebra is isomorphic to the set of elements that equal their own double pseudo-complement ("regular elements") in a Heyting lattice.

Bibliography

BALBES, R., and P. DWINGER
1974   *Distributive Lattices*, Columbia, Missouri, University of Missouri.
DALLA CHIARA, M.L.
1977   "Quantum Logic and Physical Modalities", *Journal of Philosophical Logic* 6, 391-404.
ELLIS, B.
1976   "Epistemic Foundations of Logic", *Journal of Philosophical Logic* 5, 187-204.
1979   *Rational Belief Systems*, Oxford, Blackwell.
FIELD, H.
1977   "Logic, meaning, and conceptual role", *Journal of Philosophy* 74, 374-409.
GOLDBLATT, R.
1974   "Semantic Analysis of Orthologic", *Journal of Philosophical Logic* 3, 19-35.
HARPER, W.L.
1976   "Counterfactuals and representations of rational belief", doctoral dissertation; University of Rochester.
VAN FRAASSEN, B.C.
1973   "Extension, Intension, and Comprehension", in M. Munitz (ed.) *Logic and Ontology*, New York, New York University Press.
1980   "Critical Study of Ellis (1979)", *Canadian Journal of Philosophy* 10, 497-511.
1982   "Quantification as an Act of Mind", *Journal of Philosophical Logic* 11, 343-369.

Yorick Wilks

Reference and Its Role in Computational Models of Mental Representations

Introduction

This paper is written from a standpoint that still has considerable support within that part of the artificial intelligence (AI) community concerned with modelling or simulating mental representations and processes, but which does not accord with the currently fashionable emphasis on the role of logic in those representations. I would characterise the position as procedural intensionalist: not a very clear phrase perhaps, but which is intended to capture a set of claims that mental representations, in so far as they can be modeled by computer processes are (a) essentially symbolic, (b) that their semantics are to be given ultimately by procedures and not (except in a circumscribable set of cases) by computations over sets of referents or by the standard semantics of predicate logic, and (c) that semantic decomposition to some set of primitives, which may be domain dependent or (as some would argue) universal, plays a plausible role in those representations.

The group has a low profile in philosophical terms, its members being among those in AI more concerned to make programs work, by understanding natural language, answering questions and so forth, rather than in having theories that are well-founded in the terms set by their opponents. They are thus often charged with ad hocness in their theories, and sometimes with having no more than the morals of engineers.

In this paper, I want indirectly to defend that club, of which I happen to be a member, by examining the recent claims of two writers concerning the role of "reference" in mental and computational representations. These two Johnson-Laird (1981) and Smith (1982) are not from the extreme logicist camp; on the contrary, both of them go out of their way to distinguish themselves, in their quite different ways, from the claims of the sort associated with McCarthy and Hayes (1969), or, more recently, Barwise and Perry (1983) who assume that some variant of first order logic and its semantics is adequate for the description of meaning and knowledge.

This paper, then, is in the standard tradition of political discourse, in which it is more important to set to rights some groupuscule to one's immediate left or right, than to tackle the far-off opposition with whom no serious dialogue is possible. The points of difference concern (b) above in the case of Smith and (b) and (c) in the case of Johnson-Laird: point (a) is what serves to separate, I imagine, all those mentioned from the yet newer fashion for connectionism (see, e.g., Feldman, 1985). But that is a wholly separate issue, and for a separate occasion. I shall discuss each of the two authors mentioned in turn, and then attempt to relate the two discussions at the end.

Reference and decomposition in "Mental Models"

In his (1981) Johnson-Laird defends again his theory of procedural semantics. I shall not discuss that here, since I have done so elsewhere (1982): my view remains that procedural semantics must, in some sense yet to be defined, be correct, but Johnson-Laird's version is clearly wrong.

A conspicuous virtue of his (1981) paper is that it begins by dismantling, pretty effectively, two major attacks on the notion of decompositional semantics: those are Kintsch (1974), and Fodor, Fodor & Garrett (1975). Johnson-Laird then goes on to discuss what he calls network theories of semantics (e.g. Quillian 1968) and meaning postulate theories (e.g. Fodor et al. 1975), and considers, but does not pronounce on, the issue of whether these two are notational variants of semantic decomposition theory. Johnson-Laird's real concerns then emerge: for him, all three are forms of what he calls "the autonomy of semantics":

...they assume the meaning of a sentence can be established entirely independently of what it refers to. This autonomy is self-evident because none of the theories has anything of substance to say about referential matters. (ibid. p. 114)

Johnson-Laird's purpose in his paper is to show the wrongness of such pretensions to autonomy, while mine here is to show that, whatever may be the case on that, Johnson-Laird's arguments carry no weight. However, it must be noted immediately that his is a bold and unconventional claim: if "reference" determines "meaning" in any way (and if "meaning" is held steady so that it does not slip back to meaning "reference" in the way some translators of Frege would prefer) then that is a non-Fregean claim, and they are rare these days: this is perhaps the first clear denial that "meaning" is a function, picking out referents in the world, since Putnam (1975). In his (1977), Johnson-Laird seemed to hold a much more conventional Fregean position, recast as recognition functions that actually identify classes of object, but now his positions is: "Would that it were always so, and that natural language invariably worked in this orderly fashion" (ibid. p. 115).

The present author has no desire to reassert Fregean orthodoxy in these matters, but who would be converted from it by Johnson-Laird's opening sally (ibid. p. 115)?

The interaction between meaning and reference is evident in the machinery of selection restrictions. What has to be constrained is not the meaning of expressions but their referents ... An assertion such as "It is pregnant" plainly constrains the referent of "it", not its meaning; it must refer to an idea or to a female animal.

None of this advances Johnson-Laird's position, nor does it touch those he opposes, whether semantic decompositionalists, more generally procedural intensionalists, or orthodox Fregeans; all he says is compatible with their position. The trick, he seems to feel, lies in the use of "it": that shows the topic must be reference, for it is as referential a word as you can get. But, that does not follow at all. If the sentence had been "Marion is pregnant", then we would have known, in a standard way, that Marion, whoever she is, is female and not male. But now it does not seem so revealing to say that the assertion plainly constrains the referent of Marion, not its meaning... etc. We can see the processes involved in understanding that sentence as adding information to what we know about Marion. We can also see them, at least if we are Fregeans, as aiding us in picking out Marion. There is no contradiction there; it is all depressingly orthodox. What has not been shown is that the referent in any way determines meaning.

Actual AI techniques

The early seventies produced a range of AI programs that used inference techniques, applied to elementary text representations (some decompositional, as in Wilks 1975, some not as in Charniak, 1974), in which pronouns were tied to one and only one candidate from among a number the text offered, and on the basis of feature and factual information. This task was called "resolving pronoun reference" or more pretentiously, "anaphora resolution".

So, in Charniak's program the procedures needed to decide, when faced with "He will make you take it back", whether "it" referred to one, real, child's top (say TOP1) or another (TOP2), which was purely notional, and might or might not exist. The procedures that did this were of exactly the same type and ontological status as those that decided, in my own contemporary program that in "The soldiers fired at the women and I saw several fall" the pronoun several referred to women and not to soldiers. In that case nothing in the sentence required that candidate groups be arbitrarily named (WOMEN 1 versus WOMEN 2) so as to make distinctions or perform quantifications, but nothing excluded that option. Nothing is served by describing these processes as constraining referents, as opposed to determining meanings. What they are doing in both cases is locating the stored description that best fits the features of the slot available and which must be filled.

That work was all pretty elementary by today's standards, but there was nothing about the processes that could have caused anyone to believe that "referents were determining meaning". The assumptions behind such programs were paradigm cases of what Johnson-Laird considers "autonomous". But when notions of reference were required, as when labelling groups of referents so as to distinguish them, as with this (female) Marion versus that (male) Marion, or those soldiers versus these soldiers, then that could all be done by arbitrary labelled nodes, usually called Gensyms. Nothing Johnson-Laird says shows there was anything wrong with that procedure. And nothing so far supports any claim about meaning determining reference.

Johnson-Laird continues his argument:

A still more critical weakness of the original theory is that it turns out to be impossible to state determinate selection restrictions for many verbs. Consider again the verb 'lift', which was earlier assigned the following constraints on its subject: ((HUMAN) or (ANIMAL) or (MACHINE)). ... It fails to allow for the following sentences:
The wind lifted the leaves over the fence
The magnet lifted the pins
[followed by five more examples, YW], (ibid. p. 115).

He goes on to suggest that the examples might be accomodated by ad hoc additions to the constraints, but this "suggests that some underlying general principle has been overlooked... The principle underlying the interpretation of sentences is that a listener often has recourse, not to selectional restrictions, but to inferences based on factual knowledge about referents. It is necessary to know that hot air rises, that ropes can support weights, that roots grow..." (ibid. p. 115)

Reading that sort of thing is very depressing for anyone familiar with work in knowledge representation and language understanding in AI of the last fifteen years and, more generally, it should make anyone very pessimistic about the future of the discipline usually referred to as Cognitive Science. It is clear that its principal practitioners, in some cases at least, work in total isolation from what goes on in the neighboring disciplines, even though those are, or so the story goes, supposed to share goals, methods etc.

The use of facts and inferences is exactly what the work of the general type he criticises (within decompositional, semantic net and meaning postulate approaches, whether or not they genuinely differ) has been writing programs to do for fifteen years or more. In the programs cited above, it is not possible to distinguish what is based on "features" and what on "facts": "Mary is female" is both an assignment of a feature and a statement of a fact. One can see it as one likes, and whatever view one takes need have no procedural consequences.

Work of the type described above was extended by many writers in AI to cope with exactly examples of the type Johnson-Laird lists: everyone will choose their own, and I am naturally most familiar with work like Wilks (1978) that discussed just how to generalise rules that performed as already described to cases like

My car drinks gasoline.

Such cases are exactly cognate to his own, where generalizations were derived, based both on features and facts, to imposte interpretation on "drinks" in this context. The method was to argue that in sentences like "The wind lifted the leaves over the hedge" a verb like "lift" did not have its "preference" for an agent satisfied (if it had, one type of algorithm would have come into operation) hence the broken preference in this case ("wind" not being a preferred agent of "lift") triggered a fresh set of inferences that endeavored to impose sense on "lift" on the basis of other facts known about winds. In both cases the aim was to maintain the overall coherence of sense on which understanding rests. On such a view there is no problem about disjunctions of features for agents etc, and their inability to cope with certain cases. That is assumed: the preferred cases guide one range of interpretations and the unpreferred are not rejected but guided to an interpretation by a different use of context. Such processes were claimed to be one source of our understanding of everyday metaphor (Wilks 1979).

Many other AI workers concerned with metaphor have explored similar methods and programs. What is so depressing here is that Johnson-Laird is either ignorant of such work or, more likely, is unable to see that it makes nonsense of his case. There is no opposition of primitive-feature-using procedures to those using facts.

If he persists in believing that introducing "facts", however he defines them, shifts the discussion to a world of reference and therefore establishes the distinction he needs, he should consider the following. Any formalist could, if he chose, deem that the semantic primitives of decomposition had referents themselves and, if that were so no formal distinction could be made of the type he needs. If Johnson-Laird considers this fanciful he should look at work like (Heidrich 1975) where exactly that was done. I believe it to have been a fruitless exercise, but its importance here is to show that no such formal distinction can be that as will support Johnson-Laird's point. This in fact is the burden of this part of my paper: Johnson-Laird seems to believe that there is some grounded antithesis between semantic decomposition and reference, and he is quite wrong; it is simply an issue of formal ingenuity. More seriously, a whole generation of AI programs shows there is no basis to what he says.

Johnson-Laird's key example: LEFT-OF

Johnson-Laird then moves on to his key example: spatial relations, and in particular relations like LEFT-OF which are the foundation for his recent theory of mental models. I do not fully understand how that differs from various-well known systems in AI of the last decade or so, and will not discuss it here. Let me restrict myself to the significance of his example, which is that LEFT-OF is not transitive in certain cases, particularly in situations like that of a group sitting round a circular table. Each person is to the left of their neighbour, but transitivity fails when you get round the table, since the person (directly) on your right is not also, transitively, on your left.

Now this is undoubtedly a clever example, at least as long as we ensure a fair number of people at the table, since two people sitting opposite each other at such a table might not concede that each was on the left of each other, preferring to use OPPOSITE. LEFT-OF may always fail as a transitive operation if applied enough times, and it may simply appear transitive for small numbers. It certainly fails on the globe we live on, and may fail for the universe as a whole if certain cosmologists are right. So the situation may be that LEFT-OF fails in a range of circumstances and that thought can conjure up examples, or structured models if one prefers, where that is so, thus rejecting transitivity by a form of Gedankenexperiment. The technique has been known at least since the Stoics who produced a method often called "semantic disproof" whereby a syllogism could be shown invalid by a particular choice of substituents — a world in which the syllogism was false, to speak in the current fashion.

It may be that this has something to do with reference, I am not sure. The locus classicus for Johnson-Laird's example is Kerkule's vision of the Ouroboros, the snake consuming its tail. That vision caused him to see, so he said, that a chain of carbon atoms could be a ring, and so LEFT-OF need not be transitive in that world. And thus we obtained organic chemistry. But does one want to call that a use of reference, because Kerkule plainly had the wrong referent: a mythical snake, not a chemical molecule? Until the theory of reference, so called, can produce a plausible account of the relation between the snake and the carbon referents, one might be forgiven for thinking that the whole event should be explained by a theory of metaphor or analogy, until now the province of the groups Johnson-Laird disapproves of.

But all this is totally beside the point, though our author seems not to see it: "How", he asks, "are the inferences based on ON-THE-RIGHT-OF to be handled by decompositional dictionary entries, semantic networks, or meaning postulates? The answer is that they cannot be. Such inferences destroy any theory based on the assumption that meaning is autonomous and independent of the reference of expressions". (ibid. p. 117)

But why should decompositional semantics have anything whatever to say about ON-THE-RIGHT-OF? It is itself a plausible primitive in any system: since Kant, many have believed that the difference between a right and left glove could not be expressed in any other three-dimensional terms. But again, that is irrelevant, because there is no case to answer. If transitivity of that relation fails in some models (and may in fact fail in all non-limited models, if my hunch is right), then so be it. The transitivity or otherwise of such a relation, and the scope in which it holds, cannot be easily connected to the status of the language containing the relation, and Johnson-Laird makes no serious attempt to do so. Nothing he writes shows, as he seems to believe it does, that some property of a model in which the relation fails determines the meaning of the relation. Intuitively, we seem to accord meaning to the relation in limited models where it works, and that is indeed interesting, but nothing more. For Johnson-Laird's case to succeed he would have to show that this success or failure somehow affects the nature of the vocabulary of the language over whose expressions the inferences are done. But he cannot, because that very enterprise makes no clear sense.

To put the matter at its crudest, whether TO-THE-RIGHT-OF is a primitive in a language or not can have no relation to the models in which the relation applies transitively or not. And whether it applies transitively or not in any particular model seems to have no effect whatever on the relation's intuitive meaning (which remains grounded in transitive cases). If Johnson-Laird were right, in so far as I understand him, description of the circular table case would change the meaning of LEFT-OF for anyone who heard it. A quick experiment should settle that one, and I will be happy to take the money of anyone who bets that the outcome will show any such change.

Towards the end of his paper Johnson-Laird retreats somewhat and seems to allow that, in certain circumstances, as when we ask the meaning of "name" a decomposition may be in order, and he goes on to suggest that a solution may be sought through "levels of decomposition" depending on context, and allied to a notion of "instantiation", or making a concept more concrete or constrained than a context requires. Yes, indeed, this debate is well-known in AI and, as it concerns levels of decomposition, it has been going on for some time particularly in the context of the debate about the language KRL (see Bobrow and Winograd 1977, Lehnert and Wilks 1979) and whether, as the KRL architects seemed to think, as Johnson-Laird does too, that belief in semantic decomposition was incompatible with there being levels of decomposition (it is not, of course, and many working AI systems reflect that; modesty forbids any more self references, but he really should consult Wilks 1979, or any of the MOPS papers by Schank, such as Schank 1979). Also, KRL was strongly committed to the notion of instantiating variables in discourse as items of another type, or of a more concrete type than the context forced ("seeing X as Y").

Semantic autonomy: does anyone hold it in Johnson-Laird's sense?

Jonhson-Laird ends with "My case against autonomy and in favor of an interactive theory of sense and reference is now complete" (ibid. p. 124). As I hope I have shown, he revealed no forms of reference that breached any supposed autonomy, since all the evidence he produced had long been accomodated within positions he would consider autonomist (though I maintained they were not). He showed no interaction of meaning and reference: in working systems that cover the phenomena he described, meaning and reference (in his sense) simply cannot be distinguished in his examples. They certainly do not "interact"; that is sheer muddle, and in no case did he produce a plausible example of a referent determining a meaning, however we chose to interpret those slippery terms. As I already noted, there is nothing in his conclusions that the procedural intensionalist club should object to.

It is interesting here to compare what Johnson-Laird calls the "autonomy of semantics" with what other cognitive scientists, working from very different points of view, have diagnosed as a vicious form of "the autonomy of syntax". In his (1983) and elsewhere, Fodor has argued that computational processes can only be what he calls "syntactic", and that they have no significance until given a semantics which must mean attachment to real world entities, since attachment to yet further symbols within the machine will be only more syntax, given that symbols (of themselves) can never have significance. Searle in his (1984) and elsewhere has made virtually the same point, but he chooses to draw consequences he believes much more damning for AI and the possibility of modelling human functions on a machine. This is not the place to discuss those two claims, except to say that they are profoundly muddled about the nature of formal semantics and what divides it from syntax.

I mention that work here only because of its striking similarity with the claims of Johnson-Laird we have just examined: both diagnose a vicious condition which arises when purely symbolic processes are, so it is claimed, cut off from reference and significance. Both claim that their demonstration shows up fundamental inadequacies in current theories of computational and psychological representation. Both, in my view, fail in precisely the same way, in that they fail to realise that symbolic processes can only be brought into contact with other symbolic processes (except perhaps for motor manipulations of objects, but none of our authors emphasise prostheses as our form of referential contact with the real world).

In both cases, too, claims that certain phenomena, essential to understanding, are excluded by the claimed autonomy are quite false: we saw this in Johnson-Laird with facts and inferences and access to object descriptions. These are in no way autonomous to the kind of "semantics" he proscribes. Similarly with Fodor and Searle (and this would take detailed demonstration) the formal, symbolic, access to referents is not and cannot be precluded by what they call "the autonomy of syntax". Referents in formal semantics just are additional symbols and nothing can change that: both syntax and semantics are within "the autonomy of symbol processing".

The most odd feature behind these similarities of view is, as readers will have spotted, that Johnson-Laird calls the doctrine he finds distasteful "the autonomy of semantics" whereas the others view (essentially the same doctrine) as an "autonomy of syntax". I take comfort from that fact, for their attributions cannot, on their own views, both be right — and it is essential to both their, otherwise identical, arguments that they not both be right! There is more trouble here than the well-known ambivalence of the notion of semantics, but this may not be the occasion to pursue it. What will cast further light on the problem will be to examine the views of Smith, very close in many ways to Fodor's, but coming from within the computational modelling community, thus making a double contrast with Johnson-Laird though, as we shall see, falling into the very same confusions, however they are named.

Smith on linguistic and computational semantics

Smith (1982) begins with the interesting claim that computation and computational processes are fundamentally linguistic in nature and that there are important general consequences from that if true, particularly for the formal semantics of natural and computational languages. Smith argues that they are similar, as has been noted before, but that the similarity brings both closer to the semantics of natural language, rather than to the semantics of computational/formal languages.

The position taken in the present paper will be that formal semantics, in Smith's sense, belongs essentially to the analysis of formal (including computational) languages, and has little proven application (at least for the goals of mental representation within AI and machine language understanding) to natural languages. That view would appear to be compatible with Smith's position as indicated above but, as we shall see, the thrust of his paper is really the reverse, that is to say the (traditional) assimilation of natural to formal languages.

That Smith's starting point is unconventional is confirmed by his opening observations, that programming languages "are called languages" (p. 1) and that "language-derived concepts like NAME and REFERENCE and SEMANTICS permeate computational jargon (to say nothing of INTERPRETER, VALUE, MEMORY, EXPRESSION, IDENTIFIER!)." He goes on "... in discussing computation we use words that suggest we are talking about linguistic phenomena." (ibid.) This is dangerous territory if one believes those listed words to have their primary sense in the field of language, or if to use a word is always, willy-nilly, to be talking about the object of its original sense.

The rag-bag of terms above come from every discipline: logic, psychology, but particularly mathematics. There is nothing very close to language in such terms as variable, identifier etc... Shakespeare wrote of "sermons in stones, books in the running brooks..." but was under no illusions about the linguistic nature of non-linguistic reality.

The good aspect of what Smith wants to say is that natural languages have been around a long time, far longer than logic, and almost certainly have some explicit analogue in brain structure. It may well be that the structure of our natural language does influence our formal/computational languages in many ways, ones far deeper than those noted by Russell and others. Much the same argument has been used to show that our visual faculty must influence the structure of natural language in its turn.

Whatever may be the case there, may it not also be that, as far as recent and historically datable influences are concerned, the above considerations are all outweighed by the fact that formal semantics as we now know it arose within mathematics and logic, and was long thought (e.g. by Tarski) to be inapplicable to natural languages. Perhaps the terms from the theory of logic and programming languages (variable, etc.) can be perfectly satisfactorily explained from their source in mathematics and without need of any other source further back. The foreground influence is firm and large and dwarfs all background.

Smith's diagnosis of the problem

If computational artifacts are fundamentally linguistic; and if, therefore, it is appropriate to analyse them in terms of formal theories of semantics... then what is the proper relationship between the so called computational semantics that results, and the more standard linguistic semantics?... And furthermore, what is it to use computational models to explain natural language semantics, if the computational models are themselves in need of semantical analysis? On the face of it, there would seem to be a certain complexity that should be sorted out. (ibid. p. 1)

We are now closing in on our target, but no problem is indicated here; and nothing that takes more than a sentence or two to clear up, should there be anyone in a muddle. Let us try:

1) Computational models are used in an explanatory way in many areas of science without that requiring prior explanation of the semantics of programs! (One could make the same point about mathematics in general and ask whether all mathematical modelling is useless until the foundations of mathematics are settled, as they have not yet been).

2) More seriously, there is no reason to believe the two notions even

connected: which is to say, the semantic objects in a theory, on the one hand, and the objects in the semantics of the program that is deemed explanatory in the area under examination, on the other.

Let me put that point as follows: suppose we have a set of structured objects as the program semantics of the program BLOGG, which, as a matter of fact, appears to understand a reasonable subset of English. Those objects may in fact correspond naturally to the range of objects that the language discourses is about: e.g. humanness, John, walking, the nature of art in the Florence of the 15th Century etc.

They may do, but they may not. There is no requirement that they do for the program semantics of BLOGG to be its semantics: all that requires is that there be a set of objects so that the expressions that are true in BLOGG (presumably correspondences of strings and interpretations) are provably so.

This point I have laboured here is no more than a special way of answering the "machine code fallacy" (one frequently committed by Fódor, see Wilks 1982) which one falls into whenever one forgets that the semantics of programs at different levels of translation are different and that the objects need not be in any simple correspondence across levels (Smith refers to Strachey in his paper, who made this point many times in different ways).

3) Smith's use of "therefore" in the last quotation above suggests that he believes that the original or fundamental role of formal semantics is to analyse natural, rather than formal, languages. But this view, which might make Montague the principal figure in twentieth century logic, simply turns the whole history of logic on its head (see the reference to Tarski above).

A terminology problem

...as presently used in computer science the term 'semantics' is given such an operational cast that it distracts attention from the human attribution of significance to computational structures. In contrast, the most successful models of natural language semantics, embodied for example in standard model theories and even in Montague's program, have concentrated almost exclusively on referential or denotational aspects of declarative sentences (ibid.p.1).

As we noted in the first part of this paper, it is no news that the word "semantics" creates problems: it was for that reason that Schank, for example, described his work as conceptual dependency, just to avoid comments like the above. It may be that the phrase "Montague's program" is just an infelicity and should not be allowed to distract our attention from the fact emphasised in the first part of this paper, that successful programs to understand language or manipulate mental models computationally have never been written within Montague's, or any other, paradigm. But as Smith has set his world up, there might seem to be just no place for that large body of AI work. He may be right, but that is odd for anyone who claims to be making the natural and appropriate concerns of the semantics of natural language paramount, and to assimilate other, more abstract, matters to them! In fairness, it must be said that, unlike Johnson-Laird, Smith refers to work such as KRL (Bobrow and Winograd, 1977) and Brachman's KL-ONE (1979), and his paper can be interpreted not as dismissing such work, but as setting out demands for the kinds of semantics that must be provided for it, so that it become respectable. We shall come to that point later.

Smith then sets out his general views in terms of a number of distinct (though fairly classical) mapping relationships: a Greek relation θ maps linguistic strings onto internal/computational representations, one that, in Fodorian terms, takes one from English to Mentalese or, if one prefers, to the sorts of structure we associated earlier with "procedural intensionalism". A Greek ϕ maps from Mentalese to real things out there in the world (to T.S. Eliot "the poet himself" says Smith; perhaps an unfortunate example, since an existing object is normally thought to help for explicating that particular semantic relationship). And finally a Greek ψ which maps from some internal structures and states to others, as does the derivability relationship in logic (ibid.p.2):

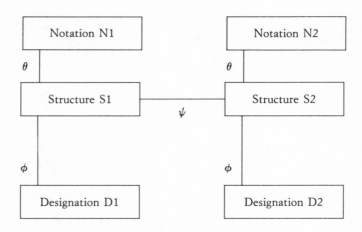

Smith adds "...we need not take a stand on which of ψ and ϕ has a prior claim to being the semantics [of a structure in the internal language, YW]".

That is to say, we can take the semantics as yielding real things out there or further symbolic expressions. It is a consequence of Smith's position, and some formalists have ignored this, that the expressions of a formal semantics themselves require a structure of denotata. Indeed, from Smith's diagram it follows that the designations D1 (of the Mentalese) and D2 (of the formal semantics of the Mentalese) can differ. This is essentially the point I made earlier to show the a priori non-coincidence of the objects "talked about" by a program and of the objects of the program's formal semantics. It still seems to me that a demonstration of that difference must tell against the initial goal of Smith's argument that computational and linguistic semantics can be in some sense assimilated to each other.

His immediate aim in setting out the diagram is to separate what he calls procedural consequence (i.e. ψ semantics, or what we have been calling procedural semantics) from declarative import (Φ semantics, or denotational/referential semantics) (ibid. p.2), and to argue that both are needed. The burden of the present paper is that, although Smith clearly considers this a very liberal concession on his part, he never makes clear why natural language, or knowledge, processing systems really need ϕ at all, particularly as he concedes that ϕ and ψ cannot be formally separated in those areas.

This diagramatic development now enables us to locate the missing body of work we noted earlier when discussing Johnson-Laird: it comes in as forms of what Lewis called markerese semantics, the "project of articulating θ , (which) cannot really be called semantics at all, since it is essentially a translation relationship" (ibid.p.3) though Smith concedes that "θ in computational formalism is not always trivial". Note the assumption in passing that a translation relationship will in general be trivial. Although Smith later makes concessions to mollify this point, here is the heart of the paper, quite different from its declared aims: most AI work in semantics is not really semantics (because it lacks ϕ mappings, just as for Johnson-Laird, that work is non-serious because it lacks reference, which should be the property given by Smith's ϕ mappings but is probably not, as we saw already).

This sort of point is a very familiar one, and has been made many times before and since Lewis. The question again is, what is it doing here in the work of one who was going to assimilate formal matters to natural language intuitions? Montague (who it will be remembered believed that "Every nice girl likes a sailor" had two syntactic structures!) had no difficulty with the assumption that linguists knew nothing about language, but Smith appeared to begin from a different position.

A crucial point here is that, for programming languages, Smith accepts that θ can be specified independently of ψ and ϕ (p.4). He refers to Fodor's modularity thesis (1983), which amounts to the same claim for natural languages (it is not explicit whether Smith accepts that or not, but it appears to underlie the rest of the paper). Yet, it is very important to be clear that that is not so for natural languages. In discussing Charniak's work I once referred (Charniak and Wilks, 1976) to effectively the same thesis as "decoupling". It was an assumption that Charniak explicitly made: that computer parsing of natural language into a representation could be separated from (subsequent) logical/inferential procedures and so, in Charniak's case, one could begin a project already parsed logical representations, or Mentalese if you will.

But that is not possible: a natural language parsing system must use inferential processes on knowledge bases in order to establish the initial representation itself. How else could one assign a structure, any representational structure to the example we discussed earlier:

The soldiers fired at the women and I saw several fall.

To do it you have to know the normal effects of such actions and who they normally damage, i.e. not the firers. The speech-act/pragmatics literature is a mine of such examples. The consequence of this is that θ and ψ are not distinct for natural languages (at least if we are allowed to take ψ as covering inferential relations on representations in general) and, since the last half of Smith's paper is an unwilling admission that ψ and ϕ may not be distinct, even though they ought to be, it is not clear how far his taxonomy can survive examination.

Terminology revisited: further problems with the diagram

Most of the problems raised for Smith in this paper concern the diagram and the fact that it bears amendment and interpretation that suggest final conclusions quite different from Smith's.

He interprets the diagram once for formal languages and once for natural languages. For formal languages, the layers of the diagram, from top to bottom in order, are code strings (on paper or screen), internal representations and designata. There is the usual ambiguity in such writings as to where the designata really are: the T.S. Eliot case suggests that they are out in the real world of people, tables and chairs, past or present, but that cannot be the case for formal languages, which may well lack designata of such a type under any interpretation. Indeed it can be argued that they must not have designata of that sort because, if the real world of objects were within the semantics of a program, then it could not run in any other world without being a priori false of it! And that is just the property programs do not have. There is no future in being a realist about the semantics of programming languages.

It seems clear that for Smith the designata in the formal language case are the formal structured formal objects of model theoretic semantics. Relations θ are translations to representations; ψ are logical relations, derivations from representation to representation; and ϕ are the mappings to formal designata. The problems with this, even for formal languages, are well known: the designata are also symbolic expressions in the machine, so if ψ is the space of such mappings, then ψ and ϕ, even if they can be formally distinguished, are both symbolic objects, within the machine. This is the special methodological solipsism of computation, however formal. Smith does not even concede the (conventional) position that ϕ and ψ can be fully distinguished in the formal case, and that is perhaps the only point in his paper that does fulfill his promise to show the influence of natural language in a formal area. But the analogy would only be fully plausible if he were to go further and concede that the designata in the natural language case are also symbolic objects, and that he does not appear to be prepared to do.

But although he concedes that it may not be possible to separate ψ from ϕ for formal or natural languages, he exhorts us that we must have both and in both areas, formal and natural. The conclusion of the paper is therefore an odd combination: an exhortation to specify two things that he believes are not independent, and without detailing the real problems that followed for so long from an "inability" to separate them.

The natural language situation

It should be clear already that it is very difficult for Smith to draw the morals he wants from the formal to the natural language case. If θ and ψ cannot be separated for natural language (which is no more than to say that what something means is what it implies, the oldest of cliches), and the ϕ/ψ distinction cannot be any clearer for natural languages than it was for formal, then it is not clear anything can follow. Certainly, those AI/natural language systems that rely on some such phrase as "procedural semantics" to support their giving of a semantics only as ψ relations have not been shown to deserve his sneers, as he seems to accept at the end when giving the weakest of endorsements of the possibility of a procedural semantics. For, if ψ and ϕ cannot be specified independently, who can say that giving a ψ is NOT giving a ϕ, especially in a system that has at least one symbolic identification of an individual (say by a Gensym) independent of its features!

Conclusion

There are strong similarities between the positions of Johnson-Laird and Smith: neither are hard line realists about reference, whether of the symbolic or real world variety. Both have sympathy with the possibility of a procedural semantics: Johnson-Laird strongly and Smith weakly. Yet both nurture forms of what I would call the "escape fallacy": that one can in language, or mental representations, or programs escape from the world of symbols to some formal but non-symbolic realm that confers significance. Yet, as one committed to procedural semantics, Johnson-Laird should not want that at all.

This formal nostalgia leads both of them to down play or dismiss the majority of work in AI in mental representation and language processing. In Johnson-Laird's case that may be more from ignorance, or from the inability to see that the expressive powers he requires for "reference" are all present within what he calls "autonomous semantics". In Smith's case the demand for ϕ mappings for systems in order that they may become respectable is inconsistent with his doubts about the possibility of such mappings independent of procedures, and his professed belief that natural language semantics should influence formal semantics and not vice-versa. He is led into this last inconsistency because of his extraordinary assumption that the semantics of natural language simply IS Montague style semantics. At least Johnson-Laird never made that mistake!

References

BARWISE, J., & J. PERRY
1983 *Situations and Attitudes*, Cambridge, Mass., MIT Press.
BOBROW, D., & T. WINOGRAD
1977 "An overview of KRL-0", *Cognitive Science*.
BRACHMAN, R.
1979 "On the epistemological status of semantic networks", in Findler (ed.) *Associative Networks*, New York, Academic Press.
CHARNIAK, E.
1974 *He will make you take it back: a study in the pragmatics of language*, Memorandum No. 3 from Istituto per gli studi semantici e cognitivi, Castagnola.
CHARNIAK, E., and Y. WILKS (eds.)
1976 *Computational Semantics*, Amsterdam, North Holland.
FELDMAN, J.
1985 "Introduction to special issue on Connectionism", *Cognitive Science*, Vol 9, No. 1.
FODOR, J.
1983 *The Modularity of Mind*, Cambridge, Mass., Bradford Books.
FODOR, J., J. FODOR & M. GARRETT
1975 "The psychological unreality of semantic representations", *Linguistic Inquiry* 4, 515-531.
HEIDRICH, C.
1975 "Should generative semantics be related to intensional logic?", in Keenan (ed.) *The Formal Semantics of Natural Language*, Cambridge, Cambridge Univ. Press.
JOHNSON-LAIRD, P.
1977 "Procedural Semantics", *Cognition*.
1981 "Mental models of meaning", in Joshi et al. (eds.), *Elements of Discourse Understanding*, Cambridge, Cambridge Univ. Press.
KINTSCH, W.
1974 *The representation of meaning in memory*, Hillsdale, N.J., Erlbaum.
LEHNERT, W., & Y. WILKS
1979 "A critical perspective on KRL", *Cognitive Science*.

McCARTHY, J., & P. HAYES
1969 "Some philosophical problems from the point of view of artificial intelligence", *Machine Intelligence* 4, Edinburgh, Edinburgh Univ. Press.

PUTNAM, H.
1975 *"The meaning of meaning"*, in *Mind, Language & Reality*, Cambridge, Cambridge Univ. Press.

QUILLIAN, R.
1968 "Semantic Memory", in Minsky (ed.), *Semantic Information Processing*, Cambridge, Mass., MIT Press.

SEARLE, J.
1984 *Minds, Brains and Science*, BBC.

SCHANK, R.
1979 *Reminding and memory organization: an introduction to MOPS*, Yale Univ. Computer Science Dept. Memoranda.

SMITH, B.
1982 "Linguistic and Computational Semantics", in *Proc. Conference of Assn. for Computational Linguistics*.

WILKS, Y.
1975 "A preferential, pattern-matching semantics for natural language inference", *Artificial Intelligence*.
1979 "Frames, semantics and Novelty", in Metzing (ed.), *Frame Conceptions and Text Understanding*, Berlin, de Gruyter.
1982 "Some thoughts on procedural semantics", in Lehnert and Ringle (eds.), *Strategies for Natural Language Processing*, Hillsdale, N.J., Erlbaum.

The author is indebted to discussion at various times with Barry Smith, Brian Smith, Ray Turner, Jerry Fodor, Doug Arnold and Pat Hayes. The errors are his own as always.